I've travelled the world twice over,
Met the famous: saints and sinners,
Poets and artists, kings and queens,
Old stars and hopeful beginners,
I've been where no-one's been before,
Learned secrets from writers and cooks
All with one library ticket
To the wonderful world of books.

© JANICE JAMES.

# A TIME TO DANCE, NO TIME TO WEEP

Spanning the years 1907–1946, this is the story of a woman, brought up largely in India by unconventional parents, who came to know the continent intimately. In her adolescence, spent largely in Britain, where she was sent to receive an education, she found instead a vocation. The story of her life after her return to India—marriage to a weak but charming man, abandonment, bringing up two children in poverty—and alone—is punctuated by the publication and success of her early novels.

# RUMER GODDEN

# A TIME TO DANCE, NO TIME TO WEEP

*Complete and Unabridged*

# ULVERSCROFT
*Leicester*

First published in Great Britain in 1987 by
Macmillan London Ltd.


First Large Print Edition
published October 1989
by arrangement with
Macmillan London Ltd.
and
William Morrow and Co. Inc.,
New York

British Library CIP Data

Godden, Rumer, *1907–*
    A time to dance, no time to weep.—Large print ed.—
Ulverscroft large print series: non-fiction
1. Fiction in English. Godden, Rumer, 1907–
Biographies
I. Title
823'.912

ISBN 0-7089-2071-3

Published by
F. A. Thorpe (Publishing) Ltd.
Anstey, Leicestershire
Set by Rowland Phototypesetting Ltd.
Bury St. Edmunds, Suffolk
Printed and bound in Great Britain by
T. J. Press (Padstow) Ltd., Padstow, Cornwall

For Jane and Paula

"To every thing there is a season, and a time to every purpose under the heaven: a time to be born, and a time to die; a time to plant, and a time to pluck up that which is planted; a time to kill, and a time to heal; a time to break down, and a time to build up; a time to weep, and a time to laugh; a time to mourn, and a time to dance; a time to cast away stones, and a time to gather stones together; a time to embrace, and a time to refrain from embracing; a time to get, and a time to lose; a time to keep, and a time to cast away; a time to rend, and a time to sew; a time to keep silence, and a time to speak; a time to love, and a time to hate; a time of war, and a time of peace."

*Ecclesiastes 3:i–ix*

A time to every purpose under the heaven —but not always . . .

This book is my life as a young writer; to me and my kind life itself is a story and we have to tell it in stories—that is the way it falls. I have told the truth and nothing but the truth, yet not the whole truth, because that would be impossible.

R.G.

# Acknowledgements

I SHOULD like to thank, first of all, the experts who went out of their way to verify details of my remembrances: Raj Chatterjee for memories of Old Delhi; Toby Falk, Consultant on Indian miniatures and painting, for recollections of Imré Schwaiger and his treasures; Sir Percival Griffiths KBE, CIE, ICS, noted for his outstanding courage in the time of terrorism; Doctor Patrick Davidson BVMS, MRCVS, DVM for checkings on rabies; Molly M. Kaye, the author, for the loan of rare maps of Kashmir; Kew Gardens for their willing exploration of the legend of the lotus.

I am indebted to Allen & Unwin for permission to quote from the late Arthur Waley's *The Temple* and *One Hundred and Seventy Chinese Poems*.

I am most grateful to my friends and family for their corroboration—or non-corroboration—of events; to the latter I must point out that this is a book of my memories, not theirs, and I have checked as carefully as I could.

I especially thank Alan Maclean, who has been my guide and touchstone since the book's first inception and all the way through; Betty Walker, who was a willing and responsive victim when she let me read it aloud to her; Sheila Anderson, who, with extraordinary patience—and perception—typed and retyped and retyped from my fly-mark handwriting; also my editor, James Hale, for his consistently skilful and enjoyable editing.

# Prologue

JON and I stood together on the quay at Plymouth watching as the luggage was unloaded into the Customs Shed from the liner that had brought us from India. It was March 1920, the chill grey of a Devon morning with a sharp wind blowing from the sea. Everything was wet and colourless and we were cold to our bones—not only with the cold; we had already had a taste of England.

In 1920 we, the two elder sisters of our family of four, were the shocking ages of thirteen and twelve, shocking because we belonged to an era in which every English or Western family of any standing living in India sent their children "home", as it was called, at five or six years old, no matter what the heartbreak on both sides; it was partly the climate, the dread of catching a chichi accent—we already had one—and partly the lack of suitable schools, so that when we, too, were six and five we had been left in London with our Godden grandmother and our four maiden aunts in their tall dark house in Randolph Gardens. It was only for eighteen months; our mother, Mam, had grown nervous of Zeppelins—this was in 1915, the second year of the First World War—and we had been reprieved for five halcyon years in the Indian sun.

Our father, Fa, worked for one of the oldest of the Indian Inland Navigation Steamer Companies which, between them, were responsible for the navigation of the great rivers of Assam and Bengal. This meant that we had not lived in cities, Delhi, Calcutta, Bombay, but in remote small towns always on the bank of a great river, most of the time in Narayangunj, a jute station in Bengal on the river Megna which, in places, was two miles wide; yet it was only a tributary of the Brahmaputra, which itself mingles with the Ganges. In India all rivers are one; indeed all water, even the village pools, even the water in your basin is the Ganges, Ganga Ma, Mother Ganges, and therefore sacred. Our

Megna flowed between banks of mud and white sand from which fields stretched flat to the horizon under a giant bowl of sky; if we children grew up with any sense of space it was from that sky.

We knew, too, perhaps more of India than many grown people even if they had spent their working lives there. I have always thanked God we did not have sensible parents; it was the custom then for women with children—there were four of us, Jon, Rumer, Nancy and Rose—to leave the plains in the hot weather, March to October, and go up to the cool of the hills; sensible parents would have chosen a hill station near us, rented a house and sent us every year to the same school; though schools in India had drawbacks, they at least provided steady education. Mam chose instead to take us to a different hill station every year so that we travelled the length and breadth of India, from Kashmir in the far north-west, four days' journey by train and road to Coonoor and Ootacamund in the Nilghiri hills of the south. In other years it was Shillong in Assam, Mussoorie near Simla and Darjeeling, more days by train.

We had travelled through the scorched aridness of the Scinde desert, lived in the Himalayas facing the peaks of the snows, seen cities and mud-walled villages. We had picked gentians and edelweiss in Kashmir and hibiscus, amaryllis lilies and bougainvillaea in our own garden. We knew palm trees, jungle thorn trees and the temple frangipani with its fragrant chiselled flowers, as we knew peach, plum and cherry blossom and birds from flamingoes, peacocks and the brain-fever bird to bulbuls and hoopoes. Our house was a mingling of religions: Hannah, the ayah, was a Thomist Catholic: the table servants Mohammedan: Fa's personal bearer, Jetta, was a Buddhist from Sikkim. The gardeners were Hindu Brahmins of the highest caste: the sweeper, Hindu too, an Untouchable. They all lived and worked together in contentment. "Why do religions have to have edges?" Jane, my daughter, was to say. We did not know they had any.

Hannah, who came from Madras in South India and spoke Tamil, could not understand Jetta if he spoke his native language Paharia; neither of them could talk to the gardeners who spoke Bengali or Hindi. India is so vast and varied that no-one, not even Indians, can comprehend it all, only apprehend it, which is quite different; children as we were, a little of the apprehension of that vastness was in us and now we had to adapt to the narrowness of coming "home". Home!

A sailor set Hathi, a small stuffed elephant on wheels, on the luggage chute; Hathi had come with us because no-one could imagine Rose without him. Wearing his scarlet flannel pad, he rolled majestically down the chute to the quay and everybody laughed and cheered.

Jon and I did not cheer; a cold realisation was creeping over us. This was the end of our childhood; soon even Rose would not want toys any more.

# 1

## Us

I SUPPOSE we are what we are because of our parents—parentage is a better word because it goes far further back than that.

I have in my house—and have had in all my houses—a little chair made for children. It is of oak with arms and a miniature ladder-back; its reed-woven seat has never worn out though six generations of children have sat in it, of whom in my long span I have known at least two of each generation, from my Grandmother Harriet and her sister Great-Aunt Minnie who was ninety-one when at the age of five I last saw her, arriving at our Grandmother's house—Number 4 Randolph Gardens—in a dark green brougham with a coachman wearing dove grey livery. I remember she had a black lace veil over her hair. After her and Grandmother came Fa and his brother and sisters, the Aunts; then I and my sisters; my daughters Jane and Paula: then Jane's four children, Mark, Elizabeth, Emma, Charlotte and, now, Elizabeth's first child, Celia Elizabeth.

The name Godden abounds in Sussex and Kent because, when Normandy and some of northern France were under the English Crown, the troops who kept order there were recruited from those near counties and their morning greeting was not, "Good day to you" but, "God d'en to you" and the French called the soldiers "goddens". Our particular branch from Tenterden in Kent were corn merchants, though, "Pirates and smugglers more likely," our Godden Aunt Mabel used to say, which was far more intriguing. The family crest is a bird sitting on a sheaf of wheat, which seems fitting for corn merchants. I had always thought they were of yeoman stock but it seems they had a coat of arms as well as a crest, and owned a manor, yet the descent of which Fa was proudest was of his mother's family, as they were in a quiet way distinguished. In his enthusiasm he traced them back through the Keys—our Grandmother's maiden name—to Sir Kaye, King Arthur's scullion. That may have been true—"scullion" brings it nearer reality; this is as it may be, but I do know that one of our great-grandfathers was Professor Thomas Hewitt Key, an eighth Wrangler at Cambridge. He was the first Professor of Mathematics and Astronomy at the University of Virginia, appointed in 1826 by Jefferson himself. He came back to London University where he had been offered the Chair of Latin, at the same time becoming a Professor of Comparative Grammar and Philology—I like to think this is where I got my love of words. He went on to become joint Headmaster of the newly founded University College School, the first public school in Britain to admit Jewish and Nonconformist boys. He was, too, one of the founders of the London Library.

In his portrait as a young man, with dark hair, sideburns and a handsome face above a white cravat, Thomas Hewitt Key looks too haughty and Byronic to be a professor; he wears a dark green velvet coat buttoned with crested brass buttons for which, as I have told in Two Under the Indian Sun, we have always called him

"Buttons". "He's like Fa," Jon used to say and certainly Fa, too, had been romantically handsome. Lady Curzon, when as Vicereine she went on tour with the Viceroy through Assam and Bengal, is reported to have said she found it all boring, except that she had met an Adonis, a young steamer agent—Fa.

Thomas married Sarah, daughter of Richard Ironmonger Troward, a rich man and patron of the arts; he owned some finepaintings, including a Leonardo da Vinci, a Rubens drawing, a Poussin—now in the National Gallery; as there is no record of its sale I do not know which it is.

Richard Troward was a solicitor and it was he who prepared the brief for the Prosecution in the trial of Warren Hastings; we still have the inlaid secretary table he used in Court. I am sure I should have liked him far better than Thomas Hewitt Key. Troward enjoyed life, as can be seen from his account book dated 1787, showing that he even had a box at Covent Garden Opera House, fifty-six guineas for the season; he is reputed to have paid seven hundred and fifty pounds for a

Chippendale dining table but he was, like Fa and me, extravagant and improvident; he lost all his fortune in a soap factory in London—now the site of the Festival Hall—and only the family portraits remain.

I do not like photographs about a room, they seem to fix the memory, but paintings are evocative and these portraits, not of course of the first rank, seem to look down from the walls as if they still were taking part in our life—perhaps they are: a great-grandmother and a great-aunt painted as *Summer* and *Winter* by Wheatley—*Winter* in a delicious hat—and one by Benjamin West of Richard Ironmonger Troward himself in the full costume of the Company of Archers, cocked hat with feathers, a long coat with a sash, knee breeches, tasselled boots and a quiver of arrows. The painting shows him ready to shoot with an arrow fitted to his bow. He persuaded Benjamin West to paint his eldest son, Richard, as *The Boy with the Hoop*. In the picture Richard has come from school but is wearing a white satin suit with long trousers and a large beaver hat with ribbons. The picture's place now is over my fireplace and might be of my daughter Paula, except that, instead of the Godden brown eyes, she has inherited Mam's, which were blue as speedwells.

There is another family picture, not a portrait but a group, a seated woman with her children. It is in finest pencilling with a background of trees, columns, urns and cupid statues against a pale blue sky; the faces, hair and sashes are delicately tinted, no more. It was painted in 1820 by Cosway, one of his few large paintings—he was a miniaturist. His columns, urns and cupids are imaginary—I cannot believe anyone in our family had a garden like that—but the people are real and the little girl with red hair, kneeling at her mother's feet, is the Sarah who married Thomas Hewitt Key.

I am sure it was Richard Ironmonger Troward who had the child chair made for Great Aunt Minnie, perhaps when she came back from Virginia in 1828. She would have been two years old.

Richard Ironmonger Troward is Celia Elizabeth's great-great-great-great-grandfather, seven generations away, not long compared to those of impressive lineage but quite a while for a middle-of-the-way family like ours—and a long time for a little chair.

Mam did not care one whit about family pedigrees and portraits; though my cousins have several Hingley paintings, the only one we possess is small, in an exquisite gilt frame, of a lady in blue—known to us as Aunt Eliza—and she was not a Hingley but a Moore. I am everlastingly grateful to the Moores because it was from them I got my name. Mam could tell us much about her father, Samuel, but nothing or almost nothing about her mother.

Samuel was the last child but one of a remarkable man—Noah Hingley—to my mind more remarkable than the grand-fathers and great-grandfathers that came to us from Fa. Of Huguenot origin, Noah began work as a "puddler" in the iron-works that dominated the Midlands Worcestershire town where he was born. A puddler is the boy who mixes the melted iron ore as it flows from the furnaces; he ended by owning the very Works where he had puddled, Netherton. With a friend, John Naismith, he had invented the Naismith Hammer which can come down

7

with such force as to crush a ton of ore, or so delicately that it will hardly break an egg; it made the Hingley fortune. I am proud to think that Noah was perhaps the first Ironmaster to have provided washrooms and a canteen for his men, and cared about their housing, those back-to-back, serried houses of the Midlands; at least his were well built and maintained, and I like another trait: for the horses in his Works, he would use only dapple greys.

Samuel was the misfit of the family; he wanted to be a High Anglican clergyman. This, of course, was not to be thought of. He was made to go into the Works, not it seems effectively; he married but his wife died leaving him a young widower with a little girl, Blanche, who came to a tragic end. She was delicate and was sent "to take the sea air" at Bognor. It was the days of bathing machines, like red and white boxes on wheels, which a horse pulled into the sea so that ladies could step down into the water without being seen from the beach. There were also ducking women who ducked the shrinking and timid females; it was supposed to make them brave enough to face the sea. Blanche was ducked and immediately had a convulsion; the nurse did not tell; the little girl was ducked again next day and died.

His family were at a loss as how to help Samuel in his grief and, whether it was his idea or theirs—I feel it must have been his —sent him to the South of France. He came back with a new wife. In her photograph she is dark-haired, dark-eyed with an enigmatic smile, and enigmatic she was; nothing seems known about her except that she was an orphan brought up in France by her Aunt Eliza, the lady in blue of the portrait. Her name was Harriet Rumer Moore.

Fa and Mam could so easily have called me Harriet as there was a double reason for that, Fa's mother being Harriet too. By good providence they christened me Rumer, a marvellous name for a writer; I have never met another.

India must have seemed remote from the Hingley Midlands English way of life but when Samuel died his big house, Fairfield, was sold and the family scattered. In those days women were "disposed of" and

Grandmother Harriet Rumer went to live with her eldest son, my gentle solicitor Uncle Alfred Edward, in Eastbourne where she was tended until her death by her youngest daughter, Aunt Mary. Aunt Mary then went out to Bermuda to another brother. Mam, Katherine Norah, meanwhile had been despatched to India where her eldest sister, Ethel, had married.

Hingley stories are far more romantic than any of the Goddens'. Samuel had engaged a tutor to coach one of his sons who was trying for Sandhurst and the Army. The tutor himself was working for an examination into the Indian Civil Service and had brains as well as one of those attractive faces, near ugly, like Gerald du Maurier and, later, Noël Coward, and Ethel fell in love with him. I do not blame her; I too fell a little in love with him when I was eighteen. Ethel, though, was Samuel's favourite—perhaps he felt she was his little Blanche come back to him—and he was furious but, as he never denied Ethel anything, he gave way on condition the young man passed his examinations, which he did brilliantly—he later became Governor of Bihar. There is a photograph of Mam taken in the dress she wore when she was "presented" to the Viceroy—Calcutta too had its Season and Aunt Ethel presented her sister. There were no feathers or trains; Mam's dress was palest pink tulle decorated with daisies; her dark hair was piled in elaborate twists and puffs on the top of her head; her eyes were the Hingley blue. She must have been ravishingly pretty and as innocent as those daisies—she remained an innocent all her life.

Mam was always susceptible to good looks and, to a young girl who had hardly been out of Worcestershire or far from her good but stolid Worcestershire relatives, Fa must have seemed dashing indeed.

His father had been a stockbroker who came a crash on the Exchange. The firm, though, must have thought well of poor old Mr. Godden because they paid to send Arthur Leigh, as Fa was christened, to Christ's Hospital, the Blue Coat School so named because the boys wore—and still wear—on Sundays and occasions, the traditional uniform of the School when it was founded by Edward the Sixth in the sixteenth century, an ankle-length dark blue woollen gown with a white ruff, a leather belt and yellow stockings. The firm also kept a place for Fa and it was understood he would, when he had qualified, become a stockbroker. He would have none of it and, when he was eighteen, ran away to India. The family influence followed him there and he was put into zemindary—land management—but, when the Boer War came, he left to go into Lumsden's Horse, a cavalry regiment of volunteers. They were unpaid and each had to provide his own two horses, his saddlery and a rifle; I do not know how Fa could have found the money. He did well, coming under the protection of the Duke of Norfolk, who offered to help him in England but Fa came back to India, abandoning "land" for "rivers" where he could fulfil his passion for fishing, shooting, sailing and horses.

Horses have always been a passion in our family; we truly rode—in a ring saddle —before we could walk. Nancy and Rose became almost professionals; both played polo, rode in races and Nancy was to run a large livery and training stable in Calcutta; my Paula was to do the same in the Sixties but in Sussex; grand-daughters and great nieces have followed, while, in her later life, Rose became a breeder of prize Dartmoor ponies.

Only I was the rabbit, but there was a reason; as children we had a white Arab pony, suitably called Pearl. Fearless then, I loved to show off on Pearl but showed off once too often; on one of Narayan-gunj's high built-up roads she bolted with me. Tearing down the hard road as I vainly tried to hold her, I saw, through the white mane flying in my face, a railway gate across the road, closed. There was no turning Pearl into the fields, the road was too high, but one of Fa's babus* placidly fishing in the dykes that lay below the road, heard the small thunder of hoofs coming and, running up the bank, he knocked me off the pony with his fishing rod.

Fa always told us after a fall, "Get up at once and ride again"; I was not able to: I was concussed and Pearl was too badly injured—she had gone pell-mell into the gate. She survived but though I still rode

---

* Babu: an Indian clerk.

—Fa's creed was "If you are frightened of anything you must do it"—I was always tense with fear which the pony or horse sensed at once.

I love horses though, and love being with them—as long as I am not on them —and love their quality; we as a family never had much money but all the same Fa always had superb horses, valuable guns and rods, and a yacht that he built himself with local mistris—carpenters.

When he—the young Adonis—met Mam, he was driving a buggy, a dog-cart with yellow wheels and a high-spirited palomino called Muffins, cream-gold with a white mane and tail. He was allowed to drive Mam alone—there was no room for a chaperone—only a "tiger", a small uniformed boy, perched up behind who, if Fa stopped, had to jump down and hold the horse's head. The drives grew longer and longer; though Fa had hardly any money, Ethel and her husband were indulgent—after all they were hardly any older and had known romance themselves.

For Mam, the romance quickly wore off. The marriage was in England and for a honeymoon Fa brought her to the silence

14

and austerity of Randolph Gardens. "After dinner," she used to tell us, "we sat round in a circle in the drawing room and nobody spoke." As it was her first visit to London —and on honeymoon—she had hoped Fa would take her to theatres and concerts, at least to see the sights, but he cared for none of these things, and it was not long before she learned what was meant by being married to a man of passionate interests; back in India, as a second honeymoon, Fa took her on a duck shoot, something that, in any case, hardly appealed to Mam. It meant getting up before dawn to steal out in a country boat among the jheels or swamps that border the river, stay motionless among the reeds for hours, and do the same in the late afternoon, towards dusk, when the wild duck fly in from the feeding grounds.

One afternoon Mam appeared in a white dress and, as they neared the jheels, the shikari, a man something between a loader and a hunter, told Fa that, seeing the white dress, the duck would never come near. Fa solved it by suggesting to Mam that he land her on a little island while he shot—he would not be more than an hour, he said—and it would be more amusing for her to walk about, "Stretch your legs and explore."

There was not much to explore, a few rocks and a solitary palm tree. Mam walked up and down, sat on the rocks quite happily, until, as the hour turned into two, then three, the happiness turned to alarm, soon real alarm. That particular river, the Brahmaputra, is tidal and the tide began to rise. The island grew smaller and smaller, and Mam remembered the river also had crocodiles . . .

Fa, quite oblivious, had turned the boat for home, when the shikari reminded him that they had not collected the Memsahib. "Memsahib?" Fa had forgotten that he had one. Mam was in hysterics when they reached her.

Mam had wanted ten boys and got four girls. Jon arrived in India in August 1906 —the middle of the monsoon's worst heat —poor Mam! I, in December 1907 at Eastbourne in Uncle Alfred Edward's house and, with my typical drama, Mam fell downstairs just before midnight and the doctor had to come through a blizzard.

I was also born with a tooth which old Ellen the cook pronounced to be lucky but, typical again, it was in the wrong place, the roof of the mouth, and had to be taken out.

Fourteen months apart, Jon and I were so close that we might have been Siamese twins, I, then, in her shadow which was natural. She was the first, while Fa and Mam were still romantically in love. There was a novel, fashionable then, by S. R. Crockett called *The Lilac Sunbonnet*, the sunbonnet belonging to his little girl, Winsome, a tot of nauseating sweetness who babbled baby talk. Mam, in a euphoria of happiness, insisted on calling the sallow sickly baby after her; Fa wisely added Ruth and Key as a family name but again poor Mam! Seldom has there been a less winsome, more naughty, highly strung and violently badtempered child.

Fortunately the sickly baby grew into an uncommonly beautiful and original girl.

Fa, strangely enough, never wished for a son; he was accustomed to a household of women, and was instinctively protective. Looking back I believe that, unconsciously, he relegated women to a different category; it really surprised him if they had passions of their own. All his "long leaves"—he had six months every four years—were spent in remote faraway places where he could shoot or fish or sail without a thought that Mam was pining for travel and the Continent, for theatres, concerts, of which there were none in India. I do not think she ever pined for shops, though she loved clothes.

He was punctilious, almost fanatical about keeping his word to a man, but women were different. When he proposed to Mam he was already engaged to another girl—that landed him in trouble—but he loved Mam, deeply and faithfully as he loved his daughters, particularly Jon and Nancy—particularly Nancy.

That may have been founded on guilt; Nancy was born in harrowing circumstances, caused by him. In Assam's country towns and tea-gardens* there were constant outbreaks of rabies, brought by jackals, and when the babies started arriving Fa had given Mam a promise that

* A tea-garden is a tea plantation. Oddly enough, I have never heard anyone say coffee-garden.

18

he would not keep dogs; not much later he bought three spaniels. They would not be in the house, he explained, they were shooting dogs; inevitably they were soon in the house and all three got rabies. Fa was bitten as were Aunt Mary, our Nanny, I and several servants. Jon and Mam, pregnant with Nancy, escaped.

At that time the nearest Pasteur Institute was at the hill station of Kasauli, two to three days' train journey away—there was no other transport—and the convoy set out, costing Fa an expense he could not meet, also terrible distress as some of the servants ran away; unless treated quickly rabies is certain death.

We had to stay in a hotel in Kasauli, of which I remember glimpses but, oddly, do not remember anything about the painful treatment, injections, two needles each time, into the stomach twice a day for fourteen days. I have had it three times.

Meanwhile Jon and Mam had gone to stay on a tea-garden with friends, who had a little pomeranian. It developed rabies, most likely from the same infection, and, springing up to five-year-old Jon, caught her on the lip. The nearer the brain the more dangerous and quick is a rabid bite, and Mam, though Nancy was some seven months on the way, had to set off at once on that long journey. It was in July's almost unbearable heat and Jon had fever, running a high temperature; no-one had told Mam that rabies has at least three weeks' incubation and she naturally thought this was the onset.

She reached Kasauli near collapse and a few days later Nancy was born, so small she was not expected to live; Mam, too, was desperately ill. Somehow she and Nancy survived but I do not think Mam ever forgave Fa.

Nancy is the only one of us I can remember Fa carrying about, petting and taking on his knee; he confined himself to teaching the rest of us how to play cricket and, in later days, to sail, fish, ride— except me—and shoot.

Nancy was charming and unfailingly attractive in her piquancy, with a head of short curls and eyes that were slightly slit; "Mam must have been haunted by a ghurka," Fa used to tease. Rose was as good-looking as Fa. All three had Godden brown eyes; I was a Hingley but did not inherit the blue eyes, only the high Wellingtonian nose.

One day at luncheon Fa came back from the office for "tiffin", as it was called, and we all had it together—he looked down the table at me and said, or rather murmured, "Where did that child get that face?" I know now he was only thinking aloud but I had heard and when we were allowed to get down from our chairs, I went out and wept among the canna lilies in the side garden; the cannas were higher than my head and, as I knelt, their brilliant colours seemed to mock me. With my instinct for drama I could have said, had I known the words, that iron had entered my soul, but it was not funny, in fact a prognostication. Later on at school, in the Senior School play, I was put out of the name part of *Jane Eyre* because the girls pointed out that my nose was too big for Jane, a fact moved, I must add, by the girl who wanted the part for herself and got it. What was saddest was that for a time, after his remark, I hated Fa.

My eyes were green—and not for nothing; I was wildly jealous.

Jon was not only the family beauty, she had unmistakable talent and, too, an almost uncanny power over the rest of us. On the rare times we went to a party and were given presents, when we came home we had to parade them; Jon took first choice, then Rumer, then Nancy. Rose was left with hers because if anything she wanted were taken from her she would bawl and Mam, to whom the baby was sacrosanct, would come flying. It was Nancy who came off worst.

Part of Jon's power was that, by contrast, she made almost everyone else seem dull; no-one could have had a more vivid imagination, often of a strangely macabre kind, which was to be her greatest asset when she became a novelist. It could, too, be sadistic.

She loved to read me Edgar Allan Poe's *Tales of Mystery and Imagination*, which made me sick with terror, particularly "The Pit and the Pendulum". I can see us now:

It must have been the hot weather because we are in our petticoats—we were allowed to go without dresses in the morning; our hair, which Mam usually let flow—she disliked hair-ribbons or slides—is twisted into a knot on the top of our heads; our feet are bare. I am still homesick for the feel of our verandah stone floors, hot from the sun and for the warm Indian dust between our toes. It is siesta time, we are on our beds and supposed to be asleep, but Jon has me pinned down, with one elbow on my chest as she reads:

"I now observed, with what horror it is needless to say, that its [the pendulum's] nether extremity was formed of a crescent of glittering steel, about a foot in length from horn to horn . . . the under edge evidently as keen as a razor . . . it was appended to a weighty rod of brass and the whole *hissed* as it swung through the air . . .

"I could no longer doubt the doom prepared for me . . ." the victim was strapped down. "Down—steadily it crept . . . relentlessly down."

"Oh no, Jon! Please no!" but the dark

eyes look down at me, bright with glee and the elbow pins me fast.

I suppose things made such indelible impressions on us because we had so little.

In that faraway Bengali town there were of course no schools for European children —in fact no European children of Jon's and my age; no libraries except at the Club, where the books were mostly memoirs with names like *Under the Punkah* or *Moments of a Memsahib* or else romantic fiction. There were no real shops, only the bazaar and though, in the hills, we went to an occasional film, except for a pantomime when we had been in London we had never seen a theatre.

There were, of course, books of our own, but though it would be pleasant to think we grew up with Shakespeare and the Bible, Aunt Mary who taught us preferred Tennyson, Longfellow and anything romantic.

Had I the heavens' embroidered
cloths

24

Enwrought with golden and
　　silver light . . .

which ended:

> I would spread the cloths under
> 　　your feet:
> But I, being poor, have only my
> 　　dreams;
> I have spread my dreams under
> 　　your feet;
> Tread softly because you tread
> 　　on my dreams.

"A-aah!" we said, but when I tried to write poetry myself, as I did continually, Jon was a stern critic. The opening of my novel *The River*, where the girl, Harriet —myself—reads her poem to her sister Bea—Jon—is true.

> "Saw roses there that comforted her heart," read Harriet, "And saw their crimson petals plop apart."
> "*Plop* apart?" asked Bea, her eyebrows clear and surprised and Harriet blushed.

In *The River*, I did not tell of Harriet and Bea going to England; it would have broken the spell; but that was a novel and, in a novel, you can do as you like.

Twelve going on thirteen and thirteen going on fourteen are difficult ages to be. "Not a town, like childhood, strongly walled, nor yet a city"—no-man's land, a transition age, difficult enough without any other transition and, "Too late," our Grandmother predicted in that spring of 1920.

Fa had run away from home and no wonder. When his father had lost his position and money, Grandmother decided that, as she could not entertain properly, she would not entertain at all and shut herself into the large gloomy house in Randolph Gardens, Maida Vale, an unfashionable part of London where she inexorably ruled her five maiden daughters, all of whom had suddenly to earn their livings. Only one had the initiative to escape by becoming, like me, a teacher of dancing; the others led an ascetic life, partly from what was then called "slender means" but also from a true holiness—they were devoted High Anglicans—which

26

made them deny themselves the little they might have had.

When Jon and I had been left with them, those five years ago, it must have been as hard on them as it was on us, the quiet of their lives disturbed by "Arthur's two eldest", but, with a strict English nurse, they had dedicated themselves to bringing us up. We had not been "brought up" before—in India children are largely left to grow—and it had been a painful process on both sides.

For the first time we had to live by rules, strict rules. To begin with we were banished to certain rooms, a night nursery at the top of the house and by day, to what had been the morning room in the basement. I remember the extraordinary silence in the house between, a silence that quelled us—not always: Jon was once driven to dance like a dervish on the morning-room table, breaking Aunt Mabel's magnifying glass which had been left in the drawer. "Why dance, dear?" asked the puzzled Aunts. Only the kitchen was lively but we were not allowed in the kitchen except now and then, when invited by the cook who had been Fa's old nurse and had a soft spot for us.

Our own nurse took us for an afternoon walk in the Park where we were forbidden to speak to other children; every day we took it in turns to have luncheon in the dining room, where we were not allowed to speak at all, and if our knife or fork or spoon made the slightest clink of noise on our plate Grandmother's and the Aunts' eyebrows were raised—I must say I wish more people had had that training. At five o'clock we were "changed" into velvet dresses—white muslin in summer—and sent down to the drawing room where the Aunts devoted a children's hour to us with music, duets on the piano, readings aloud by us, not them—I at five and Jon at six years old—and learning embroidery. We did play spillikins and sometimes cards, "Beggar my Neighbour" and, suitably, "Old Maid" but on Sundays all toys were put away and, worse, books. We went to church twice and had to learn the collect of the Sunday to say to Aunt Evelyn, who was in charge of our spiritual state and much grieved by it. We had to say our prayers to her morning and evening, something I tried to dodge. It was accepted that prayers could not be said twice and I used to rush downstairs and, kneeling on the front doormat, would gabble them to the postman who was in love with our house-maid, Emily, and welcomed any excuse to dally.

For grown-ups, eighteen months is an infinitesimal time; to children it can be an aeon and its memory was coming back to us. The Aunts were so truly good, noble and dedicated but, as Mam had found when she went there as a bride, never in all that tall dark house was there a gleam of laughter, fun or enterprise and it was there that we were going now.

Standing on the quay on that chill March morning, Jon and I moved closer together.

# 2

## The Little Fishes

THERE is a tinted photograph taken of us just before we went to school; the photographer has knocked our heads gently together—in those days that was the way sisters were posed—and we have come out as two thin small girls, cheek to cheek, with too much hair and wide open eyes. Jon's eyes were like the spaniel's in the poem "eyes like mottoes", eloquent and sincere; they impelled you to live up to them, but, in the photograph, our eyes have an appalled look and our mouths are slightly open which gives us the look of two little fishes gasping.

When Mam had driven away from the big red-brick building of St. Monica's with its steepled church topped by a cross, its playing fields and asphalt paths, we were taken by a lay-sister to the nun in charge of the dormitories. "These are the two

Goddens." As Sister Irene looked down on us, tall in her habit and wimple, graceful and cool, her eyes amused, it was obvious that this was what she saw, two odd little fishes out of water.*

We must have looked odd. The school coats were thicker than anything we had ever worn and we moved stiffly in them like marionettes; their dark blue made us seem more sallow than we were. We had not worn gloves before and we held our fingers straight out in our new brown kid gloves. "Curl your fingers round," said Sister Irene. "Unbend them." Our noses and eyes were swollen and pink with weeping and cold, and our pie-dish hats would not sit down on our curly hair. "That hair must be tied back!" said Sister Irene and, before she took us downstairs, she plaited it for us—it was to be one of our disgraces that we did not know how to plait. My hair soon adapted itself but Jon's obstinately curled in its plait; it was a real pigtail.

* Long after, I was to write the story of our time in that school for the New Yorker; I called it "The Little Fishes".

31

I still cannot fathom why, as it had been decided that Fa would go back to India alone and Mam would stay with us four in a rented house, we could not have been day girls which would have been more merciful; perhaps Fa and Mam had decided Jon was out of hand and, of course, where Jon went I went too. Perhaps our Grandmother prevailed— Mam was a chameleon in the way she took on other people's influences—and it was boarding school and not simply a boarding school, a High Anglican Convent.

In one week we collected more order marks than other girls in a term; we had order marks for answering back, for unpunctuality, for being untidy, and finally we were sent in to the Sister Superior, Sister Gertrude. "You must learn that there is a place and time for everything and a way of doing everything," said Sister Gertrude.

I have seen many headmistresses since then, some of them awe-inspiring, but I have never seen one as awful, in the old sense of the word, as Sister Gertrude. It is strange to think of a nun as arrogant and unkind but she was both. "A time and a place for everything," she said.

Jon looked at her with sincere and thoughtful eyes. "But it takes time to learn the places," said Jon.

Jon had more order marks than I, chiefly because she was more loyal to our upbringing, more honest. I found ways of avoiding trouble and I tried to help her but this was something that was not allowed. St. Monica's was a convent school founded on religion; twice a day we went to chapel, three times a day the Angelus sounded through the school and we had prayers in the big gymnasium every day. Sister Gertrude read the lessons and the girls took it in turn to read the collect for the day—not, of course, either of us because of the chi-chi accent. "Blessed are the meek," read Sister Gertrude, or "God has chosen the foolish things of the world to confound the wise." "God hath chosen the weak" . . . "things which are despised hath God chosen." A little feeble-minded girl, Florence, was very much despised; Sister Gertrude treated her with heart-rending coldness. "The first shall be last," read Sister Gertrude, but the work and life of the school, its conduct and lessons and games, seemed founded on a precept that was quite opposite; there was a scramble to be first, to be best, to be successful, and it was shameful to be last, to be slow, to be weak.

By degrees we learnt that there was something that reconciled these extremes; it was called "being sporting".

"You and your sister really must learn to be sports," said the mighty Games Captain to me. Probably no two girls ever went to school who were more feeble sports.

We were sneaks, as well; when Sister asked about an overturned inkpot or a scribble on the blackboard, "Who did this?" Jon and I answered obligingly, "Greta Robinson" or "Mary Smith". How were we to know that Greta or Mary would be made to stand on the rostrum in the gymnasium in front of everybody or be sent to bed with the Juniors or have dry bread for tea? When, in India, Fa had asked, "Who did this?" and we had said, "Jon" or "Rumer", nothing had ever happened.

All the same I achieved a certain popularity—for a while. The school went out, two by two, in a crocodile; for some reason sisters were not allowed to walk together and, as no-one else ever chose Jon or me, we would wait, hanging about with the other rejects, until a nun paired us off; Jon was either made to walk with the nun or else a Chinese girl, Ansie, with whom nobody wanted to walk because she spoke very little English. I usually had Florence who never spoke at all. I grew quite fond of Florence; I could tell her stories and, as she was silent, the stories were not interrupted; it was like writing aloud.

The girls in front or the girls behind must have listened to my stories as we moved along in our blue-coated, blue-hatted crocodile, for soon I was being asked to tell them in recreation, in the garden breaks, in sewing hour, especially stories about India. It was so intoxicating to be suddenly interesting that it went to my head and I told everything that the girls wanted to hear about India: about rajahs, elephants, howdahs, faithful brown servants, curries, tigers and snakes. It led to trouble: ". . . with his foot on the python, my father looked up," I was saying, one day. "He looked up and saw not one but three tigers."

"That's not true," said a girl with some sense.

"I swear it's true . . ." but there was Sister Irene and she beckoned me.

"Come with me," said Sister Irene. Feeling small and chilled, I went.

The nuns used public opinion as a rod and I was publicly shamed. As a branded liar I was told to wear my class badge upside-down. "All people are liars," said Jon and wore hers upside-down too. When told she must not, she still did it and was sent to Sister Gertrude.

"This spirit must be broken," Sister Gertrude told her and proud mature Jon was sent to bed with the Juniors.

I can see now that it must have been almost as difficult for the Sisters as for us.

In lessons, for instance, we were years ahead in reading and poetry. Jon, in art— both of us in geography; but we had not heard of algebra, geometry, physics, science or Latin, and so had to be put at the bottom of the bottom class of the Senior School; we were too old for the

36

Juniors. Again I managed better than Jon, having a parrot quickness that she, who was more honest, did not possess. I found that the way to cope, for instance, with literature—the *Book of Ballads* and *Julius Caesar*— was to learn them both by heart. I could gabble:

> You-all-do-know-this-mantle-
>   I-remember-
> the-first-time-ever-Caesar-put-
>   it-on
> Twas-on-a-summer's-evening-in-
>   his-tent-
> that-day-he-overcame-the-Nervii.

"Who are the Nervii?" asked Jon. "It doesn't matter," I said and began on the *Ballads*.

> He-was-a-braw-gallant
> and-he-played-at-the-glove,

"What glove?" asked Jon, "and what's braw?"

I also learnt to cheat. I used to look over at the papers of the girl next to me and copy. Sister Margaret was taken in and thought I was improving. "That's the way," she said encouragingly.

"One day you will be found out," said Jon.

It sounded all too probable but I was so miserable already I did not think it would make any difference. All the same I think I worried about it. There was a big clock in the gymnasium that chimed every quarter, like St. Joan's voices in the Bernard Shaw play:

You-must-go-on,
You-shall-save-France.

In those nights I used to lie and listen to quarter after quarter, and then to the slow striking of the hour: One—another long, long pause—Two—sometimes I heard a little sound from Jon but we dared not speak to one another. All round us girls were sleeping and breathing lustily. Tears used to trickle down my nose and soak the pillow. "Sick for home . . ." to the depths of my being I found out what those words meant.

Some of our misery was physical. Jon had

malaria of which the School Infirmarian had no experience; when Jon's temperature jumped and then sank, as malaria temperatures do, sometimes up to 105°, two hours later below normal, she was accused of rubbing the thermometer on her blanket—a school trick we poor innocents had never heard of—and she was told to get up, dress and go back to her class at once. She soon had a painful cough.

We were stupid with head colds and had chilblains; we looked at our swollen purple hands with horror. Sister Irene gave us malt and codliver oil but the taste stayed in our throats and it was as difficult to get down as was the food. From the beginning we had disliked and dreaded the school food; I shall not forget my first sight of porridge, and when at lunch a pudding was put on our table, suet, encasing rhubarb, or suet with raisins, "What is it?" we asked. We were not being captious, we really wanted to know and though we did not believe the answers, "dead baby" and "spotted dog", they made it harder to eat the puddings; as nothing was allowed to be left on our plates, we choked with dead baby and spotted dog and grew thinner and thinner.

Perhaps our greatest shock was that Mam seemed to take it for granted that we should be unhappy. "School is always like that at first," wrote Mam. "You will get used to it, then you will like it," wrote Fa. "Like it!" said Jon as if she had been stung. "I shall never forgive them for this. Never!" It was the first time we had known that a father and mother could be against their children; indeed, with great love and tenderness, they made things worse.

They had decided that perhaps it was the religious life of the Convent that was a little too strict. The religion was one of the few things we really understood though we had not known you had to pay to go to church—we went to the parish church on Sundays.

In the general austerity and chill of St. Monica's, the colour and warmth of the chapel were beautiful, with stained glass, deep crimson carpets, lit candles and music. The nuns and choir sang, we thought, like angels and the religion was romantic; for chapel we wore little round caps of blue, like medieval pages, and, on Sundays, black net veils that made us feel like madonnas or nuns. Feast days were especially glorious, with lessons interrupted and processions and chapel at odd times. Then Mam wrote to Sister Gertrude asking for us to be excused from chapel.

For the nuns this was the last straw; offended and shocked they shut us out. Now we were really outcast, horribly and conspicuously alone. Sister Gertrude's announcements would be: "Tomorrow is the Feast of the Birthday of the Blessed Virgin Mary. The whole school will attend Mass at eleven—except the Goddens," or, "There will be Vespers after tea tonight for everyone except the Juniors and the Goddens." If she had said "the barbarians" she could not have sounded more scornful and we burned in our heathen shame.

Jon and I did not stay at St. Monica's, not even to the end of term. When we were told we must not close our letters home but leave them open so that Sister Gertrude could read them, Jon said she would not write at all. Mam became alarmed at the silence and asked a friend who had known us in India to call and see us. She came when we were in class and was told we were not available but the friend was Jon's adored, and aristocratic, Mrs. Hely-Hutchinson, who calmly replied that she would sit in the Sister Superior's office until we were available. When we were produced, as we speedily were, she was so shocked by our looks—especially Jon's—by our thinness, coughs and our hollow-eyed misery that she telephoned Mam and we were taken away next day.

A taxi came for us. It was a perfect early December day of blue and sun; fallen leaves crackled under the tyres, winter colours and cobwebs sparkled with dew. It was like being snatched up to heaven in a chariot, with the taximan as the angel.

I had hated Sister Gertrude for what she did to Jon with a child's hatred which is searing because it is unmitigated. "One day I shall write a book about you," I thought with darkest intent.

Even then I was certain I was destined to be a writer—even before then. Like

Harriet of *The River* I used, in Narayan-gunj, to keep my poems and stories in a secret place, a hollow in the trunk of the giant cork tree that grew in our garden—it had white flowers and was circled by a bed of amaryllis lilies. At St. Monica's there was no secret place. Sister Irene regularly went through our lockers so that I could not even make notes but indelibly every moment is etched in my mind; yet, when that thought came full circle and I did write a book about nuns, *Black Narcissus*, I mysteriously could not take that revenge.

The ending of my *New Yorker* story of "The Little Fishes" is fictitious in that it tells that we adapted to school life, which we never really did. "Too late," Grandmother had said and I suppose we have always been intransigent and farouche. Jon and I went to five schools in the next two years.

It was altogether an unsettled time. Fa had refused to buy a house in England as he would then have had to pay English tax; in consequence we moved from rented furnished house to rented furnished house, taken for only six months, at most nine because Mam was always on the point of going back to India and Fa—and did not go. The houses had to be cheap and they were small with shabby furniture. Somehow Mam managed to make each a home. She ran up curtains; we had a few pictures and pieces of china and there were always flowers—her great joy—but it could not have been easy for her and Jon and I made it worse.

Fa had been remote from us but his very presence instilled respect; Aunt Mary of the astringent tongue would stand no nonsense but she had left us to make a home for Uncle Alfred and with Mam we did what we liked. Jon, spoiled and wilful, cowed the whole house with her tantrums; too highly strung she was often ill, sometimes seriously, while I went from one lofty scheme to another, not caring whom I penalised.

It was partly unhappiness, the feeling of being misfits; we would not ask any of our school friends to those shoddy houses, so that we saw almost no-one but each other, Uncle Alfred Edward and Aunt Mary, one or two families with children of Nancy's and Rose's age and a few female friends of Aunt Mary's—except Uncle we never spoke to a man or a boy.

Eastbourne, too, seemed to me the epitome of mediocrity. I liked extremes; I did not know any duchesses or any charwomen but I think I would have liked them equally. "Eastbourne's all middle, middle, middle," I used to moan. In this I was right; Eastbourne, in a way, was opulent with its wide roads, big houses standing in gardens, its squares, a sea front with expensive hotels and promenades; true, it had a pier but no shops along the Front, no booths or pierrots on the beach. Most of the visitors, as well as the people living there, were self-satisfyingly middle class. "Not quite out of the top drawer," Aunt Mary used to say—as if she were out of it herself. Conventions were strict; speech was refined—nothing vulgar was allowed to intrude. I suppose something in me recognised the artificiality; even today people, for me, are divided into those who like Eastbourne better than Brighton—or Brighton better than Eastbourne, dear honest Brighton, unashamedly itself, admitting—no, welcoming—all shades of life.

I pined for London, not of course the London of Randolph Gardens but of adventure. No-one, I was sure, could have adventures in Eastbourne. In adolescence things, good or bad, seem as if they would go on for ever; good or bad would at least have been interesting—for us Eastbourne was simply dull, and I despaired of ever getting away from it.

There were, though, two mitigations, more important than we knew: Eastbourne's Devonshire park with its theatre and winter garden, and Uncle Alfred Edward.

Devonshire Park Theatre was large for a provincial town and endearing with its rose damask walls, white paint, rose velvet seats and stage curtain with, over the proscenium, cherubs and masks round a painted motto: "To hold as t'were the mirror up to nature." Aunt Mary and Mam were addicts but, once again and more regretfully, it was not Shakespeare we went to see; thrilled to the bone we saw Oscar Wilde's *Lady Windermere's Fan*, we saw plays such as *The Garden of Allah*

—its camels were walked every day for a week along the Front—saw or heard *The Desert Song* and *The Maid of the Mountains*. I can still hum:

> At seventeen, he falls in love
>   quite madly
> With eyes of a tender blue.
> At twenty-one, he gets it rather
>   badly
> With eyes of a different hue.
> At thirty-four, he is flirting sadly
> With two or three or more.
> But it's when he thinks he's past
>   love
> It is then he meets his last love
> And he loves her as he never
>   loved before.

The Winter Garden famed for its concerts was a different matter and it was there that we began to have an inkling of, not romanticism, but true art and dedication; in those years we heard great orchestras and artists: Kubelik, Heifetz, Suggia, Adila Fachiri and her sister, Jelly d'Aranyi, Rubinstein—by ill luck I twice missed

Paderewski; even more unforgettably, we saw Anna Pavlova.

And Uncle Alfred Edward?

He and Aunt Mary had built a house almost on the Downs—Sussex's green hills that roll from the sea far inland. As the house was on a corner of the golf links it was named The Corner; though we thought nothing of it then it could have been called "the corner that held them", our only anchor in those uncertain years, and it was through Uncle that our obstinately blind young eyes were opened to England, its traditions and beauty.

He was a calm, quiet and peaceable man who asked only to be able to devote himself to his garden, where he toiled wearing a disreputable Burberry and an old tweed hat. Like the Godden Aunts he could not have wanted us, yet he was forced into being a proxy father, and every fine Sunday of those summers, he would come chugging up in his snub-nosed Morris Cowley two-seater, Aunt Mary beside him, to take two of us, turn by turn —there was a dicky seat that would take two perched high behind—into the country and to the river, the Little Ouse, where he kept his canoe.

Though it was difficult to believe when we knew him, Uncle had been a young blade at Oxford; the canoe was called "Dream Days" and had gold-coloured velvet cushions and paddles with his college crest. I wrote about it in my secret book—everything about my writing was secret then; it was not a diary, perhaps an attempt at a journal, often imaginary and full of clichés.

Dream Days, 1921.

With the quiet dip of paddles we drift under tangles of wild roses, meadows of buttercups and lady's lace, past swans and moor hens, with glimpses of village roofs among trees, a church spire or tower and, made blue by the distance, the rolling Downs . . .

For once the clichés were true. Uncle Alfred Edward drove us up onto the Downs to Alfriston for the cowslips; to small walled towns like Petworth and to Midhurst with its famous Spread Eagle inn, not that we ever went into it—it was picnics for us. I was born in Sussex and Sussex is where I would choose to live and did live for sixteen years, the longest I have stayed in one place, the ancient town of Rye where I came to feel, not an outsider, the perpetual "stranger" I seem fated to be, but at home; I am sure that was rooted in Uncle Alfred Edward.

He and I had a special affinity. Long before we came to live there he took me on my fifth birthday to Eastbourne's prestigious toyshop, fittingly called "The Children's Paradise" and let me choose my own birthday present. Afterwards, we had lunch in his rooms where he had provided my favourite, a pink fruit jelly—for years I puzzled over how the fruit got inside; there were no holes. Allowed to serve, while he and Mam were talking, I ate it all. Uncle would not let me be scolded.

It was for Uncle Alfred that I bought the Christmas present the family has not let me forget. With us, Christmas has always been kept in the true meaning of Christmas but still necessitated giving presents, a problem for girls who had as little pocket money as we; Jon a shilling a week, I ninepence, Nancy sixpence, Rose threepence. "It's the thought that counts," said Aunt Mary but the smallest thought needs some embodiment. The "Littles", as Nancy and Rose were called, had, helped by Mam, the monopoly of things we could make easily and cheaply, spills, pen-wipers, cross-stitch book markers. "You two big ones must think of something else," said Mam. Somehow we managed—until it came to Uncle.

Like the canoe, "Dream Days", Uncle Edward's things were unusually elegant for a provincial town solicitor; his books had leather bindings, his handkerchiefs and his slippers were hand made, his pipe and tobacco of the best. How could we give him a lead pencil, a packet of drawing-pins, a cake of cheap soap which was all our money could run to? Every year we asked ourselves that same question but our second Christmas in England it was acute. I found myself with only threepence to spend on Uncle Alfred Edward.

"Give him a card," said Jon who was happily furnished with a comb-case she had made, but cards were considerably paltry and all presents were distributed

51

with horrible publicity from the tree in Aunt Mary's drawing room.

"Nothing for Uncle!" she would say, and at four o'clock on that Christmas Eve I had nothing.

We, Jon and I, were standing outside a bookshop and I was turning over a tray of second-hand books marked "All at 3d". It was the 3d that had attracted me, not the books; they were shabby and dirty and at no moment had I thought of giving Uncle Alfred Edward a book. Books were of grown-ups' bestowing. We had been shopping all afternoon and were tired and hungry but then I saw it.

It was under the tray and under a sheet of newspaper as well; I think now, it had been put there for someone to come and fetch quietly away. Lifting the newspaper I caught sight of a book, its cover of clean white vellum, stamped with gold. It looked not unlike some of Uncle's own books and I could not imagine how it came to be in the 3d tray but, cautiously, I drew it out, opened it and took a quick look inside. It was poems with a few pictures, and obviously quite new; most of the pages were uncut. I felt the end papers which were of satiny white paper stamped with a curious little object in gold that conveyed nothing to me at all, nor did the title. I could not stop to read or look very carefully and in any case was stunned by the binding and paper. I could hardly believe my luck.

The custom at that bookshop, for a buyer from the cheap trays, was to take the book of his choice and leave the money in a saucer set on the tray; at that price one could not expect the attention of a bookseller. I had an uneasy feeling that I should have gone in and asked about this book but, "It was in the threepenny tray," I said to Jon afterwards and I dropped my threepence in the saucer, put the book under my coat and ran all the way home.

I showed the book to Jon but there was no time to do more than glance at it, because Mam was waiting for us to take our presents up to The Corner and hang them on the tree for the Christmas afternoon party.

We are in the bedroom we shared, changing in the winter cold—few people had heating in their bedrooms then. I am shivering with cold and uncertainty.

"Wrap it up," urges Jon but I still hesitate.

"Jon, there's a picture of a naked man and woman on the front."

"Probably gods," says Jon. Gods, we knew, are allowed to be naked as long as their hands are properly disposed.

Then I see there is a subtitle and read it aloud, "The Eight Attitudes and Sixty-four Ingredients of Love." It sounds strange; I had not known that love had attitudes or ingredients. "*Will* it do for Uncle?"

"Well, Mam says he is the most loving man we know," says Jon, "and it looks quite new. Hurry. Wrap it up."

Uncle opened my parcel almost at the last. I was covertly watching. He undid the string, opened the paper and looked. After a moment I began to think he was stunned, he was so still. I took this as a tribute; it was a surprisingly handsome book to come from an obscure niece. He opened the front cover, still keeping the book in its paper; not once did he lift it out proudly to public view as I had hoped. I had written a card, "To Uncle, with love", with my name underneath and he shot a look in my direction. Then I saw that he had coloured deeply—with pleasure? I wondered—and all at once I was as uncertain as I had been when I saw the naked gods. The next minute he had wrapped the book up again and thrust it under all his other presents and, his fingers trembling a little, began to undo Rose's packet of spills.

He had been quick but not quick enough for Aunt Mary. "Why Alfred, what have you got there?" she asked.

"Nothing," said Uncle with strange briefness.

Nothing! My precious book! I opened my mouth but I got a look from my Uncle that I had never had before, a look that quelled me.

"But I saw . . ." Aunt Mary began.

"It's a book of poems," said Uncle. "They are only for me."

"You funny girl," said Aunt Mary who had caught a sight of my card and immediately thought I had written them. "Poems! Uncle doesn't go in for that sort of thing at all."

There was a sudden sound from Uncle.

I raised my head and looked at him. He was quietly opening his presents but had it sounded like—a chuckle? I think it was a chuckle: the book was the *Kama-Sutra*.

When Uncle Alfred Edward died he left me a treasure, a miniature eighteenth-century tortoiseshell and enamel snuff-box that held not snuff but a singing bird that springs from a gold filigree nest when the box is wound and the catch pressed; it sings the lark, the nightingale, the thrush and the robin, moving its tiny brilliantly feathered head and wings.

Uncle had, of course, no idea of how we tormented Mam, we were on our best behaviour with him. Not even Aunt Mary knew—Mam was too loyal to tell her—but it came to a crisis the summer Jon was to be eighteen. Driven to desperation Mam made a typically Mam plan, then announced that, for the holidays, she was taking us to France.

"France! *Us?*"

For once we made no objection. We could not; our breath had been taken away.

# 3

## The Greengage Summer

"WE are going," said Mam, "to the Battlefields of France"— she said those words in capitals —"and perhaps when you see the rows and rows of crosses for those young men who gave their lives for you, it might make you stop and think of your selfishness."

Mam did not make the impact on our lives that Fa did, simply because she was always there; from the moment Jon was born, Mam lived for, and through, her children with little regard for anyone else, even Fa, even Aunt Mary, who as the younger and unmarried sister clung to her; Mam could be a juggernaut for her children, yet she was naively innocent, something she never grew out of. When Mam was seventy, my daughter Jane was to say, "Mam, you are half an old lady, half a little girl," which was true and gave her a sparkle—Mam's favourite drink was that pretty mockery of a wine, sparkling burgundy.

She hardly reached up to Fa's shoulder but he was no match for her when she made up her mind which, usually quiescent—she was the least talkative of women—she would suddenly do and often for something fey, those long trips across India trailing the four of us and now to France. Mam had never been to France or anywhere on the Continent, she spoke no French but this was a crusade; her cheeks were flushed, her blue eyes determined. "We have to change trains at Rouen and have two hours to wait so I shall take you to the market place to see where Joan of Arc was burnt"—she had read it all up thoroughly—"St. Joan, too, might make you think. And," she added, "you are not to tell Aunt Mary. She thinks we are going to the seaside."

We did not see where Joan of Arc was burnt; all I remember of the time in Rouen were our first French strawberry tarts which we ate—Rose in heaven—while we spent the whole two hours in a pâtisserie opposite the station because Mam could go no further. She had not absolutely deceived Aunt Mary; we had been at the seaside in Varengeville in Normandy for three weeks and there Mam had been bitten on the leg by a horsefly—"That's France for you," Aunt Mary was to say when at last she knew. On the train Mam's leg began to swell with agonising pain; Jon and I knew enough about fevers to know she had high fever; by the time we arrived in Paris she was helpless.

I can see us now, the four of us on the platform of the Gare de l'Est, grouped round Mam who sits on our suitcases. "Children you . . . Jon . . . Rumer . . . you must . . ." is all she can say, but though Jon and I are, to our minds, quite old, not children at all, we are oddly inexperienced and tongue-tied into shyness and dismay. Nancy, stilled for once, can only hold Mam's hand, patting it but when Rose, trying to lean against Mam, touches her leg she gives a cry, almost a shriek. Rose begins to cry too. No-one takes pity on us.

"What are we to do?" I ask.

"Go to Château Thierry," says Jon.

Mam had asked a clergyman, turned theosophist, friend for advice—always attracted by any religion that was not orthodox Mam dabbled for a while in theosophy—and he had told her that Château Thierry, a town on the Marne, had been the American Headquarters in the war. "If you want to see the battlefields there can be no better place," he had said and recommended a small pension, the Hôtel des Violettes. As with Joan of Arc, we failed to see the battlefields but we did reach Château Thierry.

Not without a private battle. "Jon, you must get a porter and ask him," I said.

"You speak better French. You ask him."

"I don't speak better French."

"You do."

"Girls," said Mam feebly, and, "Go on," commanded Jon.

I had to beard a horrible and extortionate porter like a bear in a blue blouse and station cap; at first, he could not understand a word I said—which was not surprising—until at last, "Château Thierry," he shouted; it sounded as if he were swearing and we wondered what was wrong with Château Thierry. Mercifully the train left from the same Gare de l'Est; he shouldered and swung some of our suitcases, we carried the rest, another porter almost carried Mam and, after parting with far too many francs, we found ourselves in a second-class compartment, bumping slowly through a flat countryside. Jon and I grew more and more frightened as Mam spoke not a word; Nancy as well as Rose was crying. We were dizzy with tiredness and hunger—the strawberry tarts seemed an aeon ago and it began to be dusk as we bumped towards this unknown Château Thierry.

It is difficult, with the novel I was to write about those two months in Château Thierry and the film that followed it, to know what I remember as happening, what is transposed in the novel, and what is overlaid by the film; each seems to shimmer through the others. I do not know if we really had to walk from the station, Jon and I one on each side of Mam holding her up, a boy pushing our luggage in a handcart, Nancy and Rose trailing behind as, "Hôtel des Violettes," we said over and over again.

"Si," said the boy, "Si," and nodded ahead to where trees, iron railings and tall scrolled iron gates showed, behind them, a big house with lights. "Hôtel des Violettes". We felt a tingle of anticipation. In the book and film, the hotel was called the Hôtel des Oiellets, but, as I write:

I smell the "Violettes" smell of warm dust and cool plaster, of jessamine and of box hedges in the sun, of dew on the long grass—the smell fills the garden—and, in the house, it is of Gaston, the chef's, cooking: of furniture polish, damp linen and always a little of drains. There are sounds that seem to belong only to des Violettes: the patter of the poplar tree leaves along the courtyard walk, a tap running in the kitchen with a clatter of pans and china, mixed with the sound of high french voices, especially of the chamber-maids as they call to one another out of the bedroom windows: the thump of someone washing clothes in the river sounds close and barges puff up-stream: a faint noise comes from the town and near, the plop of a fish; a greengage falls.

The river was the Marne; and beyond the hotel's formal garden of gravel paths, statues, small flower beds edged with box, an orchard stretched to a wall in which a blue door opened onto the river bank. The orchard seemed to us immense; there were seven alleys of greengage trees alone; they were ripe and in the dining room Toinette, the waitress, built them, on dessert plates, into pyramids. "Reines Claudes," she would say, to teach us their names; always afterwards we called this time the greengage summer.

Madame—I will call her Madame Chenal—was kind; few hotel keepers would have accepted a critically ill foreign woman with four children; the doctor was there that night and she comforted and reassured us, calling in an Englishwoman, a Mrs. Martin staying in the hotel who, herself, had a small girl. Mrs. Martin coaxed Nancy and Rose to eat supper and put them to bed; meanwhile Jon and I were almost overcome by the hotel.

The Hôtel des Violettes had been a

château; it had elegant rooms, a great hall from which a painted panelled staircase led up to a first and second floor of bedrooms —there were attic bedrooms above with mansard windows. The salon was panelled too, with sofas and chairs in gilt and brocade; the dining room had—what particularly impressed me—blue satin wallpaper. Our bedrooms were large with four-poster beds—it seemed at first that there was only a hard bolster, no pillows; we were surprised when we found them in the vast armoires. The windows had shutters too heavy for us to close; we could see lanterns lit along the drive and, even in that night of distress, we lingered breathing the warm fragrance and, again, felt that tingle of anticipation.

"But you were glad enough to come back," Aunt Mary was to say.

"We never came back," said Jon and that was true; for Jon and me nothing was to be the same again.

Poor Mam! How could she have known it would all turn out the opposite of her innocent plan. To begin with, Château Thierry was set in the champagne country, a luxury town to which the buyers came for the vintage. It was, too, famous for its liqueur chocolates—Jon was to be given boxes of them. As the "Littles" did not like them, we gorged ourselves, and on the delectable food, especially the ripe fruit in the orchard. Perhaps part of the feeling of being in a dream was because we ate so much; we were, too, out of ourselves from being so suddenly immersed in France.

We loved the town, I especially; Jon was too taken up with herself really to look. Château Thierry, beside its wide river, was centuries old; its upper and lower town had grown slowly, haphazardly with a maze of cobbled lanes around the Place where the market was held twice a week. In the upper town, a particular cream-washed house with marigold coloured stains on its walls bore a plaque saying that the poet, La Fontaine of the *Fables*, had lived there.

We had learned some of the fables at our last but one school and it made the poet seem startlingly close.

"He lived here!" I stand rooted, staring at the house. "Jon, do you think one

65

day, there will be a plaque on the house where I lived?"

"No," says Jon.

Château Thierry was altogether a poet's town or a painter's, with its houses, spaced along the river and crowded in the streets, showing the faint variations of shabby plaster, and the pink and grey-green of the paint that had blistered on doors and shutters. "The French don't spend much money on paint," said Jon. Up above were the ruins of a monastery's walls, their stone turned honey-yellow. As we looked down from them, the air was hazed with the town smoke against the sky. There were other colours: grains of grey or white that were pigeons or cats: the unexpected pink of an apron, a man's blue overall: a jug, a cask, a child's toy; and there were sounds, the sound of bells, of hammering and clanging from the boatyards, the hoot of a barge and, nearer, the cries of children bathing from the Plage.

Mam had septicaemia, acutely dangerous in the days before penicillin.

"Are there no relatives we could send

for?" asks poor Madame Chenal and before I can open my mouth, "None," says Jon firmly. This is a new bold Jon. In the morning and evening Mam has to soak her leg in lotion and so Jon and I have to go twice to the upper town to get the bottles refilled. We go in the afternoon too because Madame Chenal has arranged French lessons for us.

Probably Mam was trying to salve something from the expedition but she never met our teacher—fortunately. Madame Bec was a voluptuous-looking lady who lived in one of the oldest houses which smelled of damp and crumbling stucco. The lessons were non-existent; she gave us brioche and cups of delicious dark chocolate while we talked English.

Soon our feelings about the battlefields and the war grew cynical—we could hardly help it; almost every day, coachloads of tourists visited that part of France, most of them Americans come to see where their fathers, husbands or sons lay in this foreign soil and, of course, the American Headquarters were of great interest so that luncheon at the Hôtel des

Violettes was on their itineraries. The château had been under fire and the panelling of the staircase had been spattered by machine guns; every morning the kitchen boy came with a gimlet and opened the holes again. With raw liver, he freshened up the bloodstains in the billiard room that had been the guard room where men had died. Mam would have been shocked to know we thought it funny.

For us there was shock after shock.

"Do you know," asks Nancy who manages to discover everything, "Madame Chenal has a lover. What's a lover?"

From habit we squash her. "Madame *Chenal!* She can't have. She's as old as Mam or Aunt Mary."

"She has. Toinette told me," and, "I wouldn't be surprised," says Jon suddenly.

I am—surprised almost out of my skin.

That middle-aged women could make love astounded me; I cannot remember how Madame Chenal looked except that she was plump and pale but Jean Pierre, a French Canadian, was big, handsome with heavy-lidded eyes, astonishingly blue and a mass of wiry dark hair. He smelled of sweat and drink—he was often drunk. Years afterwards, I discovered he was a spy who was trading on Madame's bounty. He fell in love with Jon, at first furtively. He used to get a ladder and climb up to our window as we undressed for bed. The first time I froze with terror and let out a scream but Jon's hand came like a clamp on my lips.

"Be quiet!" and, "You're not to tell—ever."

"Suppose he comes in?"

"He won't."

"Why?"

"Because he knows that I don't like him. He keeps on bothering me," says Jon, "so I asked Toinette what to say and I said it. Salaud," says Jon with relish . . .

"Weren't you afraid?"

"No. Why should I be?" She gives a shrug. "Men do what you want them to," says this new Jon. I am speechless.

69

It was not only Jean Pierre. There was Mr. Martin, husband of the kind Englishwoman; he was English too, young, slim with lazy good manners and perfectly dressed.

They had a four-year-old daughter, Betsy, and to our relief, took charge of Nancy and Rose. Mr. Martin, Madame told us, worked in a bank in Paris; he left every morning before we were up and came back late but during weekends he was there and, in his magnificent car, drove us out into the green and gold countryside, its white roads winding between vineyards where the grapes were heavy. He took us to a restaurant overlooking the river and let us order as we liked. "Comme il est gentil," said Madame Chenal but I saw him looking at Jon, not as Jean Pierre looked, avidly but with a half-unwilling tenderness and this time Jon looked back.

The only people who seemed not to appreciate Mr. Martin were an impressive French general and his even more impressive wife who were staying in the hotel's only suite. She thought it her duty to sit with Mam, to the mutual agony of

both and, "Emil says," she told Mam—
Emil was the general—"you should not
put too much confidence in Monsieur
Martin." As she said it in French Mam
did not understand—until afterwards.

The weeks passed, the vintage began,
and everything, the hotel, the whole town
was filled with bubbling life; on our
evening errand, Jon and I saw men and
women drunk; I remember a gutter
running with wine from a broken cask and
children scooping it up to drink. The
young men were rowdy and no longer
stared at us but sometimes would not let
us pass. I knew enough now to know they
would not have given even a wolf whistle
for me—it was Jon.

Mam said often, "Jealousy hurts no-one
but yourself, don't be jealous," but if you
are, how can you help it? I do not
remember who told me it was not wrong
to be jealous, "It's what you do with jealousy that can be wrong," and that has
comforted me. That summer I was not
jealous; Jon was Jon and I was only I, but
I was sad, a contained secret sadness
because she had gone beyond me.

That August she was eighteen and, for

her birthday, Mam let her choose herself a dress which is imprinted on my memory as are many of Jon's dresses. This was strawberry-pink French voile piped with white and chic—which none of our dresses had been.

The guests clapped when she came in to dinner wearing it. There were murmurs of "Ravissante" . . . "Charmante" . . . "Adorable" and "Heureuse anniversaire!" Madame had told them it was her birthday —Madame had no idea of what Jean Pierre was doing. "Heureuse anniversaire!" they called and raised their glasses. It was the first time I saw Jon blush.

One of the buyers, Monsieur Bosanquet, sent a bottle of champagne over to our table. Nancy wrinkled her nose at the taste of it, Rose spat hers back into her glass but Jon and I sipped it reverently. We took the bottle up to Mam who could sit up now and walk a little; as she drank her wan face took on a little colour, her eyes had an echo of her sparkle. "I had forgotten how it tasted. Nectar!" she said and looked at Jon with love and pride but that was the last night of our dreams.

Next morning we woke to find the hotel

in chaos and full of police, the gates guarded by gendarmes, even the blue door in the orchard. Mr. and Mrs. Martin and Betsy had gone in the night and a Paris bank had been robbed, "Of millions and millions," said Toinette. Mr. Martin was a well-known international thief; Mrs. Martin was not his wife but an accomplice and Betsy was not their child, she was borrowed or hired to add to the illusion of their being an ordinary English family.

We were interviewed by the police, even Rose. When Mr. Martin took us out, where did we go? Did he meet anyone? Did he leave us in the car and go anywhere? Had we heard Mr. and Mrs. Martin talking? Jon was stiff and as non-committal as if she hated them but I felt like a heroine, shielding Mr. Martin and talked willingly until, out of the corner of her mouth, Jon hissed, "Stop, stop."

"But . . . don't you mind about Mr. Martin?"

"Mr. Martin!" Jon made a sound like "p'fui" and looked scornful when Madame Chenal wept, "He was such a gentleman. He left money for their bill." "A gentleman thief!" I did not know whether it was a thrill or a grief.

As if she had been alerted, straight after this, Madame discovered about Jean Pierre and Jon and told Mam.

"Rumer, what do you know about this man and Jon?"

"Nothing."

I refuse to know anything. I am like a snail retreated into its shell, not wanting to put even its horns out. Jean Pierre had climbed the ladder—I am not going to tell Mam that—and had not Jon said, "Men do what you want them to" . . . Then had Jon wanted. . . ? I recoil from that further into the shell but, in spite of myself, the horns come out. Doesn't she mind Jean Pierre's smell? I could not know.

"Nothing, nothing," and I break into hysterical sobs.

Madame Chenal was icily cold and we were asked to leave though Mam was barely able to travel; painfully she took us home where Aunt Mary had to be told—but not everything.

There was an unexpected—and touching—sequel. One day of Mr. Martin's last week at the Hôtel des Violettes, as he was leaving for work, the handle of his attaché case had come off—it would have been called a briefcase now—and Jon had lent him hers, a small case but made of crocodile leather from a crocodile Fa had shot. Jon treasured it but it had disappeared with Mr. Martin.

He was not caught but three months later the case came back, posted to Eastbourne from the South of France—he must have taken a considerable risk to send it. "Mr. Martin, p'fui!" Jon had said but when she opened the wrapping and saw the case, she burst into tears.

It was not all over; in 1958 those strange two months of the greengage summer turned into a novel. Two years later a film was another move away and yet perfect in flavour; Susannah York as Joss—Jon—seemed utterly unlike her yet was Jon to the life. The film ends after the tragedy with Joss coming out on the road between the slopes of vineyards in sun—the film was all green and gold. As she walks, tears still on her face, she deliberately kicks a little stone, sending it rolling down the hill; it has all gone—out of her way—and she lifts her face to the sun.

# 4

## In Xanadu *or* Who Paid?
## The Publisher or Your Mother?

"GO to school *alone!*" I meant, without Jon.

"Jon must get on with her painting," said Mam.

There had been a conclave of Mam, Uncle Edward Alfred and Aunt Mary backed by letters from Fa; the result was a firm decision that Jon and I must be parted. I was to be a day girl at still another school; Jon was to go to art school.

No-one has fathomed why we, Jon and I, were, even as children, true dyed-in-the-wool writers of the kind who, published or not, would write, but it is easy to trace the root of Jon's other and more obvious talent, that line of painters and patrons of art on Fa's side of the family; she seemed set to be one of those rare—and lucky—people, a writer who could illustrate her own books or an artist who could write her text, but soon it became clear she could do more than that.

In April 1917 when Jon was eleven, Fa had become due for long leave and as, because of the war, he could not go to England, we spent six months in Kashmir. In Gulmarg, the accepted hill station, an Exhibition of Art was held every summer in the Gymkhana Club to which artists, both professional and amateur, from all over India sent their work. The year we were there it happened that Solomon J. Solomon, then a well-known portrait painter, was in Kashmir to paint the Maharajah's family; he opened the Exhibition and offered a gold medal which made a special stir.

There was a Children's Section for which we all, except Rose, had entered, Jon with a water-colour of our houseboat on the Dāl Lake. When, on the opening day, agog wth excitement, we rode to the Club on our ponies, Jon's painting was not there. Being Jon, she was immediately sure it had been judged not good enough to be hung; far otherwise; it had been taken out of the Children's Section and put in the main Exhibition, not hung but displayed on an easel because it had won not only First Prize for Children but also the Solomon Gold Medal.

He talked to Fa and Mam; Jon, he said, must go to an ordinary school until she was sixteen and, "Don't let anyone teach her what they call art," he said. Then, when she was sixteen, she should go to the Slade in London.

I do not know why Fa and Mam acted completely contrarily to this sound advice but Jon was taught "art" from the moment she set foot in England. Even before we went to St. Monica's and were on holiday in Wales she had lessons by correspondence from John Hassell, a course meant for grown-ups; he did not realise how young she was until she wrote:

Dear Mr. Hassell,

Here is the pattern of St. John's Wort you said I should draw but I am afraid I cannot find a naked man anywhere.

She had special lessons from the art teachers at every school we went to and, even in the holidays, was sent sketching with a teacher; when she did go to an art school it was to Eastbourne's Art School not the Slade. Perhaps a London school was out of Mam's compass. There was no safe house in Randolph Gardens now; our Grandmother had died and the Aunts had been able to fulfil their lifetime's ambition of living in the country.

As provincial art schools went, Eastbourne was sound, even good and for a while Jon bloomed; she was a student, free to go her own way, taught chiefly by masters who wore fascinatingly unconventional clothes. She was mingling with other students, young men as well as girls and women. All at once she was grown-up.

"Jon, where are you going?"

"I'm having dinner"—with Dana or Susan or even Robert, though in Eastbourne young males of any age were scarce, while I was left to have family supper with Mam, Nancy and Rose; like them, I seemed hopelessly young—and hopeless. "What uniform do I have to wear at this ghastly new school?" I asked Mam.

"There isn't a uniform."

Not a uniform? Nor, it proved, so much else I had hated. To begin with the teaching at Moira House was utterly different, much of it centring round history, and not only of Britain as in all the other schools I had been to; Moira House taught history of the world, from the most ancient of civilisations to the present day, a cycle that took two years. Each period transformed the school so that, for instance, in the Egyptian term we were steeped in Egypt, for the Greek term in things Grecian, history, literature, art, architecture and philosophy, even to the pictures on the walls and the school play. Each of us in the Senior school wrote our own text book of the period, illustrating it as far as we could with maps, reproductions and, for some of us, our own drawings and paintings. I discovered that I loved to learn, which was a revelation as was the ordering of this school's life; we were respected as people, not children; when the teachers had taught us, they left us for their own world of the staff room and their own concerns. We governed ourselves, the older girls supervising and keeping order. I would not have believed

I could like any school but this was different.

It was not of course perfect; in that mainly boarding school Rose and I were day girls which made us, again, outsiders, walking up the hill to school every morning, back at half-past four; she, as a Junior, came out of class earlier than I and had to wait for me in the cloakroom where she had a companion, a little Russian girl, Nina, waiting for her mother who taught French. One afternoon, when I picked Rose up among the rows of lockers and hanging coats, she was unusually silent while Nina sat hunched and did not speak. We were hardly out of the gate when Rose burst into such a flood of tears and sobs as I had never seen. It was dusk but under a lamp post I looked at her; one eye was almost closed, her face was swollen. I took off her beret, her hair was soaked with blood. Aghast, "Rose! What happened?" I said. "What happened? Who did this!" Half strangled by crying she could only sob, "They."

We had all seen cruelty; having lived in India who could escape it? Children twisted and deformed at birth so that, exhibited in the bazaars, they could earn a few pice but that was grown-up cruelty to children. At St. Monica's I had seen, in the way the girls had treated poor Florence, how a child can be ostracised and despised; still they had not physically hurt her but this . . . "They? You mean the others?"

Rose could only nod.

There is such a thing as righteous anger which is good and makes you dare anything; I had felt it against Sister Gertrude over Jon but that was pale to this. We had only been at Moira House for a few days but I turned Rose round, took her back into the school and straight to what I knew was the Head Girl's private sanctum; I did not even knock but flung open the door.

There were four of them—at Moira House no girl, however senior, was allowed to act alone—and the four heads lifted in amazement as I stormed, "Look at this. Look what your school has done to my sister. Fetch Miss Ingham"—she was the headmistress—"Fetch Nurse. Do something."

They did, and promptly Miss Ingham,

Nurse, were fetched—both appalled and, more appalled, the Junior Mistress. "I left them alone for just ten minutes . . . ten minutes," was all she could say.

Her class had been in the art studio at the top of the house where they had been modelling in clay when she had been called to the telephone. "I trusted them," she said in bewilderment. Our family was bewildered too. "Little girls to behave like that," said Uncle Alfred Edward, "Little *girls*." They did not know that when girls are cruel they are more fiendish than any boy. Rose and Nina had had clay rubbed in their eyes, put up their noses and down their mouths half suffocating them, then had it soused away by being held under the studio's cold tap. Worse, two girls had taken a pair of calipers—sculptor's measuring tongs—put a tong each side of Rose's head and hammered them in. Nina they had used as a battering ram, running her head against a wall of drawers; no wonder she did not speak, she was concussed. The bell had gone before the mistress came back; with the children pouring past her on the stairs, taking Rose and Nina with them, she had not seen anything amiss.

A taxi was sent for; she accompanied us home and had to break it to Mam; then Miss Ingham came—poor woman. Her illusions—and the school's—had been shattered. "But they were not your older girls," Mam typically consoled her.

One child's parents were asked to remove her; that much we knew but punishments at Moira House were, as far as possible, private. Rose was brave and came back to the school; though she was to be there for eight years, she was never reconciled to it but I had not been there a fortnight before it became a turning point.

In our close and doting family, it was as strange as it was salutary that my endless poems and stories were dismissed as "only Rumer". No-one saw in them any talent or promise until in my second week at Moira House I met on the stairs the Vice-Principal, Miss Mona Swann, who taught English, choral speech and drama. She stopped me and asked if I sometimes wrote in my own time. "Oh, *yes*," I said with all the conceit of fifteen, "I have had a book of poems *published*."

Mona has the most percipient of eyes, dark, expressive almost to eloquence; they looked me up and down, head to foot, then, "Who paid?" she asked. "The publisher or your mother?"

It was not quite as bad as that. I had read an advertisement from a publisher—I will call him Mr. X—in which he asked for poems to be submitted to his firm. I was too naive to know that publishers do not ask for poems—most would do anything to avoid them—and under a pseudonym, thank goodness, I sent him mine and was not in the least surprised to have a letter back saying they were truly gifted; I thought so too. The only snag was that, though he was anxious to publish them, he would need fifteen pounds against the cost.

In those days fifteen pounds was a large sum, as far out of reach for my kind of schoolgirl as the moon; it should have been daunting but I am not easily daunted. We all had a touching faith in print and, once the poems are printed, thought I, and get into the newspapers, as of course they would, to burst upon the delighted public, they would sell by the hundreds if not thousands. "Mam, will you lend me fifteen pounds, without asking me what it is for?" I said. "It's for something I can't tell you about yet, something you will like. I'll pay you back, I promise. Will you trust me, Mam?"

Mam, as I have said, was not a sensible parent—or was she? She asked no questions and lent me the money. Mr. X was afterwards exposed in the monthly *Truth* but he did print the poems, sixteen of them in a pamphlet with stiff covers, as cheaply as possible and only fifty copies. All the same they were printed, no-one could deny that but, apart from Mam's surprise—or was she surprised?—and Aunt Mary's and Uncle's amused congratulations, nothing happened at all. Fa was half tickled, half appalled, by my initiative—females should not have initiative. He wrote to Mr. X who promptly sent him all the copies, remaindered. Thankfully they were lost or thrown away, thankfully because there was not the least spark of interest in any of them, but I remember the acute disappointment and the letter I wrote to Mr. X: "You'll be sorry. One day I shall be a famous author." Oddly enough, it was not Mr. X's glowing approval but Mona—Miss Swann to me then—and her coming castigations that made me sure that I could really be what I had always felt I was born to be, an author.

Mona herself has written about what happened:

I was first introduced to the Godden saga at a pre-term Staff Meeting in 1923. The two new day-girls, we were told, had come from India where they were brought up.

Rose who had given trouble at her own first school came to Moira House with me; Nancy followed later.

Rose, the younger one [*wrote Mona*], is a horse-aficionada, but the fifteen-year-old Rumer, might be more of a problem. She had already been a misfit at several schools. She would I realised with some trepidation be in my form. I wish I could remember precisely the theme of my next week's English assignment; it was something commonplace concerning the seasons. When I looked through my usual crop of undistinguished efforts, I found one that was far from commonplace. Rumer had created a Red Indian's alert-sensed record of his varying seasonal experience. When I asked her how the idea had come to her, "I had to write it that way, it just came," she said. Further reading of Rumer's work confirmed my first assessment that she was unusually gifted. If I was right, each of us faced a challenge: to achieve her goal had she the humility and strength of purpose to learn and submit to the essential disciplines of the writer's craft? Could I introduce her to them and familiarise her with them without impairing the creative spark which already illuminated her compositions?

Mona must have decided that I could because, a few days after our encounter, she asked me if I would like to omit most of the school curriculum, taking only a few subjects, literature, history, French, music. "I see no sense," she said, "trying now to teach you mathematics and science." How I agreed. "No sense." Instead would I like to work privately with her on my writing?

Would I like? Had heaven opened I could not have been more astonished and exalted—too exalted. Now, I thought, *now* there will be someone who will really appreciate my stories! In the two years I worked with Mona I did not write a single story.

I spent the first term reducing the leader in *The Times* to fourteen lines; anyone who has tried précis will know what gruelling work that is. Another term went in comparing the consonants in "Il Penseroso" and "L'Allegro" to show how Milton achieved the melancholy of one poem, the gaiety and lightness of the other —it is a tribute to Mona that I do not detest Milton! I had to write articles without using an adjective, others without adverbs: reviews in which she rationed the use of "I"—what a pity some of our reviewers have not learned that lesson. I did write poems but always in some strait-jacket form: sonnets, rondels, triolets, even haiku. I studied and wrote Anglo-Saxon riddles . . .

Anything I could devise [*wrote Mona*] to increase linguistic control and to curb verbal wastefulness. Voluntarily Rumer rewrote draft after draft and was ever ready to discuss and learn from the most ruthless criticism. She was mature too in her awareness of and compassion for deprived humanity, and in her rather patriarchal devotion to her sisters; immature however, in three characteristics that deprived her personal (non-family) relationships of empathy: intolerance of ordinariness in people or situations: a veneer of imperialism from her childhood upbringing in India and also, submission to a novelist's urge to endow everyday facts with fictive interest, consequently fascinating listeners by her colourful reporting of them while exasperating and alienating realists.

What even Mona did not understand—and what no so-called realist can understand (and is their "seeing" more real than mine and my kind's?) is that, for us, life itself is a story, its happenings fall into stories so that we can only tell of it in this way.

This is our gift and no-one, not even a "guru" as Mona had become, should persuade us from it—as long as we keep to the rules, because there are rules. Long ago, Jon and I had discovered what we called "truthful writing" which does not mean the stories or studies had to be true, only that credibility was not distorted or manipulated, even in fantasies. A master of this was Hans Andersen; in his *Tales*, a tin soldier can speak but he must speak and act as would a soldier: a daisy like a daisy, which brings me to another thing; it often seems that writers do not see things as they are but as they would like them to be; a daisy is not just the wee modest crimson-tipped flower of Burns's poem but a tough strongly rooted plant—have you ever tried to pull one up?—and it has a pungent smell. Now, for the first time, I was made to look honestly at what I wrote and it was Mona who gave me the confidence to do it. "If you don't respect your work," she said, "no-one else will."

There was something sad in that. I have fathomed, though she never said it, that Mona would not have chosen to be the headmistress she became; she loved teaching, not administering, and her greatest love was for the theatre; she had taught at Michel St. Denis' Theatre Studio and written and published plays as well as books on choral speech.

I never hero-worshipped Mona; that did not occur to me, nor did I know if she particularly liked me; from the beginning I was treated as a professional, which I found infinitely soothing. Once I had to tell her I had not finished the essay she had set me.

"Why not?" asked Mona.

"It was nine o'clock. Time to go to bed."

"If you are a writer and you have work to deliver next day, you don't go to bed until it's done." That made me feel inches taller.

She told me, long afterwards, she sometimes wondered how much more I would take but, rebellious and opinionated as I was, by some marvel I had the wit to understand what she was doing for me. No-one can teach anyone else how to write but one can teach them basic technique, give them a firm grounding; that is what she gave me. And for her? Years after she wrote saying:

> Our time proved to be one of the most rewarding commitments of my teaching career: a rare opportunity to observe the evolution of an embryo author both as a writer and as a character. Week after week until Rumer left school she completed my rigorous assignments and never failed me.

Reading that brought tears to my eyes.

It was not only my writing, it was all of me; unthought-of successes came my way. Eastbourne seemed transformed; the very pavements became benign as I trod them. I see myself walking home after one of Mona's drama lessons in which we were acting *The Canterbury Tales* and she had chosen me as the Young Squire.

> "Embrouded was he, as it were
>    a mede (maid)
> All ful of fresshe floures, whyte
>    and rede.

Singing he was or floyting (fluting)
    al the day,
He was as fresshe as is the month
    of May . . ."

In my head I am saying those lines with a
vision of a youth in hose and a doublet
with puffed sleeves, embroidered with
rosebuds. "As fresshe as is . . ." and I
bump straight into a lamp post.

As if anything more were needed to make
that a halcyon time, the second summer I
fell in love.

Shelagh was a year younger than I, the
only child of a widow, a sensible and
worldly mother if ever there were one,
who knew exactly what she wanted for her
daughter—she made Mam seem inept.
"We like her inept," Jon would have
said but I half-envied Shelagh, half-
commiserated with her over all the codes
and ethics. "Even if I only have one nut,"
Shelagh's mother would declare, "I am
going to have dessert after dinner—with
the cloth properly removed." We did not
have dinner—unless Uncle Alfred Edward

came—only supper round the kitchen table.

Shelagh was outstanding among the other girls, at sixteen almost statuesque, with something Grecian in her beauty; the proud way she stood, the straight eyebrows, short straight nose—which I did not envy but adored—black bobbed hair, dark blue eyes. Shelagh was tall, cool, almost laconic, the opposite of my five foot two impassioned self. I did not know I was in love—that, I would have said, would be with a boy—I only knew I loved and was loved, only that we wanted to be with one another, touch one another, steal hours to be together, talk or not talk it did not matter. Instinctively we tried to keep it secret, we were not "best friends", not friends at all; it was genuine "first love" with all its ecstasy and aching, pain and joy. Perhaps it owed something to Chaucer's Young Squire but whether I was the Squire or Shelagh I do not know—and it had the purity of a chorister's voice before it breaks.

In the 1920s, with people of our background, it had not occurred to most of them that a man or woman could enter seriously into love with someone of their own sex and find it binding. The very words had not dawned; I had a second cousin who was christened Lesbia, which seems incredible, but "What a pretty name," said Mam and Aunt Mary. Mercifully, no-one interfered with Shelagh and me.

I learned a good deal about love in those two years; a smaller steadier one had come to me, beginning a lifetime of pleasure.

Most girls pine for an animal of their own but, even as a child, for me the longing had not been simply for a pet but for an extraordinary or fabulous animal. I would have loved a unicorn rather than a pony, or a salamander or that mythical monster with the head of a lion, the body of a dragon, a kylin, if I had known about them then. A Persian kitten was the nearest Mam could get to this—she always tried to let us have everything we wanted —and, on my sixteenth birthday, not long after I came to Moira House, Mam had given me five pounds, a handsome present, to choose and buy a Persian kitten.

In the pet shop there was a rusty old

bird cage and in it sat a puppy, small, square, black with cream paws and vest. He was of a kind I had not seen before but his eyes, which took up most of his face, looked at me compellingly. I bought him, my five pounds being accepted as a down payment. I now had an allowance of ten shillings a month and pledged myself to pay half-a-crown from that for a year.

I am sure now that the pet-shop owner did not expect me to come back as this puppy was flawed; for one thing, his lower jaw protruded, a fault the Chinese call "Earth covers Heaven". He also had two rows of teeth and was worth precisely nothing—to anybody else—but how glad I am that I met every one of those monthly extortions so that my lifetime of pekingese is founded on fidelity, however slight. I called the puppy Piers, the most aristocratic name I could think of.

He was extraordinarily clever and extraordinarily brave. I had to go to school and he had necessarily to amuse himself through those long hours, which he did; one Saturday I took him to catch the bus up to the Downs—buses were open-topped then—and the conductor asked, "Is that your dog?"

"Yes."

"Then you owe the Corporation at least ten pounds."

It seemed Piers was in the habit of taking himself to the terminus and boarding the bus; he got off at the Downs, spent the morning rabbiting and took the bus home. He was perfectly all right if people left him alone but, often, seeing a small unaccompanied pekingese, they took him to the police station and a bored policeman would have to come and tell Mam, "Piers is in quod again." It cost five shillings each time but again I did not grudge it.

I had six terms with Mona—they seemed amazingly short—then Mam, and the family, decided the time had come when she must go back to Fa and Narayangunj as, except for one leave, he had been alone all these years. Jon was nineteen now, in their eyes fully-fledged. It is odd that no-one considered her painting; it seemed not to have dawned on them that she could be a professional, not on Jon either but then, in our family, we did not have women professionals. She could paint just as well at home in India, they said and, as she would be the only girl of her age in Narayangunj, it was decided that Nancy and Rose would be left at school under the guardianship of Aunt Mary but I was to go with Jon.

Jon? All that time, though we had lived in the same house, or rather, houses—we had three rented houses in those two years —I had scarcely thought about Jon.

Our family seems to have grown apart [I wrote in my book that autumn]. Mam and the Littles—Nancy and Rose—Jon by herself—and me.

"Me" could have been written in capital letters.

Best of all about that time, for me, was that it was private; no-one could enter into it—not even Jon—particularly not Jon.

Perhaps I had to lose Jon in order to find her and also to stand equal with her in the way that mattered most to us, our work—art seems too pretentious a word but, yes, I suppose it was art. Now, suddenly, it seemed she needed me.

This was to be put to the test. Shelagh's mother intervened. Shelagh, too, was leaving Moira House. "The time has come," said her mother. "Moira House, too, is very middle-class"—to us it was the height of aspiration. "I am taking Shelagh to France. A girl must have French. Cela va sans dire, n'est-ce pas?" As Mam did not know what "Cela va sans dire" meant she thought it best to acquiesce. "Not to Paris, to Tours, the best accent in France. Shelagh will study at the Lycée but live at home," which meant, "under my strict eye". "I am taking a modest apartment. I can't afford it but . . ." To our immense surprise and gratification she offered to take me as well.

"Perhaps she needs a lodger," was Uncle Alfred Edward's dry remark.

For two days I trod on air. I would be with Shelagh, live with Shelagh! Then I started to feel Jon's silence; she did not say a word against it, which was all the more potent and I began to waver. "If you don't want to come say so," said Shelagh, "I don't mind," which showed me how much she minded. Mam was no help. She said I had to choose but it was not Jon or Shelagh that decided me, it was India.

All the nostalgia had come surging back —things I had almost forgotten; the sun, the hot sweet scent of flowers in our garden: my cork tree: the warm dust . . . the river . . . it was all too strong. There was, too, excitement in the air. Fa wrote of giving a dance—there were "cohorts of young men"—and there were the clothes; Mam had always spent too much, for Uncle and Aunt Mary to approve, on our clothes but now we were to have trousseaux: four or five evening dresses, afternoon dresses, cotton everyday dresses, riding clothes, tennis clothes—"You'll need them," said Mam, which sent a thrill down our spines—and first there would be board-ship, a three-week voyage. Anything could happen on a voyage!

If, when I was born, there had been a fairy godmother and I could have chosen her gift, I should have asked, like Solomon, for good judgement. I always wonder what my life would have been if I had gone to Tours. It is one of my deepest regrets that

I did not; quite apart from Shelagh I should have been able to speak French which I love, instead of mangling it.

I was not to see Shelagh again for years, nor did we write—letters would have been completely useless—and strangely enough when our separation came, it was not as tearing as was my parting from Piers. He went of course to Aunt Mary—with Aunt Mary it was always "of course"—and to his own end. His very cleverness was his undoing; overlooking Eastbourne's golf course, The Corner was close to a high green surrounded by gorse bushes to which the golfers had to play up without being able to see onto it. Soon after Piers went to The Corner, when they followed their shots onto the green, mysteriously no balls were there, nor were they anywhere in the rough grass around. One day there was a tournament and the umpire, walking along the high edge of the course, saw when the two competitors had played up onto the green, a small dark object come out of the gorse and, swiftly, one by one, remove the balls. A cache of more than fifty was found deep in the bushes. Aunt Mary said she gave Piers away.

I did not know when we left that I would not see him again but I wept all the way to Liverpool where, that October, Jon and I and Mam boarded the *City of London*, of the City Line, bound for Port Said, Colombo and Calcutta.

# 5

## Flat Roofs

I pace backwards and forwards, round and round; sometimes I climb up to look out over the parapet to other houses with flat roofs where, in the evening, Indian women and girls often pace, looking down on the bazaars and lanes where they cannot go unless a father, brother or husband takes them. Are they, I wonder, as frustrated as I? From the parapet, Narayangunj looks an ugly squalid little town; how had it once seemed enchanted? The river that had been its whole meaning, now has only one meaning for me—it leads, to the outside world. Here, there is nothing for me, nothing.

IN Bengal, if a house is built of brick and stucco, sign of the well-to-do, it usually has a flat roof with a high parapet because this is a much used part of the house, families sleep on the roof in the hot weather; it is where boys fly their kites, boys, never girls, though we four used to trespass. Made of coloured paper and fine bamboo, Indian kites are as brilliant and light as butterflies, sending a thrill down the string to the bamboo roller in our hands as the kite wheels and soars; we even glassed our strings with a mixture of flour paste and ground glass so that we could challenge other kites, bobbing the kite three times and sending up a battle cry which sounded like, "Dhari. Dhari. Dhari," but I was too old for kites now.

What is needed is constant work, day and night; constant reading, study, will. Every hour is precious for it.

That is what Chekhov wrote more than a hundred years ago to a young writer seeking his advice. Mona made me promise not to try and get anything published until I was twenty-five; she had debarred me from publishing, not from writing, but how could I work and study here in this place of idleness? It had not dawned on me to look at what lay around me. "Every hour is precious for it," and I did nothing but waste the hours. Chekhov went on, "You are not a child. It is time."

I should have been warned; for one thing our garden that had seemed a world to us looked small; the stretches of green on which we used to drive our herds of guinea pigs, pretending we were David and Jonathan, were bald and shabby lawns; the flower beds held only cannas. Of course Mam had been away for five years—she, who made a garden anywhere she was, and quickly remade this. Besides being ugly, Narayangunj was dull, filled only with jute works up and down the river, while Dacca—called Dakha these days—eleven miles away, had the usual hierarchy of colonisation: the Indian Civil Service Commissioner and Collector: the Chief of Police: Chief of the Public Works Department: of the Railway: the Bank: the Chancellor of the University: a woman Schools' Inspector: the Doctor: the Vicar —it seemed somehow odd to find a vicar in India. There was not an artist or, it seemed, anyone interested in painting, music or poetry among them.

Jon and I had never heard the

contemptuous term "boxwallah", which most of the Europeans and Americans in Calcutta and Narayangunj were, any more than we had heard of the "fishing fleet", girls and young women who were then taken out, or came out, to India for the cold weather "season" in the hope of finding a husband. Had Mam, unconsciously, been one of them? We remembered the tulle dress with daisies. Does almost every Westerner who comes to India come in the hope of gain in some sort or another? For Jon and me, India was home but we were at once caught up in that pastiche. We had had a taste of it on board ship but board-ship times are not meant to last. It is part of their charm; in India, for many people, especially women, the pastiche was their life and nearly was mine.

October 1925.

We have landed in Calcutta. Fa met us with other old friends—and we are in the Great Eastern Hotel for a few days. I am sad to say goodbye to the *City of London*. I liked the ship's doctor but don't suppose I shall see him again. Jon is glad. I think she has left some damage behind her. What now?

Fa and "other old friends"! By Christmas, to everyone's astonishment including my own, I was engaged. "You mean Jon," everyone said when it was announced, but quite long before that we had overheard Mam say to Fa, "Arthur, is it *possible* that Ian Finlayson is serious over Rumer?" and, "He has spoken to me," said Fa.

Jon and I laughed. We had known Ian as children and, because he had so haunted our house, we had thought he wanted to marry Aunt Mary—poor Ian, he was only thirteen years older than I. Then, suddenly, we stopped laughing. Jon drew away as if she would have no more to do with it and I was left, mesmerised, like a little pigeon on a chalk line—a dishonest little pigeon.

I was only just eighteen, still in my dreams, and had lived such a wrapped-away private life in Eastbourne that, except for Mona and Shelagh, people in books were more real to me than people in actual life. Also I knew no young men;

in Château Thierry it was Jon who knew them, I was merely an onlooker; added to which, from the time I first read *Pride and Prejudice* I have loved Mr. Darcy so much that no actual man has measured up to him.

Psychiatrists would, I am sure, have found undercurrents of meaning in this, or at least that I had an inhibition against men. For a while I had; it still amazes me that Mam, when she heard our bedtime prayers—in those days prayers were said aloud—let me plead every evening, "Please God let me grow up good enough to be like the Virgin Mary and have a baby without being married." The reason was simple; the only married couple I knew were Fa and Mam and, even then, something in me rebelled at Fa's Olympian ways; I did not understand then that Mam could twist him round her finger.

Neither Fa nor Mam said a word about my being too young which was strange, particularly of Fa because, though he had helped and advised innumerable young men in their careers and difficulties, he could not abide them coming near his daughters. When, on those balmy nights of stars in our first cold weather, after dancing to the gramophone, we used to sit up late talking to our "cohorts"—chiefly Jon's—Fa would get up in his pyjamas and chase them off the verandah. Ian was different; a senior man, not Fa's contemporary of course, but his friend and high in business rank.

And it should have been romantic; it appeared Ian had singled me out when I was eleven and had patiently waited for me to grow up—as he thought. He wasted no time, met the boat in Calcutta, came continually to Narayangunj and, at Christmas, planned a duck shoot for us and other guests, going far upstream, where his firm's roomy launches and Fa's made a little island of luxury in the loneliness of the vast river.

On Christmas night, after dinner, Ian took me apart onto the high foredeck of the furthest ship and, under those glittering stars, asked me to marry him. I must have known it was coming yet, when it happened, the deck seemed to tilt and run away from me up into the stars. I had no chance to say "Yes." Ian said it for me. "No" would have been unthinkable. "It is yes, isn't it?" he said and kissed me. All his love and longing was in that kiss but I think I only blinked—Ian's kisses never went further than my skin—but back in my cabin I kept feeling my lips. This was happening to me and it was wrong.

I was quite unable to say it: Fa was so tremendously pleased and I, of course, was flattered but when I was asked to show my engagement ring—a big solitaire sapphire —and the cohorts pretended to salaam and called me "burra Memsahib"—"chief, big or great, lady"—which I knew I could never be, it made me recoil; and there were pangs, especially when one called Monty did it. Monty, thin, dark, moustachioed, was said to be a scallywag and I have always liked scallywags; there was certainly nothing of the scallywag in Ian with his kind grey eyes, serious face and small clipped moustache. Though Monty probably never gave me a thought he was the nearest I ever came to Mr. Darcy; he was killed soon after, driving a car when he was drunk, which Mr. Darcy, if he had lived nowadays, would never have done but I knew in my inmost heart if there could have been a chance of the most modest ring from Monty I would thank-fully have given my magnificent sapphire for it.

Then why did I let it go on? I think I did not know how not to and I was immensely flattered: to be a chosen girl, for a while even Fa's—it did not occur to me that, in a different way, I had been "chosen" already so that there was bound to be conflict. There was not time to think of that; Ian arranged for me to come to Calcutta "to meet people"—Jon, too, of course and we were plunged into the whirl of the Calcutta season of dinners, dances, balls, parties, picnics, racing. Hostesses beamed approval on me. "Ian is such a nice man," which he was. "He deserves to be happy," which he did. Flowers came every day and Ian would take a case out of his pocket with a smile and there was a brooch—or a bracelet—once a string of pearls. I had a car and a driver to use as I liked and Ian had borrowed a polo pony for me to ride, so well trained even I was not afraid; he understood my fears and promised, if I liked it, he would buy it for me, "When we are married."

"When we are married." I was taken to

see a possible house; Aunt Mary wrote about sending out linen and all the time I was watching Jon free to go out, dance, ride, play with whom she chose; other men had to ask Ian if they could dance with me; I rode, raced, went out under his protection and I did not want to be protected, I wanted adventure. Perhaps it is Mam's Quaker upbringing, passed in a way to us, that makes me seldom want possessions; now I felt as if I were weighed down with them. I wanted to live light and free—I have always wanted that.

I hurt Ian abominably but not as much as I would have hurt him had I married him; somehow I was saved from that or saved myself because I found the fortitude to break it off, to Fa's dismay and for a time anger; he would never have forced any of us to marry against our will but I had betrayed his friend and behaved badly.

Mam, as usual, said nothing censorious but I knew she was sorry it had begun and for a time I felt in disgrace, rejected by everyone—except Jon. "You were right," she said, "but don't go on about it."

"Would you like to go home?" Mam

asked. "You could train for something" —but home meant Eastbourne. "Perhaps Tours? I could write to Shelagh's mother . . ." but it was too late for Tours. Shelagh after Ian? So I stayed, in a way comfortable again, back in Jon's shadow, but becoming more and more of a misfit in that—does it have to be called "Raj"? —way of life. "Raj" was another word we did not know, but I lived it for two years because I did not know what else to do.

It was not all frustrated and barren; other girls of eighteen start training for a living, go abroad to study French, few go where Jon and I went, saw what we saw.

Those hot weather summers were spent in Shillong, the hill station for Assam, a place of gently rolling hills, red roads and white bungalows with red-painted roofs, a Club on a hill overlooking an ornamental lake, spanned by an equally ornamental bridge. The roads were bordered by white-flowering may trees and blue hydrangeas.

Shillong's people were Khasias, a distinctive tribe, gold-skinned, flat-nosed with heavily lidded slit eyes; the men were skilled archers, the women diminutive and strong, wearing old-fashioned print dresses and a fine shawl over their head and shoulders, tied around the neck so that the two ends stood up behind their heads like rabbit ears. We had a little Khasia ayah to wait on us; she was called Butterfly.

Twice we went into camp with Fa to fish and shoot on the border of Bhutan.

Of those early camps I do not remember much—they have become fused with others that were later—but glimpses break through: a half-circle of tents pitched round a huge camp fire that sent sparks, it seemed, up to the stars and threw a glow into the tents as, with the tent flaps turned back, we lay in bed, smelling the camp smell of warm jungle grass and trees, of woodsmoke and, faintly stuffy, the smell of the tent canvas. From the darkness beyond the fire, a pair of eyes, shining in the dark, would look at us; a jackal? a wild cat? It might even be a leopard. The eyes would look and vanish. Jackals, though, usually went in packs and howled, a fiendish sound; hyenas laughed which was even more satanic and made the "tsswick, tsswick" from a jungle cock sound almost homely; he gives his cry as, suddenly, he flies high, chasing his hen with a loud clatter of wings. There would sometimes be a sudden swift shriek, something caught and killed and, once or twice, in the distance we heard a tiger roar. Even far off the sound brought terror.

By day we fished on the wide pebbly river; there is a snapshot of Jon in khaki shorts and shirt, with tousled hair and look of sheer delight as she holds a giant mahseer she has caught. We rode on the chief camp elephant, Bata Scully, into the greenness of the jungle, its great trees creeper-hung.

Elephants have always seemed my familiars; before Fa went to Narayangunj, he was stationed in Assam on the edge of the jungle and as an extremely small girl I took my airings not in a pram but with my ayah on an elephant inappropriately called Birdie; when we came back and Birdie obediently knelt to let us get down, I always picked her a bunch of grass and she would take the infinitesimal offering with the end of her trunk and stuff it into her mouth.

In later life I adopted a young elephant, almost a baby, who had arrived at the London Zoo from India. He had rickets, was weakly, and had the overlong eye-lashes of a delicate little boy, but my favourite of all time was another camp elephant whom I grew to know well as she and I were both in a way camp followers, I because I did not like shooting, she because she was under-sized and not "staunch"—she would not "stand" but ran away at the sight of a tiger or wild buffalo. I thought this was sense. Her name was Mooltiki and she was the only elephant I have known who amused herself; she was used in the camp as a kind of "tweeny", sent to fetch loads of sugar cane and leaf for the other elephants, carry visitors' luggage, take the cook to market and bring his shopping back; if he had bought a crate of live chickens she would turn her head and lash with her trunk as they made their aggravating clucking. To do all these commissions she had, each time, to cross the river, wide, shallow with pebbled pools and, to pass the time, would put the end of her trunk just below the surface and blow bubbles.

Mooltiki also had to build the camp fire.

The fire is burning low and Fa claps his

hands; there is an answering rattle of leg chains from the elephant lines and, presently—as "presently" as she can possibly make it—Mooltiki comes muttering elephant curses under her breath. She gathers and fetches bundles of wood, even knocking down small trees and breaking them off, her mahout schooling her with fierce cries of "Ari!" When she has brought enough he makes her kick the fire together with a fore-foot. Sometimes she squeals and turns away but is usually cajoled and scolded into doing it but sometimes big Bata Scully is called up to spank her, which she does thoroughly with her trunk.

Bata Scully was a noble and sagacious elephant, always taking great care of her passengers—we did not, of course, ride in howdahs but simply on a pad strapped to the elephant's back. If Bata Scully thought a branch was too low and might hit us, she would put up her trunk and break it off; if a piece of ground seemed to her treach-erous—a swamp or a hidden pit—she would stop and test it carefully with a

119

forefoot before she ventured over it. In those camps she took us for long rides.

We go through jungle undergrowth and tall grasses broken by open spaces where thorn trees grow, with tiny yellow fuzz flowers smelling of honey and peacocks strut and roost. Peacocks are sacred in India, no-one must shoot them though Fa does, now and then, take one for the pot; the taste is delectable. There are barking deer, and red spotted deer. We come on a scarf of butterflies fluttering over the carcase of a doe and Fa has a machan—a platform—built in the tree above it and we sit up all night waiting for the tiger to come back and eat its kill.

The tiger did not come. It was strange that Fa, a magnificent shot—who even shot, in Kashmir, that most elusive of creatures, a markhor, the wild mountain goat of the Himalayas—never got a tiger.

In our second camp something uncommon, if not unique, happened.

Getting up one morning, after we had

dressed and opened the tent flaps again, Jon sat down on her camp bed to put on her shoes; her foot felt something in one shoe; she put her hand in and drew it out, not hastily but with curiosity; on her palm was a small thin black snake, asleep.

She was looking at it when Jetta, Fa's bearer, brought our morning tea. Crash went the tray as he screamed, startling Jon so much that she dropped the snake. "Up on your beds," screamed Jetta and ran for a stick but the little snake had woken, unwound and was moving across the tent floor matting. The stick came down and missed; the snake flicked and, in the flash of a second, showed how dangerous it could be; it was like a whip but Jetta sprang back and it was gone. "Jon Miss Sahib a little lucky!" said Jetta shaking. The snake was a krait, most deadly of all Indian snakes. That same year, a krait dropped from the stable roof onto the flank of one of the horses and bit him; the horse died in half-an-hour.

Jon and I went back to Assam for the Race Weeks that were held in all the tea-garden districts every winter, each district holding its own Week of racing, polo, tennis tournaments and dances. It was a golden opportunity for the "fishing fleet" as there were few girls and, again, cohorts of young men who often led the loneliest of lives in isolated bungalows and were doubly susceptible. Jon, as was to be expected, cut a swathe through them; if she had been the kind of girl who counted "heads" she could have numbered a dozen but, even with the shortage, I did not greatly appeal.

Jon was loyal and saved me from that most desolating of all experiences, being a wall-flower, especially in the days of programme dances when, your card half empty, you spent hours in the cloakroom or pretending to be admiring the night-sky from the verandah. "I won't dance with you unless you dance with my sister," Jon would say. I had to pay by listening to paeans of admiration about her and pleas for intercession. "Couldn't you ask her to be in my party tomorrow?" . . . "Sit at my table?" . . . "Let me drive her home?" Saints are valuable for intercession but I did not feel at all like a saint!

The Assam tea-gardens have their own beauty; their spacious thatched or tin-roofed managers' bungalows and the workers' huts are set on stilts because the monsoon churns the earth into liquid mud, so that they stand high among the acres and acres of tea with red earth roads running between the serried rows and shade trees spreading their lace-like leaves above them; at night, in the cold weather, the roads are lined with glow-worms shimmering in the dark.

Did you know that tea has flowers like camellias, small, white, waxen with a splash of gold in the centre? They grow on the underside of the bushes and the top of the bush is cut to an even spread of green, table-pruned so that the flowers are hardly seen; but they are there and balls of fruit as well. The tea is made from the leaf. The pluckers pick two leaves and a bud at the tip of the spray.

Of all the places of that time, Delhi was the beginning of a lifetime's fascination— if I were rich I should spend every winter in Delhi. Jon and I were asked there one Christmas to stay with John Blomfield, the architect who, when New Delhi was being built, was responsible, under Lutyens, for the Street of Princes; there were princes, rajahs and maharajahs then, each of whom had his Delhi palace: Baroda House: Mandi House: Hyderabad, Patiala, Jaipur, Jamnaghar Houses and many more.

The Blomfields' own home was in one of the wide tree-shaded roads of New Delhi, with spacious houses and gardens, even the roundabouts set with fountains and flowers, all seeming so rich that it was a shock to see an old woman, in a tattered grey-white sari, sweeping up dust and leaves with a little twig broom; to see among the gleaming cars and carriages, rickshaws pulled by straining little men, sweat pouring down their faces, muscles over-bulging on their poor thin legs; few rickshaw men survive after they are thirty years old.

In December, Delhi is cold, a cold of clear sunlight with a sky of palest blue. The gardens are filled with English flowers —sweet peas, cornflowers, sweet sultan, roses, violets—while over walls and up house-fronts rise riots of orange-creepers and bougainvillaea; there are great mounds of bougainvillaea too on the lawns, with hibiscus, poinsettias and the white raht-ke-rani, queen of the night with a scent so fragrant that it is said to make people swoon.

Delhi, then, was still fabulous; for instance on Christmas morning, John Blomfield's rajahs brought him presents:

We hear a horn blow and come out onto the courtyard where, ranged in a half-circle, huntsmen in blue and buff livery with gold epaulettes, turbans of blue gauze threaded with gold, are standing with, at their feet, a magnificent black buck, those deer that are grey-black with twisted corkscrew horns and great dark eyes, eyes glazed now in death, the horns lying in the dust.

There have been seven Delhis and history is in every corner; in the carved red sandstone buildings, in a blue-domed mosque —the famous Delhi blue that had come with the Moghul Emperor Babur from Samarkand. We went of course to the Red Fort.

"Here the Peacock Throne was kept."
"This roof used to be silver," intones
the guide. "Look at the inlay in the
marble," an inlay of morning glory
flowers in lapis-lazuli, carnations in
cornelian. "This is the Emperor's winter
bath which took, for each bath, eight
hundredweight of wood to heat." "The
Queen's bath, see, the floor is inlaid
with so tiny fountains jetting warm rose
water."

"What are those niches for?" asks
Jon. "For soap?"

"Indeed no. Flowers were put there
by day, lamps by night, so that water
flowed over colour . . ."

History for me could not compare with the
excitement of the living Delhi. I particularly loved the Old City with its labyrinth
of narrow streets and alleyways, seething
with people, naked babies playing in the
gutter among goats, skinny cows, pai-
dogs, chickens, while a sacred bull,
meandering through the crowd, helped
itself to grain and sweetmeats from the
open-fronted food shops. I liked the
hubbub: bicycle bells, rickshaw bells even

more shrill, the incessant hooting of cars, shouts from the tonga drivers—two-wheeled carriages whose horses wore head-dresses of feathers and beads. Street vendors shouted, beggars whined, the air was filled with shouts, cries, laughter. I even liked the cooking smells, frying in mustard oil mingling with the stench of human sweat, of animals and, always, cess.

The tall old houses with their shutters and fretted balconies had once been gracious but, broken up into flats and letting rooms, these fronts were hung now with notice boards: "Goodwill Electric Company": "Perfume, Incense, Chewing Tobacco": "Happiness Coffee and Tea House": "Paradise Hotel".

The streets led off the Chandi Chowk, Delhi's Moonlight Square, as famous as London's Bond Street or the Parisian Rue de Rivoli. We shopped in the Ivory Mart; the chess sets, in ivory or sandalwood, exquisitely carved, were too expensive for us but there were ivory elephants, small figures of the Gods and, especially fascinating, ivory balls that had other balls intricately worked inside them. How did the craftsmen carve them? We bargained of course as we had learned to do as children —Nancy was a champion bargainer.

"I'll give you thirty rupees."

"Thirty rupees!" The shopkeeper pretends to faint. "Miss Sahib, I tell you, because you are new customer, because you come from England. I give this ball, *give* it to you for ninety-five."

"Let's go to the ivory palace," says Jon.

"I give what it cost me—no profit— I take ninety." We get up . . . but he flings himself between us and his door.

"At least take a little lemonade. Mohan, Mohan, bring lemonade . . ."

We got the little ball for forty rupees. It is in Nancy's house now, the ivory still as white as when we bought it.

We had the privilege of going with the Blomfields to call on Imré Schwaiger, the great connoisseur of international fame among antique dealers, with not shops but houses for his antiques in London, Paris and New York as well as Delhi. He was more elegant than any man we had seen, thin, almost shrivelled with a nut-brown skin and strangely quizzical but kindly eyes that smiled; no matter what the season or what city he was in he always wore a cornflower in his button-hole. I think he was glad that we were too shy to be enthusiastic. In his hall stood a dancing Shiva in bronze of such beauty that, ignorant as we were, we stood spell-bound in front of it. The Shiva was sold to New York and, he told us, two security guards were coming to fetch it.

He took us into an inner room that had steel doors and showed us some of his treasures that were not for sale. "No-one could buy them," he said. "They are priceless."

Some were from the Moghul Emperors. I remember Shah Jehan's inkpad-stand of jade inlaid with rubies, the watercup made of a single emerald. Jade is cold to the touch and curiously heavy; I have the feeling of that penstand in my hands still.

On one of those days of cool sunlight, the men went out at dawn shooting and we, women and girls, joined them for luncheon, driving out in full panoply, much as with English Edwardian shooting parties. In Delhi they were dressed-up occasions but far away from tweeds and caps and heavy shoes; I had a pale pink dress and a hat to match that I thought pretty, white, straw-brimmed with a chiffon crown patterned in pale colours. As we sat under the trees eating curry puffs, game pie, cherry cake, peaches and ice-cream, small brown monkeys peered down at us from the branches. Suddenly, one of them let fall a stream of shit on my precious hat.

"Now you will be lucky all your life," said John Blomfield. As if the monkey had given me a benison, shaming and stinking as it was—and ruining my hat—I have had extraordinarily good luck and extra-ordinarily bad, as if I had been born under crossed stars. I sense now that it is not luck or in our stars but the working of a pattern we cannot see yet have to trust, a providence, in my case bringing ups and downs so unusual it has often been diffi-cult to believe they were happening.

In those two years, though, as I paced our flat and parapeted roof, it seemed, as it had seemed in Eastbourne, that nothing would ever happen, that I should never find myself; as eighteen turned to nineteen, nineteen to twenty, I was sure my life was over.

Jon seemed content not to paint. She had fallen slightly in and out of love more times than I can tell. Then, in our second summer in Shillong, she met Nigel Baughan—there was no question after that.

As I look at Nigel's photograph now it seems so stiff and posed that it is better to go back to him in memory because he always seemed more vividly alive than other people; his hair and eyes were almost sorrel brown and the eyes lit to show golden brown flecks when he laughed. His skin seemed to glow and I remember, particularly, his hands, strong and gentle, and his voice that had a cutting edge to it when he was angry, as had Jon's, but that could be coaxing enough to have won over even Fa.

He and Jon were a match in looks, charm and tempestuousness; there was one fierce quarrel in Shillong when Jon gave him back his ring, an Australian opal, darker than most opals, deep blue and green with glints of gold. Nigel threw it from the Club's whiterailed bridge into the lake. They were engaged again next day.

It could not be official; Nigel was in the Imperial Tobacco Company, which did not then allow their young men to marry until they had done two three-year tours; he was only mid-way through his first and, as he had no private money, they would have to wait four years.

It is difficult to realise how governed we were in those days by shibboleths, cruel shibboleths. If it had been nowadays, Nigel would have broken away; he and Jon would have made a life together, no matter how poor they would have been—or might not have been; both had talent and Nigel encouraged her to paint. As it was, the tragedy which seems to have been the fate of many of us Goddens was waiting; Jon was to be blighted while I, who by contrast, seemed to have come to a full stop, was steadily making my way.

I still do not know how, in that isolated Bengali town, Jon and I found our way to at least a fringe of what was happening in

London, Paris, even America. We probably read about it in the papers in the Club where we used to go perhaps twice a week in the long evenings—women segregated from the men—when there was nothing to do but turn over the pages of the *Illustrated London News*, the *Tatler and Bystander* and *Vogue*, but where did we get the books? There were none of any pretension in the Club Library. I had not thought of asking Mona to send me books; certainly Aunt Mary would not have done so and we had no account or even connection with any bookshops, yet I remember our delight in the Sitwells, especially *Troy Park* and *Façade*, in Virginia Woolf, especially *Mrs. Dalloway* and *A Room of One's Own*; T. S. Eliot, D. H. Lawrence, Constance Garnett's translations of Chekhov . . .

It probably began when, on my nineteenth birthday, a young woman out from England gave me Katherine Mansfield's *Journal* which, she said, she could not read, it was too depressing. To me it was a revelation and a springboard; I lived and breathed Katherine Mansfield. Not long after that I read *A Passage to India* and, as if I had been a kitten born blind, my eyes were suddenly opened. Were we, the English in India, really like the Turtons, the McBrydes and the Callendars, those righteous, insensitive characters? Was this how people saw us, those people in London whom we had set up almost like gods? I know now that E. M. Forster for all his truth was biased and, too, ignorant of the best and valuable role of the British in India but, at that time, the shock was complete. Once again, a character in a book was more powerful than anyone actual; Mrs. Moore of *A Passage to India* changed my life.

It was the scene when she, the mother of the young City Magistrate of Chandrapore, had stolen away in the moonlight from the amateur theatricals in the Club—how often had I not stolen away from Clubs and parties—and was found by Doctor Aziz in the Mosque.

"Madam! Madam. This is a Mosque, you have no right here at all; this is a holy place for Moslems, you should have taken off your shoes."

"I have taken them off," said Mrs. Moore.

Here was someone, new to the country, who innately and, it seemed instantly, understood its values and gave them respect. I was ashamed of my blindness and ignorance, ashamed of how little I knew of India or had tried to know.

As usual, impetuous, I went about trying to salve this in the wrong way, first by blaming Fa and Mam. Mam had accepted, as most wives then did, that she and her children must be kept apart from Indians but Fa had never, for himself, made a barrier; he spoke not only Hindi but Bengali and some Assamese. In all his working life he never had a strike but was honoured, loved and trusted by all his staff, from the captains—serangs—of his ships, his babus—middle-class secretaries and clerks—to the lowest coolies. He knew their ways and their ideas which he respected but I ranted at him, "Why didn't you give us Indian books to read?"

"What books?" Mam would have said but Fa knew of the *Upanishads*, the *Mahabharata* and *Bhagvad Gita* just as he knew of the Quran, though it would not have occurred to him that a girl should read them. "Why didn't you make us learn Hindi properly?" Mam and the rest of us spoke what is now known as "Johnston" —Memsahibs' Hindustani—with none of the right tenses or proper modes of address. My insistence ended by a babu coming from Fa's office three times a week to teach me in Fa's study but, when I asked questions about Hinduism and its customs—some of which are crude—I do not know which of us was the most embarrassed and the lessons were futile. "Everything is futile," I raged.

Oddly enough it was Fa, to whom I was the family enigma, who helped me. He had not read *A Passage to India*, it was not the kind of book he would read but he sensed I was unhappy and thwarted; he could see no reason for this; all the same he acted. Though he loved his work for the Steamer Company he had four daughters, either at expensive schools or living in luxury at home, and he was perpetually trying to find schemes that would make some extra money. Most were disastrous; he bought an orchard in Tasmania, unseen, which turned out to be a desert infested by rabbits. There was, too, the button machine; our river abounded in mussels of a dark blue sheen, lined with mother-of-pearl. "They would make beautiful pearl buttons," said Fa, with visions of buttons in his eyes, and he bought a button machine, large, black and shining with steel, which was set up in a shed in our garden, to Mam's dismay. Unfortunately no-one had thought how to separate the mother-of-pearl from the shell; they proved to be welded so rock-hard together that this could not be done without shattering the pearl, and the machine vanished from the garden. Now, though, he had found something not only lucrative and promising but of importance to India or, rather, Bengal and in which the Government supported him: the propagation of improved jute seed which would give the peasants a better crop in the myriad small jute fields, spread around their villages and in water dykes along the road.

Fa was allowed the use of a big Agricultural College and Farm outside Dacca, impressive with its colonnaded buildings, straight well-sanded, white-railed roads that led through model fields with experimental crops of jute, paddy-rice, grains and pulses, fruits, sugar cane and wheat, acre after acre. It was slow work. The Indian peasant, like all peasants, is rooted in deep, slow prejudice but unlike Western peasants he is convinced that it is his "karma"—"fate"—to live and die in monotony and poverty, toil and debts, probably hunger and still more toil. Fa talked endlessly to them of 85% germinating seed; of bigger crops, better crops, different crops, and crop rotation—it scarcely made a dent. "It does not matter how we farm," they said. "If we farm well in a bad year, still we get bad crops. If we farm badly in a good year, still we get good crops. What is to be, is to be. What does it matter how we farm?"

Fa pushed on but sometimes he said he felt as if he were pushing the whole of India before him. Now he asked me if I would like to come and help him work in the office and in the seed sheds. I was enormously flattered and pleased; ironically if Fa, who so often seemed my enemy, happened to approve of anything I did or tried to do, it meant more to me than praise from Mam or Jon, Uncle Alfred or even Mona.

I drove to Dacca with him in the mornings. Sometimes he left me in the College all day, keeping records, making charts, diagrams, testing. I knew it was important work and Mona had taught me to be thorough and careful.

I met and worked with the students, in those days all young men, no girls, and irrepressibly impudent and merry. Soon I was accepted; they forgot to be careful how they spoke in front of me, and I learned the precious anonymity of work in which there are no distinctions except that of merit, though sometimes I was chagrined when they lapsed into Bengali or even Hindi, so rapid that I could not follow them.

I rode out with Fa among villages to which there were no roads, only small built-up paths of earth between the fields; sometimes I rode alone, which is astonishing when I think of how women or girls in India now are rash if they adventure unprotected into the countryside; they are safe in a car or bus but not alone, yet we, all four of us, rode out almost every day, two of us or even one, without a groom. We thought nothing of it.

Riding, as part of my work, though, made me look with different eyes as I went cross country among the little humble fields, walled with mud to hold water necessary for rice and which was ladled, from field to field, by clumsy wooden scoops worked by hand. There were bigger fields, yellow with mustard and, always, jute growing high. In the villages I saw small intimate scenes that in the mysterious way of sights and sounds were to come back later in my books.

It was only for one cold-weather season. Fa was due for long leave and we all went back to England in April, but it was an indelible time and has stayed woven into my work. I was not writing then, nothing was stirring—or so I thought—but a small episode happened that was to affect that writing for the rest of its life.

There was, in Dacca, a young married woman—I will call her Dodo—who was Dacca's acknowledged literary queen; it was said she had been a journalist on the

*Daily Herald* or *Daily Mail* and Mam, in her naiveté, told her about my aspirations. Dodo, kindly I am sure, patronised me, no matter how I squirmed. She did not, thank God, ask to see anything I had written but showed me some of her short stories, not asking my opinion which would have been embarrassing because I thought they were punk. She told me, impressively, she was sending them to a literary agent in London. It was the first time I had heard of a literary agent.

Time passed and, at last, I asked Dodo if she had had an answer. "Yes, indeed. Such a kind letter and helpful advice. A true gentleman!" She could not have been a journalist or she would have known what the letter implied; it was kind but firm; the gentleman thanked her for sending the stories but regretted they were not of the kind his firm dealt with and suggested she sent them to *Titbits*. Even I knew the level of *Titbits* and could not help a base little feeling of triumph, whereas I should have been grateful to poor Dodo because, "Those are the agents for me," I said.

The agents were Curtis Brown; I sent my first attempt at a novel to them and they have been my agents ever since.

# 6

## The Little Stick

MY godfather had left me a small legacy which came to me when I was twenty and, back in England, I used it to train as a teacher of dancing. Why? I still ask myself that question and still cannot answer it except that most writers want to do, or have to do, something quite different in their early days; most are wise enough to refrain from things for which they are quite unsuited, as I with dancing and yet, for ten years or more, I lived for it, and from it; it has haunted my books.

> The instruments of music are
> made ready . . .
> Up rose the fair ones to the
> dance . . .
> The wielder of his little stick,
> Whispers them to their places
> and the steady drums

Draw them through the mazes
of the dance.*

That was written in China more than two thousand years ago but, no matter what the country or the style, the wielder of the little stick who is, of course, the conductor, has only to raise his baton in London, Paris, Milan, Monte Carlo, Copenhagen, New York and the overture begins, the lights in the auditorium dim to come up on the stage curtain as the music swells and I, with the whole audience, am excited, stirred and quickened.

"Quickened" means "shaken into life"; that is what dancing does to all of us who have any spark of gaiety and response and perhaps it is what we all need, certainly what I needed at that particular time, though I was only to discover its finer shades far later.

What is mysterious is that Anna Pavlova

* From "The Dances of Huai-Nan" by Chang Heng: born AD 78, died 139. Translated by Arthur Waley.

144

was the only true dancer I had seen. It had been with Jon in Eastbourne. When we came out of the theatre we had not been able to speak even to one another, and that evening has stayed with me as one of the most momentous of my life. It was the beginning of what I can only call a spell. When Pavlova died at The Hague in 1931, I shut my School in mourning.

She was the only one because, in the Twenties, ballet companies did not come to India and, too, for us dancing was not yet synonymous with ballet as it was to become. It certainly was not honoured and loved as it is today; to most people, if they thought about it at all, it was an interlude in opera or the inevitable "transformation scene" that interrupted a pantomime, or even music hall.

Arnold Haskell, that great balletomane, once wrote of the ballet *Petrushka*:

Your ordinary unimaginative theatre-goer will enjoy it as a brightly coloured nursery tale, the love-story of three puppets. Someone with imagination will read into it the story of the awakening of a soul—and souls are more interesting than puppets.

At the end of *Petrushka*, the magician throws down on the stage a toy of rag and straw but we have seen the poor puppet, the clown, shut in his cell by the cruel magician, beating on its wall with his fists, tormented by his love for the doll with her rouged cheeks and tin trumpet; seen the agony of his dance, his poor twisted face, and it is no surprise when he rises renewed behind the magician on the roof of the booth theatre, as the snow falls and the last eerie strain of Stravinsky's music dies away.

I think I break my heart every time I see *Petrushka* but, in 1927, he was a long way off.

In top ballet schools, the history of ballet is taught so that boy and girl dancers grow up in line with a great tradition. I had to teach myself. People, even critics, have thought Marie Rambert was the prototype of Madame Anna Holbein in my novel, *A Candle for St. Jude* but, though she had opened her school long before I came to London, I never met her nor, for years, Ninette de Valois. She had not then started her Company at Sadlers Wells but Cechetti had settled in London, while the Russian influence had not been broken but as it were fused, as with Serafina Astafieva, the Russian ballerina assoluta who taught Anton Dolin, Diaghilev's "English dancer" and Alicia Markova, born Alice Marks, who had danced the Nightingale in *Le Rossignol* when she was twelve years old. As he was dying Diaghilev had said, "Take care of my little girl."

I never saw a Diaghilev ballet—he was to die in 1929; the great names, Nijinsky, Tamara Karsavina, the two Lydias, Lopokova and Kyasht, Fokine, Mordkin, Massine, Legat were only names to me, besides these great dancers taught—if they taught at all—other dancers who might follow in their footsteps, professionals, while I only wanted to give ordinary, everyday children a chance to dance for the joy of it, and did not aspire to teach anyone over the age of ten or eleven. I wanted to use the dance as it has been used time out of mind by ordinary, everyday people in festival, ceremony and religion, bringing rhythm and movement into their lives, vitality and warmth. I have seen shy children transformed by dancing, inhibited children released and, incidentally, faults of posture, legs and feet helped and cured, but I knew, if I were to teach at all, it must be honest—what could be called "truthful dancing".

Mam had always been bewitched by dancing and was determined that all her four daughters should dance. Jon and I started in London as little girls, for the short time we were there, with the Godden Aunt who had escaped from Randolph Gardens. In Narayangunj we could only practise—Aunt Mary at the piano—but, in the hills, even though schooling was intermittent, Mam always found us a teacher of dancing. There was something then called "fancy dancing" and I tremble to think what our cavortings must have been like.

We are butterflies in yellow with yellow muslin wings spotted in black velvet, the wings tied to our wrists. Jon and I circle round one another, each holding the end of a long pink chiffon scarf which we send billowing up in the air, or circle again as Serbian peasants, arms akimbo, feet in red boots stamping, red caps on our heads, full blue sateen skirts, white blouses and boleros. Mam and our dirzee—home dressmaker— must have been kept busy. We are rosebuds, one of forty, in a ballet where a bouquet came to life by moonlight, as a tenor sings "Roses are for loving in the month of June", pink muslin petal skirts, green bodices, wrinkled green stockings—there were no tights in those days.

We danced at charity matinées, in hospitals "for the wounded soldiers"—the soldiers must have been abysmally bored —even in cabarets for fund-raising dinners. Nancy was our star; she could have been a professional character dancer and once danced "Tom, Tom, the Piper's Son" opposite the small Vivien Leigh as "Bo-Peep" in a nursery rhyme ballet.

Mam used suddenly to become highminded, regardless of the torments she inflicted on us. It was the custom at the end of these matinées or cabarets for flowers, boxes of sweets, even toys to be handed up for the child performers; Mam said we were not to have any—we were dancing for the war-effort, to give not to get—and so we had to stand on the stage, shamed in our nakedness—not as much as a chocolate between us—until the last day of the nursery rhyme ballet when a friend defied Mam. "*Poor* little toads!" she cried. "It's not fair. I'm going to give them a bouquet *each*." I shall never forget the relief and gratification of having a bunch of hydrangeas, blue to match my dress; I was Lucy Locket.

None of this was what I wanted now. I shrank from its very memory.

It is curious, considering our worse than philistine background, that Jon and I were never content, with any of the arts, simply to practise them; it always had to be to professional standards or else we would rather not do it at all. The amateur has a great advantage—he does it for love—seldom facing the acid tests of professionalism and probably knows nothing of the real artist's "divine discontent" which feels anything but divine—it is searing. With music, I reached a reasonable standard in piano playing but, for the same reason that I could not truly dance, my left hand was not as strong as my right; I could hear and feel the unevenness and so stopped playing. In dancing I could teach—and teach well—but after that quite promising start, I could not dance.

When I was seven, I fell off a swing. It was in Shillong where, as in later years, we had gone for the hot weather and, like Katy in *What Katy Did*, Susan Coolidge's children's classic, I did what was forbidden. Our swing hung from a branch of a great tree standing in a dell at the foot of a small cliff in our hill garden; on the other side of the dell was a chasm bounded far down below by the road. Not content to swing tamely back and forwards in the dell as we were supposed to do, the "dare" was to take the swing up on the cliff, higher than the branch, sit in the swing while a sister held it and, with a kick, take off swinging at high velocity past the tree out over the chasm, the giddy terror being a part of the "dare" and exhilarating. I did it once too often, the swing hit the tree and I fell with a thwack on my back on a root at the tree's base.

After the first bruising wore off I could walk, even run again, and no-one realised that there had been deep injury; X-rays were rare then and it seemed even doctors had not learned about slipped or crushed discs; when I moaned from backache it was put down to a kidney infection that had become my familiar and gave me bouts of fever every four weeks. It was only when it was noticed I was dragging my left leg and failing in dancing—I had been scolded for being lazy—that Mam realised there was real trouble. Even then it was not until five years later, when we came back to England, that I had any treatment and though specialist after specialist saw me it was too late; the vertebrae had ossified.

I learned to live with it, helped by the marvellous clairvoyant, Michael Thomas, who used infra-red lamps and physiotherapy in the days when there was no recognised physiotherapy. He made it possible for me to do things I had not been able to do for years, not play games—in any case I had no interest in them—but to walk and run naturally, to row, ride, ballroom dance, and to disguise so well that few people realise I have a hurt back. It was unlikely it could be reconciled with a career in dancing, yet that was exactly what I set myself to do. The only person who encouraged me was Michael Thomas himself. "You must, you need to do something physical," he said. "You have missed out on so much," but, "I have never heard of anything as idiotic," said Aunt Mary. "To waste money training for something you know you cannot do." At the time that seemed sharp but, always the most sensible of our family, I think she foresaw, and in her love for me, shrank from, the difficulties and distress I should have to undergo.

I knew enough to realise that behind the success of any art lay years of gruellingly hard work—had I not learned a little of that with Mona? I was ready to work, but perhaps not quite ready for the humiliation. The other students openly despised me; to be the only one in the class who, in an arabesque, could not get her leg more than three feet from the ground and that with effort and pain; who could never do quick relevés, or pirouettes or jump or leap. They were mystified as to why I was there at all but the School knew my purpose and, after we came to know one another, did not think it was idiotic though, "You are always going to find it physically hard," said Madame, which was proved only too true.

For instance, I could not really demonstrate—a bad handicap; as the Japanese say, "One glimpse is better than a hundred words." Only last year I was privileged to see Alexandra Danilova taking a workshop for the American City Ballet. She stopped one of the girls. "No! No! Look, darling. This way . . ." and pointed her foot. A teacher's shoe is not a ballet shoe, it is a sandal of the softest leather with a low heel but there, still at perhaps seventy, was the famous Danilova arch, strong as steel, the foot exquisitely pointed, eloquent in its beauty; the girl looked earnestly, then yearningly stretched her own foot and achieved at least a small echo.

One reason, maybe the chief reason the School took me, was that I paid. There were then no schools offering teacher-training courses as the Royal Ballet and the Royal Academy of Dancing do now; nor were there any grants; you had to be an apprentice and put down a yearly sum. The leading school for non-professional children in London then was Miss Vacani's; she taught the royal children and most of society but, even if she would have taken me, that was not what I wanted. Madame Vandyke, relatively obscure, had a much wider scope, offering Greek dancing, tap and ballroom as well as ballet and had innumerable classes for children of all ages and kinds, from pantomime children who needed to earn money to rich little Jewish girls from Golders Green— Jewish children were always the most responsive.

For quality there was Miss Minna Vandyke for whom I ached with pity. She was a little dark wizened woman with eyes that could flash with temper, grow wide in wistfulness. She was a passionate teacher, even inspired. "If you can teach one child to do one step properly you have done your work," she would say, but few dancers of promise came to that school; she was Madame's sister-in-law and tied to her but spent her days, day in and day out, teaching mediocrity. I have seen her close her eyes to shut out the sight of us.

While I was there, a child came who had more than a spark of talent and I saw what Miss Minna did with her. The child did not stay long—Vandyke's was too ordinary to hold her; she needed to be with her peers and left. For three days Miss Minna had a migraine and could not—or would not—teach.

"For what you need I should have thought there were good enough schools in Eastbourne," Mam had said, almost piteously. I am sure there were but I knew it had to be London. I had finished with Eastbourne.

That autumn Fa, on long leave, had taken a shoot on the Isle of Mull in Scotland, some three thousand acres of rough shooting; he was allowed three stag and there were two rivers for salmon and trout. Jon especially revelled in this; she had become an expert fly-fisherwoman. The house was a low white shooting-lodge on the edge of a loch, ringed with hills and facing a mountain that, in October, was purpled with heather and often capped by cloud and snow. The nearest village was the hamlet of Pennygael that had a small post office shop selling everything from mutton to shoe laces. The school had seven pupils from five years old to fourteen; its teacher was still called a "dominie". It was our first taste of Scotland, beautiful and magical as only the Hebrides can be, but I had to leave it for London to start the autumn term at Vandykes, for the time being living-in at the School.

The big house in the Finchley Road could not have been more grimed and shabby; Madame seemed not to care in the least about appearances. My bedroom was up in the attics, with a narrow iron bed, a piece of old carpet on frayed linoleum, a chest of drawers—the drawers usually stuck—a chair and a few hooks behind the door for clothes. The students' common room, there were five of us, was even shabbier and dirtier but I was ecstatic.

I could feel myself growing, my mind and vision stretched as was my unlucky body. I was impatient with it as I always have been—how right was St. Francis of Assisi when he called his body "Brother Ass"—but I did not let the aches and pain impinge as every day brought me fresh discoveries.

I discovered London.

I love every flagstone of every pavement, every scarlet bus and pillarbox, every taxi: the plane trees and London's myriad flowering trees—to me, magnolias are always associated with London. I love the streets of houses—from my window I can see thousands of chimney-pots; I like the different front doors, the window-boxes and glimpses into basements down area steps. I love the shops, especially the little ones: the bridges over the Thames, the lamp posts, the pigeons and sparrows, even the close, petrol-smelling air.

I was too tired in the evenings to walk so I spent all my money on bus fares riding, if possible, on the front seat on top, to the termini and back again.

I discovered Bond Street where the School had a studio. I discovered hotels; as part of our training, we were sent to tea-dances, fashionable then, to dance with professionals—before the examinations we were forbidden to dance with other men; the tea-dances were held in the ballrooms of great hotels. Madame, too, was often given tickets for the theatre, especially first nights which she passed on to us and, even more rapturous to me, for concerts chiefly at the Old Queen's Hall which had an atmosphere entirely of its own and wonderful music.

The work did not cease to be hard, but, slowly, I also discovered that I had not been as wrong as first it had seemed; I was an innate teacher, which Madame saw at once. I have always been good at telling people what to do, equally bad at doing most things myself.

Teaching needs authority and that, mysteriously, I had yet it is dangerous, leading people to think you know far more than you do and I was not, then, above taking advantage of this; bitter experience brought more wisdom but then, when I was singled out to deal with a difficult child, even stand in for a teacher, naturally I—a new girl—aroused the resentment of the other girls. They knew how little I knew.

I also discovered that I was a ballroom

dancer; in six months I passed the examination and became what I had not thought possible, a qualified teacher and member of the Imperial Society of Teachers of Dancing, the only examination I have ever taken. I have to say, too, that if I had nothing else I had initiative. In my second summer season, I rented a studio in Mayfair's Hertford Street for a few hours a week—it was inordinately expensive— and taught Court curtseys to debutantes; Madame Vandyke had the most dignified and perfect of curtseys and I copied her.

The week before I left Vandykes her daughter came up to my bedroom and asked me, in Madame's name, to stay on as a pupil teacher. "If you consolidate yourself you have a career ahead of you." It was a moment as gratifying as it was touching, I felt I had vindicated myself. Once again I perhaps made the wrong decision—London had become my "place"—but I thanked Madame with deep gratitude and said I must go back to India.

There had been a dark shadow over this time; Jon and Mam had followed me to

London, Mam as thrilled by it as I, though our pattern was the same; as we had rented furnished houses in Eastbourne, we now rented flats in London. It had been intended that Jon was, at last, to go to a distinguished Art School, though not the Slade. Whether it was the prospect of this —she had been away from painting for a long while and knew her drawing was weak—or whether it was the separation from Nigel we did not know but she had a bad nervous breakdown which lasted for months, over a year.

None of us or the doctors—Jon had innumerable doctors—could fathom what was the matter; she shut herself in her room, wrote letters to Nigel, paid no attention to Mam's worries. I paid no attention either and was too absorbed in what I was doing, all this new life, to be anything but so callous that I hate to look back on it, but perhaps young people need to be callous if they are to achieve anything.

Next April Nigel came on leave and we moved to a delightful ground-floor flat in Chelsea opening on to Sir Thomas More's mulberry garden, and, surprisingly, Jon and I had our first work published

together in the *Illustrated London News*;
as my part was poetry it was not breaking
my promise to Mona.

### In the Realms of Fantasy★

#### The Death-Dealing but
#### Well-Intentioned Monster

In the curve of my back I carry
  a lake,
Silk green with floating
  waterflowers
And a laddered house with
  pink-tiled towers . . .

#### The Country Cousin
(He comes to town and finds
himself not elegant enough.)

Streets filled with sun and
  drinking wells,
Wheelbarrows and rickshaw bells,
Catsmeat and twisted fishing lines,
Sweetshops with painted market
  signs,

★ The *Illustrated London News*. Christmas Number.
1929.

162

Flags and dogs and wooden towers
And girls with faces like white
flowers
On sturdy stalks
The wicker sandals that I wear
hang heavy on my feet . . .

Poems and illustrations were mannered chinoiserie—it was the day of art nouveau and chinoiserie was in the air. The first book I was to have published was also chinoiserie of a whimsical and affected kind of which I now blush to think, but the poems had a certain crispness and wit; the illustrations were sharp, in clear colours —and both had charm, than which to a serious artist nothing could be more deadly.

It was an odd little interruption—or a reminder.

If Mam and Fa had known what was in my mind when I went back to India that autumn, they would not have been as complaisant; it was to open my own School of Dancing in Calcutta.

Once again the family was split up. Mam and I, with Nancy this time, sailed to India. Jon, mysteriously, elected to stay behind and go to Paris with Rose who was to be "finished", as girls were then, at a school in Bellevue while Jon, spurred on, I am sure, by Nigel, was to start painting again—there were still two years to go of the four years' ban on their marrying.

I started my teaching in a modest and safe way in Darjeeling, safe because it had few of the barriers I was presently to encounter in Calcutta. Indians and Europeans mingled at the Club and at Government House—the Bengal Government, then, moved to Darjeeling in the hot weather. They met, too, at one another's homes and Mam, for the first time in her years in India, made firm friends with two Bengali sisters, Mrs. Majumdar and Mrs. Chaudhuri, who had been among the first women to go to Cambridge University, to Girton. Mr. Majumdar was a barrister and had a house, Point Clear, high above Darjeeling's town. Point Clear became the focus of bountiful entertaining for young people and was the beginning, for Nancy and me, of a friendship that has gone into the fourth generation, the daughter Tara having herself two daughters who went to school in England and became, in the holidays, extra daughters of mine, fitting exactly in age with my own Jane and Paula. When they had children these, too, knew one another. Mrs. Majumdar was godmother to Paula whose second name is Janaki, after her godmother; Janaki means firefly.

The Majumdar household was strange, Mrs. Majumdar and Tara being Christian while Mr. and the two sons, Jai and Kuran, were Hindu Brahmins. Jai was in the Hussars, wonderfully handsome especially in the dress uniform of scarlet, dark blue and gold; Nancy almost married Jai though I do not know what Fa and, equally, Mr. Majumdar would have said. The younger, Kuran, was in the air-force. Both brothers were killed in the Second World War but their cousin, Muchu Chaudhuri, also in the Indian army, became Commander-in-Chief after Independence and later High Commissioner to Canada. I have a memory of Tara riding side-saddle in a sari; they were all superb horsemen.

I loved Darjeeling, Bengal's hill station below the snows, the great peaks of the Himalayas. I liked the little town, its small roads so steep that cars were not allowed; people went by pony or in rickshaws, pulled or pushed by five men, two in front, three behind. The red-roofed houses had names like Marjorie Villa, Cabochon Villa. It had its Mall, one of the few flat places, where ponies and rickshaws waited for hire and which had a bandstand. Darjeeling's Market Place looked, from above, like a game of mahjong, the tiles, flat-roofed houses, set round a square with hardly a space between. The people, Nepalese or from Sikkim or Tibet, were ruddy-cheeked, slit-eyed and merry, wearing Tibetan clothes, loose robes with a wide sash. The men had small felt hats with perhaps a jaunty peacock feather: they wore a single large turquoise earring or wound plaits round their heads as did the women, whose outer robes were sleeveless, showing the full coloured sleeves of their under-dress, sometimes of silk; the married women had striped aprons, oblongs of brilliant colour woven in silk.

It was a successful season for me and when, in October, I braved Calcutta I had a nucleus of pupils with whom to start and, more importantly, the beginning of a reputation that had gone before me, but still Fa and Mam did not like it, I had broken right away from home. They had reason to worry: it was two years before I was able to write to Jon,

At last I have found the studio I want; it is, of course, not perfect but the first that is possible and at least with a room that is big enough; we have been so cramped. It's in one of Calcutta's oldest houses.

These had been built by Indian landlords for the once-upon-a-time nabobs, men who came out to Bengal from Europe, chiefly from Britain, to make their fortunes from opium, spices and muslins in earlier days, later from jute, tea, hides, shellac, coal and jewels. The houses were built in Palladian style, with porticos, pillars, deep verandahs and vast rooms.

Upstairs the house has been divided into flats but on the ground floor there is a quite imposing entrance which leads into a large oblong hall. I have had barres put at two heights along the walls with low benches painted pale blue for the children to sit on. Its serious drawback is that it has a stone floor: any ballet dancer would shudder at that.

As I was not proposing to teach even the earlier stages of true ballet, only the basics, the dark red stone would not harm barefoot or flat-shoe dancing; in any case I could find no room that did not have a stone floor though, later, I was allowed to use the ballrooms of the Grand Hotel and the Saturday Club.

The room opens, at its far end, onto a wide verandah where the mothers and nurses can sit without seeing too closely; I have put the piano across one side to block the view. The verandah is furnished with wicker chairs and tables, a durrie—Indian cotton carpet—in stripes and I have pots of flowers, at the moment violets, on the steps where the ayahs sit and gossip while they wait. There is a small garden with trees and bougainvillaeas which is mine—unfortunately a goat wanders in from the servants' quarters and their hens come round and scratch which rather destroys the image.

For the first time too I was independent with my own flat—a sitting room, bedroom and bathroom.

I have a cook-bearer, Rashid, share a sweeper with the other flats—but he has to clean the big floor twice a day—and a little Christian ayah called Lena. It is so good to be alone,

but Jon knew, as I knew, that it was unheard of for a young woman, not much more than a girl, to live in an Indian city alone.

I am surprised, Jon, that I am allowed to be here in a desirable residential quarter. However The Little Sisters of the Poor have their Home just opposite; perhaps I shall end there.

The two years had been a true struggle. I had had to begin in a smallish room, with a side office, a hired piano, and had perhaps twenty pupils and one pianist.

When you are battling there are things you do, are forced to do, that haunt you all your life. That happened to me with Miss de Souza.

For a teacher of dancing the most important person, next to the pupils, is the pianist; I was later to have two, both brilliant, especially one, Monisha, half-Indian of a distinguished family, with an exquisite heart-shaped face, expressive eyebrows—Monisha could lift them in laughter or disdain—a creamy skin, her hair coiled in a knot. For all her breeding and elegance, Monisha was poor; I hated to see her walking home in the blazing midday heat. The other, Muriel, was officially white but still Anglo-Indian—which to us meant Eurasian—belonging to a large indigent family under the rule of a matriarchal Mamma who came to see me in fury if she thought I worked Muriel too hard.

These though were later; to begin with I had to look for someone more modest, whom I could afford to pay and who would be content to come when I could provide classes. I found her in the YWCA, the Young Women's Christian Association, where she lived in one room.

Miss Agnes de Souza—I never called her anything but Miss de Souza—was anything but young, probably in her late sixties; she was tall, thin as a clothes prop which she looked like in her Edwardian clothes, decrepit blouses frilled with lace, skirts that swept the ground and were frayed at the bottom. I remember the face powder caught in her wrinkles and remember, too, her eyes made bigger by the stained flesh around them, stains of worry and indigestion from poor food, but eyes that could still light up. Could she play? Yes, she could. Would she play? Would she not.

It was obvious she was in seventh heaven. Years ago she had been pianist in Mussoorie to a dancing teacher, Mrs. Shackle, who by coincidence had taught me in our one summer in Mussoorie. Miss de Souza had admired and revered Mrs. Shackle but no-one had asked her to play since and that meant a long long time. "These Calcutta schools!" she said and sniffed. "I would never play for them, m'n?"—probably they had thought her too old—"But you!" and she threw herself heart and soul into the new dancing school.

I knew that the few rupees I paid her were, to her, like manna, and she did not mind how hard she worked or if there were only two or three children in the class. "It will grow, m'n. It will grow," she said and when I was down-hearted it was she who encouraged me. I was offered a class in Dum Dum, the Military Cantonment outside Calcutta which meant a weary drive, bumping along in the second-hand car Fa had helped me to buy, a highwheeled Chevrolet with a hood that let in the glare and dust. After two months of those afternoons as we drove along, circumventing bullock carts, driven nearly off the road by lorries and other cars, dodging cows loose on the road, children, pai-dogs. "I don't think I can do this any longer," I said. "It isn't worth it."

Miss de Souza was silent for a while, then she said, "If you were Mrs. Shackle, you would never never let a class like this go. Mrs. Shackle had courage!" I went on teaching at Dum Dum and soon the classes were so large I could take an assistant and a car with a driver was sent for me.

Miss de Souza was as devoted as she was wise but soon I had to acknowledge there was too much heart, far too much soul. In the days of silent films she had played in cinemas and her music had not recovered from it; when she played Moments Musicaux, for instance, it sounded like a triumphant march; a Chopin nocturne swooned in sentiment. She could not keep time or adjust to the children, could not follow what I wanted. She adored the children but wanted them to call her Auntie —the Eurasian child's name for any grown-up woman friend; worst of all, when the smallest pupils had nursery rhymes to mime, she would lift up her old cracked voice and sing loudly.

She had to go and I had to tell her; it was like hitting an innocent child a shattering blow. "Go?" she whispered. "You mean . . . not come any more?" She made a grimace as if she were trying to swallow what I had said. Then her face lit up. "Is it the money? My dear, I'll come without the money. Didn't I manage before, m'n? I'll come *willingly*."

"No." It was too sharp, and I tried

more gently. "Thank you, but I'm afraid . . ."

She had seen the pity. She drew on her darned cotton gloves—Miss de Souza always wore gloves in the street—then looked me in the face though her eyes were full of tears. "You are quite right," she said. "I am not suitable." Her fingers pressed my arm. "You deserve to succeed," and turning, went out of the door, opened her sunshade and walked away down the street.

In those first years Fa had nobly underwritten me, more than nobly when he strongly disapproved of what I was doing. I had heard him say, "It is more expensive for Rumer to earn her living than to keep her at home," which was true at first— money seemed to ooze away with little return—but that remark added to the pricks of that time, sharp pricks; the struggle was not only one of money; Fa had warned me of what would happen and he was right.

In Calcutta's then almost closed society, "nice girls" did not work or try to earn their living. There were women doctors, school inspectors, matrons of hospitals, missionaries, but they did not rank as "society", whose girls should stay at home, perhaps do some charity work or amateur acting or painting, strictly unpaid; anything else was taboo, a taboo into which I blithely stepped, and stepped even more deeply than if I had opened a kindergarten or a studio of painting. It seems unbelievable now when dancing, especially ballet, is held in such reverence, that it had for Calcutta a connotation of disreputableness, partly because its schools of dancing were run almost exclusively by Eurasians.

The exception was the Aenid Ballon School which had a monopoly among the Europeans. Although Aenid, beautiful as well as a beautiful dancer, was not Eurasian but Armenian and, if Calcutta had known it, of high birth, when she married an Englishman, Frank Hunt, he was told to leave his firm whereupon she trained him to be a dancer. They made a superb couple for exhibitions of ballroom dancing but they were not "accepted", which in Calcutta terms meant ostracised.

"We have always been in and out

of Calcutta," I protested to Fa. "They couldn't suddenly . . ." They did and I quickly learned who my real friends were.

A short while before I came to teach in Calcutta the Ballon School had brought out from England Frank Hunt's young sister, a dancer known as June de Vigne, whom everyone called Jimmie.

Jimmie did what she wanted in complete innocence of taboos and shibboleths. To her, people were people, white, brown, yellow or black, rich or poor, learned or simple, it did not matter and she had an enormous circle of friends whom she cheerfully mixed together—her only criterion being that they should be people she liked. The Mems had to accept it, as did the Indians, particularly as she soon married Gilbert—Jay—Simon who was the only son of Sir John Simon of political fame; Sir John became Lord Chancellor and was made a Viscount.

When she married Jay, Jimmie had stopped dancing—or perhaps was stopped —but in any case was absorbed in being married with a husband and flat of her own. They had little money and took me in as a lodger.

In spite of my anxieties it was a hilarious six months. Jimmie was like a child let loose in delight and playing at housekeeping; we had chocolate ice-cream for breakfast, strange meals at odd times, and always interest. She had an uncanny gift for finding unusual people and bringing them together, a gift that is with her still and, through much adversity, she has never lost her bubbling joy in things and people—nor her utter disregard of time. I remember, staying with the Simons in England, waking at four in the morning and seeing Jimmie planting bulbs in the garden by the light of a table lamp, plugged in through a window. She was, too, ready to go anywhere, join in at a moment's notice; I can see now how her brown eyes would light at a new suggestion, a new adventure, which sounds impulsive, yet Jimmie was often most wise; she and Jay were an inspiration and a constant reassurance to me.

"I am surprised", one influential lady told me, "that you are allowed in the Saturday Club."

"Calamity of calamities!" said Jay and laughed. As Fa had been one of the founder members they could hardly have put me out but, for a while, invitations ceased; most of Calcutta's ladies, if we met by chance, pretended not to see me, their daughters were kept away; even some of the young men with whom I had ridden and danced did not ask me now. I pretended, of course, not to care but it stung when I innocently dropped in at a house where we had always been welcome to be told the family were "not at home".

It would not have been as outrageous if I had taught only "nice" children— English or Indian, but,

To Jon [in the early days]:

This evening, just as I was going home, an Eurasian grandmother appeared bringing her little grandson. "I thought it would be better, and all, if I came after hours, m'n?" she said.

"Why?"

She evaded that. "I am ver-ee shy"; but I knew why.

She was a shapeless bundle in a grey-black striped cotton dress with sweat marks under the arms. Her legs, painfully swollen, were bare in black Chinese slippers; her hair, thin and grey too, was pulled tightly back into a knot, her face the colour of a walnut shell, wrinkled like the shell, but it was one of the sweetest, kindest faces I have seen. The grandson was a pale little boy so thin he was almost transparent; his eyes were pale grey and deep set, his hair cropped. He did not speak but watched us, looking from his grandmother to me, from me to his grandmother; I could see his small dusty toes curling with excitement in his sandals. "Did—could", she asked, "a boy ever dance?" Here she pushed him forward. "He is mad to dance, m'n, Thomas?" Thomas only looked at the floor but a smile of radiance came on his small face. "How much would it cost?" At that he breathed deeply, looked up at me as if he hoped to read the price on my face. "Three—five rupees, m'n?" She had a shabby little purse ready as if to pay for each lesson in advance. Would I take him?

That was the rub. I tried to think of this grandmother among the nannies—some of them in crisp uniforms—even the immaculately dressed ayahs; the assured mothers with their easy manners and well-cut clothes and the fact that they took it for granted they all knew one another but, "Will you take him, m'n?" I put Thomas into the next class I opened for six- and seven-year-olds. "If I lose the rest of them, I lose them," I wrote to Jon. I did not lose them. The grandmother tactfully kept out of the way. Thomas was brought by their houseboy in the cleanest of clothes—and I did not regret it because Thomas, like too many of these delicate Eurasian children, died of a low fever when he was eight. At least he had two years of the dancing he adored.

It was not only children, though; eventually that was accepted as my own affair but, in my indignation, I was tempted into doing something that seemed everyone's affair; I trained a troupe of Eurasian girls for cabaret.

I had always been uncomfortable about the way these girls were treated in Calcutta society. In the hot weather they were allowed to be brought as guests to some of the Clubs; if you met a man you knew with one of them, it was taken for granted that you behaved as if you had not seen him. The men, themselves, had to be careful; under Indian law, adultery is a criminal offence and, if a girl had a husband, consequences could be severe; in any event if a young man became serious, as some inevitably did, he was immediately shipped home. The girls were there for exploitation as I was to show in the novel, *The Lady and the Unicorn*, I was to write some years later—it must be remembered how poor they were.

In the novel, a young man, Stephen, had just come out from England, and his cousin William, well accustomed, invites him to a party.

"It's a B party," said William.

"What's a B party?"

"There are A and B girls. These are B."

"Oh I see," said Stephen and began to wonder about these girls of whom he had heard so much, who were so alluring and so dangerous.

"What happens?" he asked.

"Usual thing," said William. "They

behave very well and we behave very badly and then they behave worse."

"You should not have written that book," an old friend of Fa's was to say to me, "showing how much you know about Eurasians. People might think you are one yourself."

I would not have cared if they had but, at the time I started the troupe, I put my whole School in jeopardy.

The girls were almost all Eurasian—as was Phyllis, my assistant. She had French crossed with Indian-hill blood, a good mixture; no-one could have been more loyal and devoted; through all those years we never had a quarrel. Trained by Aenid Ballon, she was an excellent little dancer, expert in tap and acrobatic dancing, and it was she who brought the idea, and the girls. Many of them had the beauty of so many cross-bred girls, were sweet, loyal and touching in their eagerness to dance and make a little money. Why not? I thought. Even then, there were plenty of respectable and esteemed examples of this kind of chorus dancing; on a famous scale, the Rockettes in New York, the Bluebell Girls in Paris, but this was Calcutta.

Jon, have you ever had an anonymous letter? I had one yesterday and can't describe the sick recoil—though you know you must not feel like that as it is the very thing the writer wants—but it is dreadful to believe an unknown someone hates you so much that he or she—I think it is a she who has, or has had, a dancing school—can pour out such obscenity and filth.

I had telephone calls, Indian and others, asking if I could "supply" girls for the evening, all the more hurtful because I had come to love and honour mine.

The worst thing though was that I knew this work had no appeal for me and that I did not do it well; it was this that was degrading.

Never, never [*I wrote to Jon*] should we do what goes against our instincts, not for sympathy, certainly not for money.

I do not think I would have done it over

writing but wish it had not given what was a falsity to the dancing.

If only I had kept to my original purpose of teaching small children. There I was safe and had joy in the work, which was rewarding and responsible—ambitious teachers of dancing can do such lasting harm to soft small bones. I loved seeing my classes, little girls in their short white tunics, hair tied out of the way; a Chinese shoemaker learned how to make soft ballet shoes—I barred dancing sandals, now mercifully extinct. The few boys had white shorts and singlets. The children mostly ranged from four to ten or eleven years old but I had one class where nobody was yet three years old!

I taught Indian children, little princesses—then still royal—and several children of Marwaris or rich merchants, their wives often in purdah so that they could only come and watch their children if I made sure no man were present. These children, though, were Westernised, but one year I was asked to start a class in an Indian School of Music; the Principals decided that Greek dancing would be the most suitable, and full of enthusiasm I began but the enthusiasm waned.

In an Indian School of Music the pupils, many of them children, sit on the floor or on a daybed opposite their master who has his seat of honour on a mat as, with a tabla —small drum—or a pair of tiny cymbals, he gently marks the rhythm; the Indian scale has many many notes or tones, with infinitesimal changes of pitch which the pupils sing piercingly, it seems as much through their noses as through their mouths. As often in Indian houses, all the rooms opened onto a central courtyard, no doors or windows were shut and the noise was deafening—yet still the piano that had been hired for me seemed an intrusion.

I had some twenty girls, fourteen- and fifteen-year-olds, to whom what I taught was far removed from their idea of dancing, such as the classic Bharat Natyam which comes from the temple dancing of Southern India and has a completely religious background. It needs an extraordinary control of the muscles, especially the face, neck and eyes; every gesture has a specific meaning and the movements of the face and eyes have to correspond. The traditional "mudras" or hand and finger gestures and the expressive thumb movements have names like "lotus bud": "deer's head": "swan's neck". More intricate and subtle even than ballet, it takes years of training and my girls at first could not accept the simplicity and flow of Greek dancing but they came to enjoy it as if they were, in a way, liberated.

They were so quick to learn and so graceful that when it was suggested they show an example of this new dance at the School's Open Day performance I agreed, arranged a dance for them and designed a classical costume of Greek simplicity in fine muslin. It could not be white, a sign of mourning, so I chose pale blue and laid down that the girls should have bare feet, their hair loose, bound only by a small fillet and should not wear jewellery. That was too much for the girls—more particularly for their mothers—and I arrived on the day to find my flowing blue muslin wound and tucked and pleated to make a dancer's pantaloons, while ankles, arms, neck, ears and head were covered in jewellery, the hair plaited with gold cord and flowers; hand-palms and foot-soles had been patterned in henna, and each face had a heavy make-up with a scarlet tika mark on the forehead. The dance was, naturally, a failure and it seemed useless to go on.

Slowly, in those years, I gained experience and, I think, brought my School something a little different; Moira House had specialised in Dalcroze Eurythmics and that was invaluable, as was my gift for story-telling. After the first years I put on an annual school performance, not the usual display of dances, instead a danced story—I could not call it a ballet—among others, "The Water Babies", "The Sleeping Beauty", not attempting of course to follow the Tchaikovsky ballet, "In Noah's Ark" and "How Harlequin Got his Clothes", in which I had more than a hundred children under ten. Each story ran for three matinées.

I had, quite apart from the choreography and the music, willy-nilly to do everything from finding the theatre to arranging printing and publicity, doing the decor and lighting, designing the costumes and having them made, as well as training the children. I was lucky in getting to know a small orchestra whose conductor,

Teddy Frangopoulo, was adept in arranging music. My Wardrobe Mistress was a towering black-bearded Sikh—most Sikhs in Calcutta were either taxi drivers and mechanics or else dressmakers and tailors. Each year my Arjun Singh moved his whole shop to part of my verandah where he could fit the children's costumes as they came for rehearsal.

I do not lay any claim for these dance stories except that, probably, thousands of such home-made small dramas are going on all over the world and are, after all, the beginnings of imagination, even vision, which is where all gifted people have to start. Of all the children I taught, and there were several hundred of them, though two went on to the Royal Ballet School, only one had real talent, outstanding talent and, ironically, she was the only child who had no chance of further training.

Jean came to me at four years old, and when she was nine, seeing her dance Harlequin, the governors of a cultural Trust in Calcutta raised a private fund to send her, with her mother, to London for training, arranging and paying for everything. Jean was overjoyed but her mother was an Indian hill woman, humbly acquiescent, the father a fiery Irish mechanic who not only would not let Jean go, but stopped her dancing altogether. I never knew what became of her.

Middle-aged ladies come up to me now and say, "I am Mary-Ann," or Caroline, Susan, Cynthia, Gita, Sushila. "Don't you remember me? You taught me dancing in Calcutta . . ." and, "Yes," I say. "Long, long ago," but to me it feels like yesterday and I have only to be in the auditorium at Covent Garden or dear shabby Sadlers Wells or the Paris Opera House or New York's Lincoln Center and see the conductor lift his little stick as the house lights go down and rise again on the stage curtain as the music begins and the old spell is back:

So dance to dance
Endlessly they weave, break off
    and dance again . . . in unison,

189

> Of body, song and dress,
>    obedient
> Each shadows each.

# 7

## Calcutta Dust

JON, for her second marriage, Rose and I were married in the full panoply of the Cathedral of Calcutta, Nancy in the tiny Dartmoor church of Holme in Devon, in the early morning with only Mam, Fa and Dick's father present and, afterwards, a breakfast in the village inn. Her marriage endured, ours ended in rupture.

Old Calcutta was built around the Maidan, a vast flat space of green spreading from Chowringhee, Calcutta's principal street, to the Strand that runs beside the river Hoogly. The Maidan is bordered by flowering trees—Calcutta used to be a city of flowering trees—and is broken by the hummocks of the moat and ramparts of Fort William—still a military fort—and by the white marble Victoria Memorial with its domes and flying figure of Victory;

beside Chowringhee and set apart in gardens carefully railed, is the Episcopalian Cathedral, its spire rising high. It has an impressively long nave up which the bride had to walk, I with bridesmaids, ushers, choir. We all had a reception afterwards, wedding presents and a honeymoon which was, for me, a travesty.

There is an Indian proverb that says, "If you put a bag of Calcutta dust under the bed of a good woman she will become corrupt" and certainly Calcutta, even in the Thirties, had a startling record of broken and discarded marriages, exchanges of husbands and wives and affairs not whispered about but "bruited"; even so I cannot understand now how we could have broken those vows we made, though then there seemed nothing else we could do—Rose especially was helpless. Also two words had never come into our orbit, "sacrament" in all its meaning and "duty", though I think we had an innate sense of the last because we had such pangs over our divorces. I am sorry for the bridegrooms. "Never marry anyone unless you love them so much you feel you cannot imagine living without them," an old friend had told me, but you do not know what love is—or is not—until you marry.

On my desk is a letter from Nigel to Jon. It was written in their first long separation, he in Dacca, she in London when she was so ill.

> I am numbering my letters [*he writes*]. This is number one hundred and eleven. I have just come back from touring and found your letter.

The Imperial Tobacco Company sent their young men out alone, deep into the countryside for weeks at a time, buying and testing tobacco leaf.

> You can't imagine how I have been longing for that letter, pining for it the whole time I was on tour. I see you so vividly it is painful . . .

The next spring and summer he came on leave, first in London then in Dorset where we took a cottage for the holidays to be near him.

Nigel's family lived in Chideock, then an unspoilt little Dorset village. His father had been a composer who began his musical life as a choirboy of the Savoy Chapel Royal; he wrote songs, more especially, operas and lost a great deal of money over their performances, more money by his passion for restoring old houses; the Baughans once owned the beautiful Clock House, centre of Chideock and the fifteenth-century Chimneys, but had been reduced to living in one of their own cottages. There were three sons, fortunately all grown-up and working but also two little "after-thought" girls, then seven and five years old, all of them more than good-looking.

For those weeks of Nigel's leave in London Mam had bought Jon clothes such as we had never seen, taking her to a couturière; we others gasped but in Mam's eyes nothing was too good for Nigel and she had her reward in seeing Jon recovered and restored, caught up in a whirl of dancing, theatres and dinners. In Dorset, Nigel had a big white Vauxhall car and he and Jon disappeared all day. They had May, June, July, August together, then

Nigel was posted to Delhi and had to go back.

Jon as I have told had stayed in Paris but she had never shared my visions of the Left Bank and the Latin Quarter, the ateliers, and street cafés—I had read *Trilby*. With a timidity that seemed incongruous in her of all people, she elected to stay with Rose in the finishing school at Bellevue though she, Jon, was now twenty-three; nor did she venture into an atelier—her lessons were private—nor once explore Paris alone; afterwards we learned she had been almost paralysed with unhappiness.

It was in June, the next year, that Nancy and I, then in Darjeeling, had a telephone call from Fa, speaking from Delhi. Fa in Delhi! The moment I heard his voice I knew it was something grave. Nigel, playing rugger, had been kicked on the ankle, making an open wound, and septicaemia had set in. When he knew he was dying he asked for Fa to be sent for —the only time in his life Fa flew. Nigel told him that he and Jon had been secretly married in Dorset. Fa stayed all night with Nigel, who died the next day. Mam luckily was in England. She went over to Paris at once and brought Jon back home to India.

I can write about Jon and Nigel because they are both dead; shibboleths, taboos, separations, scandal cannot touch them now. Nigel ended that letter, number one hundred and eleven:

I have your carnation by me and it still has a scent. I am sending it with this. I still have one of the roses left that you gave me. All my love.

Mine was the first of our ill-fated weddings in the Cathedral.

"Is it true," an interviewer on radio asked me last year, "that, in your first season in Calcutta, you went out sixty-seven nights running?" I cannot imagine who told him this—but it was true and not uncommon in Calcutta. It was in 1929 when I was taking my first tentative steps towards a dancing school, and it was all comparatively harmless, no more than dinners in chummeries, dancing, moon-light picnics, sitting out in cars—fun, none of the real viciousness of that "poison dust"; all the same, I soon had a reputation for being "fast". By the next cold weather, staying with the Simons, I had not the inclination or the time to be fast, I was working too hard. I saw few young men but one was always constant.

I do not remember when I first met Laurence Sinclair Foster, he seemed always to have been there, strayed, as it seemed, out of his own world. Coming from the Worcestershire branch of Fosters, well-known cricketers, Laurence was a brilliant athlete—you did not know how graceful he was until he moved. Small and slight, his hazel eyes seemed always happy, as if there were no worries in the world; he was immensely popular, especially among older men and no wonder, because it was not only in cricket he excelled but tennis, as well as old tennis, which he had played for England and, especially, golf—he had a plus-two handicap. At school—he went to Malvern as did all those particular Fosters—his outstanding prowess at games let him dodge lessons so that he was a cheerful philistine; he truly thought Omar Khayyam was a kind of curry and on the rare occasions we went to a concert, or once to an opera, he would take his seat and say, "Wake me up when it's over." All the same he could have gone to university, Oxford or Cambridge, where he would undoubtedly have been a double if not a triple blue, but his parents could not afford it; his father was doctor to a teagarden district in Assam, not highly paid, and Laurence's games were expensive—in old tennis, alone, a ball was used for only one rally. Instead they brought him out to India where he went into Calcutta's most prestigious firm of stockbrokers.

I still cannot imagine why Laurence chose me; perhaps it was because he had not met a girl like me and it piqued him but, when other young men fell away, he was still there and was unfailingly kind, which I have been told is my favourite epithet. In all our years and in all our troubles, I never knew Laurence to lose his temper—perhaps he did not care enough—but through those hard-working years he faithfully came, especially in the evenings, coaxing me away from the practising and accounts I should have been doing—and how pleasant it is to be coaxed

—to have a drink, go out to dinner, or for a drive and soon it was more than that. Now and again I thought of Fa and felt a prick of misgiving, but, Oh well, I thought, no-one knows—Calcutta's anodyne for troubled consciences. Then I found I was going to have a child.

Laurence and I were married in March 1934. If I felt a sham in my white satin dress and veil nobody knew it, not even Jon, but there is a moment in the Church of England marriage service when the priest, as the bride and groom kneel before him, takes the end of his stole and symbolically binds their two hands together; in that moment I had the first real inkling of what we had done.

We could have done other things. "Your doctor . . ." Laurence had begun, then thought again. "*Your* doctor wouldn't but he could get somebody else, probably an Indian." It was not legal then to take a baby away but to Laurence every Indian had his price. "No!" the whole of me cried out against it. "It's our child." I should have had the courage to have the baby on my own and face the consequences; go back to England so that "Nobody would know" but Fa and Mam would know, must know, probably Laurence's parents too, that honourable little doctor, and his kind wife. "You'll have to marry me," said Laurence, and added with a percipience I had not given him credit for, "and pretend you like it . . ."

It was not all pretence; I liked being married, having someone to think of and plan for, someone coming home in the evenings with whom to talk over the day, have a drink and dinner, someone to go out with. For a while I tasted again how beguilingly pleasant life in Calcutta could be—as long as you stayed on the surface. One of the best things about Laurence's golf, for instance, was that golf is always played in attractive surroundings—he used to go out early on Sunday mornings to one of the Country Clubs, the Calcutta Golf Club or the more exclusive Tollygunj and I used to drive out for lunch. Sunday lunches were usually prawn curry—Calcutta's prawns were delectable—after it there would be a long siesta until it was time for the cinema. Sunday cinema was almost a ritual, with a supper party afterwards at our or somebody else's house. We were often out to dinner, often dancing, though oddly enough Laurence was not a good dancer; he did not mind my dancing with other men. We entertained and I have always liked planning dinner parties—preferably small.

I enjoyed, too, running the house—I always have and believe a house, a home, is enormously important.

I liked my servants, principally our head servant, Ears. When I married Laurence, Ears was already his bearer; Laurence had a gift for attaching people to him and no servant could have been more devoted than Ears. He was a Lepcha, one of the hill tribes of Sikkim, noted for their fineness and gentleness until roused. Ears had a kukri, the Ghurkha traditional weapon, a short curved wide-bladed knife with a razor-sharp edge; when, before we were married, Laurence went on leave to England, he left Ears with me; to him I was Laurence's woman and Ears thought it his duty to sleep across my doorway at night—with the kukri.

He was golden-skinned with a flat merry

face, slit eyes and almost always a smile. He wore white trousers, a white mandarin tunic with brass buttons, a black pillbox hat with black embroidery. He was the head of the household and proud of it. Lepchas, like all hill men, are inclined to drink, and when I found our whisky was disappearing—I always thought it unfair that Indian servants are required to pour out drinks from a bottle that cost at least half their monthly wages—I had to act.

How can I do this, I thought, without making Ears lose face—which he could not have borne?

I go to the Club and borrow a drinks measure and tell Ears to put it on the tray. "What is it?" asks Ears.

"A measure. I shall tell the sahibs I have to use it because the servants steal my sahib's whisky."

Ears's face is expressionless; presently he brings the measure to me. "Take it back to the Club."

No drink is stolen again.

All this Laurence and I could share and delight in but for me, at least, the savour went out of life as we began to realise how much, together, we spoiled things for one another and, as had happened when I was a girl, more and more I found I was a stranger in his society, a stranger who could not talk "small talk" which was all the talk there was. I gave up going to the golf clubs; at drinks parties which I dreaded but thought, then, it my duty to go to, I might have been an iceberg spreading chill around me from the way people avoided me. "Can't you just be chatty?" Laurence used to say. Somehow I could not.

I was, too, appalled at their complete ignorance of India until I realised that, like many of their kind, they had never really been there; they were still in Britain, adapting their exile to as close a British pattern as they could, oblivious to everything Indian except for their servants to whom they were benevolent and of whom they were often very fond—and for their Indian clients. Laurence was popular with his but when, once or twice, we were invited to their homes it was to meet the business-man only, never his wife or wives and children, and I felt estranged. More and more I took refuge in the School, which Laurence did not mind except, "I wish you wouldn't teach those 'half and halfs'," he said.

All round us in this evil city, India was pressing; you had only to go out into the streets or the bazaars to see its misery and teeming distress. "Half of the people don't have enough to eat," I raged and the answer was a shrug and, "I'm sorry, but what can I do about it?"

What could I do either? At least I could care.

There was, too, the political ferment; the fight for independence was growing and, with it, terrorism especially among the young. I had seen it in Dacca where we were closer to Indian life than in Calcutta; a young policeman friend was stabbed in the back by students as he was playing rugger with them; a girl at University going up to get her prize—ironically for English—from the Governor tried to shoot him in the face. Yet I could not help sympathising with them. Who would not want, I thought, to be free? "Idiots. They're far better off under the British," said Laurence and his friends.

It slowly dawned on me that not only did they not know, they seemed unable to feel any sense of wonder, ecstasy or awe.

Indians have a custom of taking "darshan" which means, with a temple, a palace, a holy cave or a renowned view such as the sight of the Himalayan snow peaks, Everest or Kanchenjunga, or a notable person—for instance Gandhi or the President—they will travel miles, make pilgrimages simply to take "darshan" of that person or place, not trying to make contact or speak—certainly not taking photographs as we do—but, simply by looking, to let a little of the personality, sainthood, holiness or beauty, come into their souls. They go away, usually without speaking and so keep it for the rest of their lives. Innately, from the time we were children, we had done the same thing; it was perhaps our deepest delight.

On our honeymoon to the Coromandel Coast we had stayed at Puri, an Indian version of a seaside resort. Only twenty miles away was the Sun Temple at Kanarak, of all Hindu temples the most stupendous and most perfectly proportioned. Built of stone—it is a wonder how the stone was carried there— it stands on the beach and the huge carvings of wheels and horses show that the temple is the chariot of the Sun god, Surya; its entrance, where two lions sit on the backs of elephants, one paw raised in salutation, faces the rising sun, so that the first rays strike it at dawn, which was when I longed to see it. I had only known it through pictures and reading but I realised, with a new dismay, that I would rather not go there at all if I had to go with Laurence. He had not heard of Surya, nor wanted to hear and, if he had seen the carvings, as powerful as they are exquisite in their age-old grey-green stone, he would have been shocked. It is true they are erotic—the guide books call them licentious—but at the same time they are innocent because, to Hindus, the act of sex is holy; the most sacred symbols in Hinduism are the yoni, the female genital organ, and the lingam, the male. Among Laurence's friends either this would have been thought disgusting or they would have been titillated.

It is frightening what intensity of feeling

is aroused when anyone derides or desecrates something holy or simply beautiful—I still cannot stop myself burning with anger. Worse, I soon began to see that we are known by the company we keep and with my own friends it was as if, tacitly, we had agreed they should keep away, which was grievous for me—as was my growing loneliness. I longed for Jon but Jon was even further away in Assam, there was no more Narayangunj.

Fa, for his last five years in the Company, should have gone to Calcutta where he would have become a partner and made money, but he had always done exactly as he wanted and, "I will not, cannot live in a city," he had insisted. Instead, he asked to be sent to the remote little river town of Tezpur in Assam.

"That's where you started!" said his chiefs, amazed. "Our most junior post."

"Exactly," said Fa. "I can do the work in a couple of hours and have a shooting and fishing camp out in the jungle and spend the rest of my time there."

The family was more scattered than ever; Australia had been added to our travels; Nancy had gone there for the hot weather—their winter—staying with the Skenes of polo-playing fame, helping to train their polo ponies. She was to work her passage back by looking after some of the horses on the cargo boat that in October brought the horses to India taking six weeks on the way. Every year five or six hundred horses were imported from Australia for the Indian Army and Police but the Skenes' horses were picked and trained polo ponies, some eighty or ninety of them, some for their own team but most for the Maharajahs, many of whom Nancy came to know well.

Fa forfeited most of his pension and it died with him—which was hard on Mam—but for five years he had an elysian life.

The camp was a "basha" camp, not of tents but of more permanent bamboo-woven huts above his loved Bareilly river; we could look across the river to Bhutan and in those years saw wild life few people have seen. I remember a great stag being brought down by running red dogs, a sight that has haunted me; wild elephants ranged all round us. We saw cheetahs, those beautiful animals like leopards which the Moghul Emperors used for hunting. It was a paradise of animal, bird, reptile and insect life for those who came and went but Rose, when she finally came out to join me, had to live in its remoteness.

It is not always lucky to be the youngest in a family. Rose had left India when she was seven and had little idea of what its life was like but she must have heard much of this fabulous Calcutta; always thinking the least of herself, she did her best to make a good impression but she had forgotten what sisters are. Nancy and I had met her at Howrah, and I can see her now descending—the only word for getting out of those high-wheeled Indian railway carriages—an anxious smile on her face.

My most vivid memory of Rose, until then, was of a rebellious teenager, lying down on the floor of our last Eastbourne rented house refusing to go to school—it was during Fa's last leave, before we went to Mull and I had had, in the end, to drive her to school, tousled and furious—but now! Nancy and I gave a gasp.

Our little sister is taller than we are,

poised and most elegantly dressed, her hair up. Then our gimlet eyes see that on her left leg, just above the ankle, she is wearing a silver bracelet—if we had known it, this was the height of fashion. "Take that off at once. At *once*," we hiss.

The smile abruptly faded and I do not think it ever came back. Rose has always been one of those rare people who are content to "be" rather than to "do", who have no desire to make their mark in any way, to live rather than to work. She hated teaching and the School and soon gave up, retreating to Tezpur, but in those days she liked people and parties, dancing and, particularly, racing; Fa, on smaller pay, could not give her what he had given the rest of us when we had "come out"; that must have rankled and, though she revelled in the animals, she could not bear the constant killing and must often have been bored and restless.

Engagements were in the air: Jon had become engaged again and went back to England. Nancy was on the verge of hers and, among the many men Rose had met in Calcutta, was C. D. Smith—his name was Clive but he was always called C.D.; he had not been known to look at a girl before but now he was courting Rose openly. We waited to see what she would do.

I think Laurence and I would have managed—we wanted to manage—each sensibly going our separate ways, if it had not been for money or what lay behind the money.

Most junior married couples in Calcutta, unless they have private means, have to settle for living in a block of flats but I had had a friend, a Mr. Mehta who had originally come to me for ballroom dancing lessons, two half-hours a week, though I had been cautioned about elderly and lonely gentlemen in Calcutta.

Mr. Mehta was lonely, he told me so —his family were in Bombay—but all he wanted was to dance with a sympathetic partner, to keep himself "in health", he said and to talk a little, particularly about books and music. No-one could have been less presumptuous and more courteous, sometimes refusing to dance because

I looked tired; sometimes we talked in French, he gently correcting me and, always, when the half-hour was ended, he said, "Goodnight" and left me. Now, hearing I was to be married and thinking, I am sure, he was taking us under his wing, he offered us the lower half of one of his houses, a gracious one that had a garden with upper and lower lawns shaded by flowering trees with roses and flowering creepers growing up them and long beds of English flowers, bordered by violets and pinks. As the people in the upper part of the house did not use the garden and Laurence was not interested in gardens, it became peculiarly mine—the beginning of a long love—until suddenly Mr. Mehta stopped coming for his ostensible lessons, was "not available" on the telephone, and I had an uneasy feeling that Laurence in his insouciant casualness might have offended him.

Though Indians liked him, Laurence had little idea of their "izzat" or "standing" —important to them; certainly he had no idea that Mr. Mehta's "izzat" was considerably higher than his own. "Our Indian landlord," he called him. Mr.

Mehta was not Indian, he was a Parsee. Parsees originally came from Persia—they are Zoroastrians; when they left Persia, some went west to the Danube, some east to India where they lived chiefly in Bombay and are perhaps the most cultured, rich and exclusive people in the world; Mr. Mehta was not only offended, he was irredeemably hurt because, as I discovered, not one anna of our benevolent rent had been paid.

What could I do? Somehow, from somewhere, get money. That was my first thought, but how? I was too proud to go to Fa—he had always said he had no use for Laurence. As the months went on I had got heavier, more clumsy so that I could not consider extra teaching; in any case not many pupils wanted to dance in the hot weather.

I know now that I should have gone to Mr. Mehta and explained; he would have understood and, more importantly, not have been hurt. Instead I panicked and did two stupidities—worse than stupidities— one of them was criminal for which I have felt indicted ever since. I had a string of pearls; they were Ian's, which made it worse; when I had given him back the jewellery he had given me he had insisted I keep these. If I had sold them they would not have realised half their worth and I decided I would lose them—which I did—and claim the insurance. I also had a scene with Laurence, a real scene which neither of us forgot. Goddens have poisonous tongues—Jon's was wicked. We know exactly how to wound and how to say it and, though Laurence shrugged it off, "Lots of people don't pay their rent," it made him afraid of me; perhaps the rest of our failure would not have happened if it had not been for that fear—and it was all of no use. Though the rent was paid Mr. Mehta remained hurt and was never "available" to me again.

If there is any time in my life on which, looking back, I feel sorry for myself, it is in the lonely unhappiness of those later hotweather months. It was the baby I clung to and, in those stifling long afternoons—there was no air-conditioning then—I tried to sew for him or her. I see myself in an oppression of heat, that seems to be pressing down on me:

It is worse outside, with a white hot sky and merciless sun. I have tied my hair up out of the way, my neck and arms are covered with prickly heat—I am one of the luckless ones who cannot sweat and the heat burns in me. I am beginning to grow out of my clothes and there is no money for others; I look a sight and my hands are clumsy.

I wonder if any young mothers sew for their babies now—baby clothes are so sensible and comparatively inexpensive but I think I must have read J. M. Barrie's play, *Mary Rose*. He was fashionable then; after being in the Hebrides it would have appealed to me because for all the play's sentimentality the "island that liked to be visited" has the Hebridean magic. In the play, the soldier son asks to see his baby clothes, knowing that, if his mother, Mary Rose, had sewn them herself she must have wanted and loved her baby; perhaps a little defiantly, I wanted to show how much I wanted mine.

Long ago the Godden aunts had tried to teach me to sew and embroider but the linen in the frame was always marked by more blood and tears than stitches. I was not much better now and for this infant dress,

> I am trying ridiculously to sew strips of lace and fine broderie together. The needle gets sticky, the thread damp but I keep on and like mothers-to-be in books, or in *Mary Rose*, sew into it hopes and dreams.

The dress was for a little girl because daughters run in our family; I dared not hope for a son.

The baby was a son. I was still holding classes as, in the early mornings and evenings, it was cool enough to dance; a child, doing exercises at the barre, caught me in the side with a vigorous kick. Our little son was born prematurely and only lived four days. We called him David.

The death of a new-born baby is a peculiarly piercing grief, not to be compared, of course, with losing a child in its later years but piercing; everything seems for nothing and I still see that tiny grave in Calcutta's new cemetery. "We can have another," said Laurence, which showed he knew more about human nature than I did. For me, the best and only splint was work and presently I had an added reason for wanting to give up dancing: I was twenty-six, Mona's ban was lifted, and I had written my first novel.

# 8

## The Cockatoo

MY first novel to be published, *Chinese Puzzle*, was accepted on the same day that Jane, our daughter, was born.

"It occurs to me," says the hero of the book, "that we were put into this world as part of its making, as a stitch or a thread is put into the weaving of a cloth or tapestry. When we die we leave a little hole and it is our duty, before we die, to see that the hole is filled and so strengthen the weave."

I had written that when Jane was on the way and I wonder if it was why I longed so much for another child.

Not wanting ever again to see the doctors who had looked after me before, I had found a German Jewish doctor who had taken refuge from the Nazis in

218

Calcutta; still dazed by what had happened to him, he was a gentle, kind, clever and tolerant man. He needed to be tolerant; the first moment I suspected I could be having a baby again I rang him up, though it was a Sunday, "Can you come at once?"

"Now?" It was a hot day after luncheon, the hottest time. "Is it an emergency?"

"No, but *please*." When he had examined me he smiled and said, "I congratulate you, Madame." I can still hear those words.

Jane arrived, again prematurely—I was not good at having babies—in Laurence's parents' little house in one of London's new suburbs. There must be dozens of men and women born on the Assam tea-gardens who are called Thomas or Belinda because when Doctor Foster delivered a baby he would say, "You've had a little Thomas," or "a little Belinda". Doctor Percy was the dearest, kindest as well as bravest of men; small—he was far shorter than Laurence—and, when I knew him, with white hair and alert blue eyes. With only a year to run before he had been due to retire, he found he had cancer of the face; without any fuss or ado, he and his wife, Florence, left India and went straight to London where he was cured at the Marsden Hospital but, after almost twenty-five years of faithful service, because he had left before they were quite fulfilled, the Company refused to pay his pension. Doctor Percy was nearing seventy but, with what savings they had, he and Florence bought a small house in a developing suburb and he put up his plate to start again.

We were in England because Laurence was on leave. I had hardly dared to hope I could have a well baby but I was in Doctor Percy's experienced hands. He had especially bought a new anaesthetic machine which did not work, and I was fully conscious as the baby arrived. "Is it all right? Is it?"

"Listen," said the nurse and I heard a sound, at first fitful, like the chattering of sparrows in a chimney, then growing louder, lusty and it was Jane. Doctor Percy was so moved he forgot to say, "You have had a little Belinda." It must be strange to deliver your own grandchild and Florence, weeping with joy, took her, when she was cleaned, wrapped her in an eiderdown and put her in the drawing-room fender by the fire—it was in the middle of a November night.

When they brought Jane to me I said she could not be mine; she had a feather of red gold hair on the forehead and no-one in our families, I thought, had had red hair but I was wrong; in the seventeenth century, there had been a red-haired Foster girl, who fell in love with a highwayman; her father was a vicar and, naturally, would not consent to the marriage; when he was taking matins, or morning service, the highwayman and his friends rode into the church, held the congregation at gunpoint and forced the vicar to marry him to Maria, and rode out of the church with her on his saddlebow.

If I had known that story Jane would have been called Maria. It was Nurse who named her.

The novel was not *Gōk*. That had been a long untidy book about the making of one of the earliest Indian tea-gardens; tea, in India, was originally planted by Moravian missionaries, on the foothills of the Himalayas below Darjeeling, a setting I was to bring back in the first of my books that was a success, *Black Narcissus*, and again in the Himalayan diary, *Rungli-Rungliot* or *Thus Far and No Further*. *Gōk* had not found a publisher, nor did my next novel, an attempt that was eventually to become *The River*; one publisher said he would accept it if I re-wrote it from the mother's point of view, instead of the child's, which would have spoiled the concept. This third book, accepted immediately, I had thought would have little chance as its hero was a pekingese. In the publisher's words:

"A Pekingese tells his life stories"—the plural was right—"first as Wong-Li, a Chinese gentleman of perhaps a thousand years ago, then in his reincarnation as Ting-Ling, a pekingese dog, Black Face, Full Feathered, Cream with Flowerings of Gold."

I do not like dogs except very large ones and one or two with such character that they cannot be denied; pekingese are not dogs but something more. The legend is that,

222

Once upon a time a lioness grew tired of the brute attentions of her mate and yielded to the delicate attentions of a butterfly—if you have ever been give a butterfly kiss you will know how titillating that is. The result of this unusual union was a pekingese, and always afterwards pekingese have to be as brave as lions and as dainty as a butterfly.

In actual fact they go back to the Han Dynasty in China, 2000 BC, where they are described as "short-mouthed hunting dogs". When Buddhism came to China, they became sacred as they were thought to be the lion which is Buddha's familiar; it can become so large it can fill the sky and shrink to such smallness that Buddha can carry it in his sleeve—hence the term "sleeve dog". Marco Polo, in his travels, describes "the golden-coated nimble dogs" he saw frequenting palaces. In China, no-one not of royal blood was officially allowed to own one—the penalty for smuggling a pekingese out of the palace was execution.

They came to England from China after the first Opium War in 1826 when five were found by the British in the sacking of the Summer Palace. One of those was given to Queen Victoria who unashamedly named her Looty. Looty's portrait was painted with a bunch of pansies to show how small she was—on the voyage home she had slept in her soldier captor's forage cap. The portrait now hangs in the Lord Chamberlain's Office.

Everyone needs a bit of nonsense in their lives: my nonsenses are pekingese, beginning with, long ago, Piers—and now, as I write, the spirits of some thirty gambol and make carnival round me as they did in life and it was at that time in England, while I was waiting for Jane, that Jon gave me my second pekingese puppy.

I called him Chini—Hindi for sugar— and needed him, in fact needed every crumb of companionship, nonsense and gaiety I could get.

When I see young husbands now, the way they share and care in the advent of their children, I realise how much wives then were left on their own; having a baby was women's work and the fathers only appeared when it was all over. I was peculiarly alone.

For Laurence, going on leave meant, chiefly, the chance to play golf on famous courses up and down Britain from Scotland to Somerset where, that year, the Amateur Championship was held and in which he was runner-up. Taking a pregnant wife with him was no part of his plan; I hated the suburb where Doctor Percy was struggling to make a practice but there was nowhere else for me to go; I was not well enough to be on my own, nor was there enough money. Fa and Mam were still in Tezpur. True, Jon—who had not yet married again—was spending the summer in England, occupying Uncle Alfred and Aunt Mary's only spare room, but she was ill and could not come to London. Once or twice Laurence reluctantly consented to take me with him to small golfing hotels but he was out playing all day and spent all evening in the bar, which seemed exclusively male. Poor Laurence! I could see how at ease and satisfied he was among his peers and saw, more clearly than ever, what a mistake Calcutta was for him—with no-one there of his prowess. Clearly, too, I saw that my presence spoiled it for him and it was better to stay out of the way with Percy and Florence, I and Chini whom in their goodness they welcomed; he was "Black-Faced, Full Feathered, Cream with Flowerings of Gold".

I wrote *Chinese Puzzle* in Doctor Percy's surgery.

To Jon: September 1935.

Percy lets me use his surgery when he is out on his rounds and, mercifully, in the evenings, otherwise I could not very well not sit with them in the drawing room after dinner when Percy, bless him, goes to sleep and Florence knits. I can't even listen to music on the gramophone against the clicking of those knitting needles, which drive me mad— horridly ungrateful when she is knitting for the baby. I can't go to bed and read because there are no books. Do you know, Jon, it seems that in all these suburbs round there isn't a single bookshop; this one is too new to have a library and Percy does not want me to risk going to London. The surgery is the only room in this "villa" sort of house where I can feel at ease; I think it's the professionalism of its glass-fronted cabinets, the rows of instruments—Florence keeps them beautifully—the examination couch, the smell of surgical spirit and disinfectants and bandages and the big desk. I am careful not to disturb notes or papers, and I can help by answering the telephone and taking messages . . .

There, forgetting my fears, and my money worries—Laurence had bought a magnificent golf bag, a new set of clubs and a car —forgetting even my cumbersome body, I wrote with the small original of my chinaman asleep in his basket at my feet— always, over the years at least one pekingese, sometimes three or four, have borne me company while I write—and so this absurd small fantasy, *Chinese Puzzle*, was spun, and how I loved the spinning of it!

With the usual trepidation I sent it to Curtis Brown and this time a letter came back, not from David Higham who had left the firm but from Spencer Curtis Brown, telling me he had immediately placed *Chinese Puzzle* with a publisher called Peter Davies of whom I had not heard.

I was still in bed when the letter came but later, in the spring, I was able to meet Spencer and I think I must be one of the agency's few authors left now who remember Spencer's father, the original Curtis Brown—Curtis was his "given" name—who had founded the firm.

Spencer took me to see him at his house in Cheyne Walk, the first time I had seen that famous place; old Mr. Curtis Brown describes it in his autobiography:

Perhaps Cheyne Walk is one of the most fascinating little streets in London, partly because it looks out over the Thames and across to Battersea Park, but more because of its literary and historical associations. Henry the Eighth's Chelsea Manor, or palace, as it was sometimes called, had adjoined the palace of the Bishops of Winchester, torn down in 1820 to make way for the group of houses of which ours, No. 27, was nearest to the site of the royal residence where the future Queen Elizabeth [I] spent much of her childhood to the age of sixteen. It was to this place that Admiral Seymour came to make love to the widow of Henry the Eighth, and it was here he lived for a time after the marriage, and here that he was declared to have romped riotously with the fifteen-year-old princess—the crumbling back wall separating our stuffy little garden from the grounds where the palace had stood, was almost certainly standing in Elizabeth's day, and is all that is left of the palace property. Anyway, I took much pride in the thought of little Elizabeth bouncing her ball against our garden wall. It was under the shadow of this wall, according to legend, that Seymour used to approach the palace from the back, coming along from King's Road. To the east of the palace, at what is now No. 16, stood a house said to have had as interesting a history as any in London. It was here that Dante Gabriel Rossetti and Swinburne lived, and here William Morris and the Pre-Raphaelites for-gathered.

George Eliot died at No. 5 and No. 18 is apparently pretty much the same building as that in which Addison, Steele and Swift and the Spectator group used to forgather.

The Carlyles lived around the corner, in Cheyne Row, and Whistler seems to have lived all up and down that stretch of the Thames Embankment . . .

No wonder I was awed. All I can remember of the old man was that he was sitting in a great red chair and spoke to me most kindly but I do not think I took in what he said. I kept thinking of Dacca and Dodo, of the short stories dismissed to *Titbits* and here was I—admitted.

I have never understood why the publishers, Peter Davies and his brother Nico, thought as they did of *Chinese Puzzle*. "Your exquisite little book . . . which is without doubt a masterpiece," wrote Peter, and Nico, "Among the loveliest [books] I have read." Looking at it now, I know it is a piece of whimsy chinoiserie, the whimsy made worse by my having used capitals for all the nouns and adjectives in a mannered affectation; they had not been too noticeable when hand-written—in those days publishers would accept a hand-written manuscript—but as soon as I saw them in proof there was a sickening recoil and I realised I had spoiled the book. It was too late; *Chinese Puzzle* was printed.

It brought me an advance of twenty-five pounds, normal for a first novel then, and almost the best reviews I have had, including two columns and a reproduction of the jacket in the *Sunday Times* where it was reviewed by G. B. Stern whose own dog novels, *The Dark Gentleman* and *The Ugly Dachshund*, were for connoisseurs:

> Our favourite character in this book is Citron, the cat, with his lewd and cynical comments on every situation, romantic, pompous, or philosophical.
>
> Rumer Godden in his [sic] book, "Chinese Puzzle", has plausibly got over the usual difficulty of "I like a dog to be a dog" by allowing the spirit of a wise Chinese presently to inhabit the body of a Pekingese. Wong-Li fell in love with his cousin, the Lady Little Finger;

insisted on marrying her, by a subterfuge, and had no son. He was sorrowful and died: "A Heron flew from the River. I flew with it. It was like a Great Sigh, like passing under a Bridge in a Boat from Sun to Shade and from Shade to Sun." When he was reborn as a pekingese in an orchard in England he clearly remembered his past life as a man; and it bothered him with curious persistence, between normal puppy occupations with his companions—the mastiff, the spaniel, the French bulldog, and other delightfully drawn characters —as to why this incarnation should have happened: "They called me 'Funny Little Dog'. I was not funny. I was beautiful and tragic, if they had only seen it." (We know that feeling!) The spattering of contemptuous French idiom from Manon, the French bulldog bitch, acts as an excellent astringent when Ting-Ling ("They called me Ting-Ling saying it was Chinese . . . It was a pretty Name, but it was not Chinese") was apt to get a little lush about blossom and superior about his Previous Existence.

In later years I came to know G. B. Stern well and she still persisted in liking this book!

Other critics followed. *The Observer*:

> It is a simple story. The publishers label it a Chinoiserie. And since we have been sophisticated by the Chinese exhibition, Chinoiserie is surely something at which right-minded people should turn up their noses. And yet there is a quality about the book which is very difficult to define. There is something that lingers in the memory like the after-taste of a good wine.

and, surprisingly, *Horse and Hound*:

> Written with the deft, delicate, sweetly humorous touch that makes of it just as much a masterpiece as the most lovely of Chinese pottery or brush painting . . .

Peter Davies advertised it lavishly with no success; my first royalty after six months was nine pounds, one shilling and threepence. After another six months, the threepence was all.

Laurence went back to Calcutta in December leaving Jane and me behind.

The two things I remember most about that winter are the Chinese Exhibition at Burlington House and that I could not go and see Peter Davies, because I had no winter clothes, and could not buy any, barely being able to pay the Fosters for our living.

The Chinese Exhibition made an indelible impression on me; it was the first major exhibition of art I had seen—India then was cut off from such feasts.

Did that earlier Chinese Exhibition surpass the later one of 1980? It would have been difficult to exceed that in beauty and yet I think the earlier exhibition did. To me it was a revelation; the ceramics, especially the white porcelain of the Ming Dynasty: the jade and silk: the bronzes, the calligraphy, scrolls and paintings on silk and rice-paper.

Things Chinese have always held a particular fascination for me—as has already been shown. I had discovered

Arthur Waley's translation of Chinese poems with their economy and ironic wit and loved the emptiness, or frugality, of Chinese painting which is anything but empty, being like the pauses or silences in music which are almost more important than the notes. That exhibition transformed those cold dark months for me.

There was no-one to share its joy; the only person I knew, then, who could have was Jon and she was housebound still in one of her strange bouts of illness which nobody could explain.

January 1936

I should rather go to an Exhibition with Jon than anyone I have known; as if you share her eyes, she makes you see what you would have missed without her but, perhaps, it is even better to be alone because then nothing can come between you and what you are looking at and, unless you can share without words, how explain why you find rapture in a white china bowl with a faint tracery of leaves? In a miniature horse in pearl green jade, lying curled on a stand—you

235

could hold it between your finger and thumb if you dared touch it? Or in a painting of pansies on a silk scroll?

And so I went alone, every time I could scrape the money for the fares, though I shivered in my thin coat.

The rapture should have lasted but jogging back in the suburban train depression and loneliness always overcame me. "But you've been to the Exhibition," Florence used to say, mystified. "Why do you want to go again?" It was rather like someone who, asked if they would like a book for Christmas, said, "I've got one," and "What am I doing here?" I asked myself. Soon, as I walked up the road between the neat villas, with names like Mirzapore or Pollards, The Laburnums or Whispers, each with its neat front garden that all summer had been bright with American Pillar or Dorothy Perkins rambler roses and patches of bright aubrietia and where now the first signs of aconites and crocuses were showing around a concrete bird bath or sundial, I could not help the old anger waking in me and, seething, I used to mutter under my breath, but through my teeth:

> Sent as a present from Annam
> A red cockatoo.
> Coloured like the peach-tree
>   blossom
> Speaking with the speech of men.
> And they did to it what is always
>   done
> To the learned and eloquent.
> They took a cage with stout bars
> And shut it up inside.*

It was not, I hasten to add, that I thought of myself as the cockatoo but he represented all the wisdom and beauty I had been revelling in and for which these people seemed not to care a whit—which was probably unfair; how right Mona had been to censure my intolerance of ordinariness.

To despise ought to be one of the seven deadly sins and the psalmist's "coals of juniper" were waiting for me; I had

---

* "The Red Cockatoo". Po-Chii. Translated by Arthur Waley.

thought the Fosters had no idea why I would not go and see Curtis Brown or Peter and Nico Davies who had repeatedly asked me but, one evening when I came back, Percy called me into the surgery, gave me a cheque and told me not to be silly. "Of course you must go and see your publisher," said Florence. "Go and get yourself an outfit." "Outfit" must mean "fit to go out", fit to have lunch in the West End with Peter Davies, who in actuality would not have minded if I had come in a sack.

Peter was Peter Llewellyn Davies who, with his brothers, was a protégé of J. M. Barrie and the original Peter Pan; a wry look would come on his face if anyone mentioned the book. Understandably, he shrank even more from the *Little White Bird* which is so unabashed in its sentimentality that it is difficult to comprehend how the man who wrote plays of the wit and calibre of *The Admirable Crichton* and *What Every Woman Knows* could have perpetrated it. Nico Davies has told the Llewellyn Davies story in his book *The Lost Boys* but I knew nothing of it then and, of course, committed the solecism of talking about Barrie.

You would think, for an author, her first celebration luncheon with her publisher—in my case two publishers because Nico was there—would be remembered as long as she lived but it is vague now and merged with other lunches which must have been two or three years later. I remember that Peter seemed to me young to be a publisher, though he was a good deal older than I and, I fathomed at once, equally shy and even more sensitive. In his obituary he was rightly called an "artist among publishers . . ."

"Witty, astringent, with a brilliant and remarkable knowledge of literature." We made such a bond that, though we did not often meet, words and letters were hardly needed. When back in Calcutta I was to send him the manuscript of the second novel he published, *The Lady and the Unicorn*, some three weeks later—the time it would have taken to reach him—one evening in the garden, I seemed to hear his voice and knew exactly what he felt about the book, confirmed by the letter of acceptance which came later.

*The Lady and the Unicorn* was not to do well either and I am glad to think Peter Davies was eventually repaid for this and the losses over *Chinese Puzzle*.

For years I have kept a letter Peter wrote to me; it is my talisman. It must have been written after another luncheon together when we walked back from the Ivy to their office. Dear Ivy! It was then the restaurant where you saw most well-known writers and theatre people, and where to get a table was an achievement. I loved its dark panelling, the red plush, the small intimate foyer, as much as I later disliked the more fashionable Caprice.

We had been talking about what I should do next and Peter wrote:

Looking back on our conversation at lunch, I feel an impulse to repeat to you what I think I said at the time, namely that I feel violently convinced that you ought not to be deflected from whatever from time to time seems your natural inclination, by any ideas about conventionality or the public demand. Just write whatever the spirit moves you to write, and forget every other consideration. I think you are one of those writers who will appeal to a section of the reading public no matter what approach you make to them.

One way and another, I do not think an artist such as yourself either ought to compromise with the general public or would be able to do so, and that it will be best for you to write to please yourself and arrive at a sale of 10,000 copies rather than to write a book to please the public in the hope of arriving at a sale of 100,000 copies.

And I do not admit that the proper interpretation of this letter is that I have no business to be a publisher!

"Or would be able to do so". After Mona's training, I suppose I could, if challenged, write anything in any form but it would not "breathe"—you need a more journalistic instinct to be able to accomplish that; several times I have been tempted by some offer or idea to write something alien to me but always knew it would be wiser to go out and—almost I wrote "scrub floors", which is not true because I would be useless at scrubbing floors—but do anything, no matter how menial or humdrum rather than put my writing under duress and write, as it were, in chains. "An artist such as yourself", those were words to give a warm lift to the spirit and, in the innumerable moments of self-doubt—what my agent calls "Godden gloom"—I read them over and over again but in that my first, in a shy way literary summer I was not ready to be Peter's whole-hearted artist yet.

Once again, it was the lure of dancing; as if the Fosters' cheque had given me a key of freedom, I could come and go in London almost as I liked; they were able to afford a maid now so that Florence could look after Jane and asked nothing better—she and Percy adored their grand-child; at least we had been able to give them this.

In the world of dance that summer, Colonel de Basil's Ballet Russes de Monte Carlo was in London with the young dancers, Lichine and the "baby ballerinas" beauteous Baranova, Toumanova of the eloquent dark eyes, both under sixteen and, to me, most exquisite of all, Tatiana

Riabouchinska who seemed more spirit than mortal. There, too, a little older, was Danilova of the long legs and Volkova who had come from Russia via China and much hardship. It was a renaissance of ballet after several attempts to create companies after Diaghilev's death, and I was lucky enough to come into the orbit of Merlin Severn, an extraordinary photographer of ballet and forerunner of much of the technique used now.

Merlin was big and burly, more man than woman with short brushed golden hair and sharp shrewd blue eyes. She lived with a young woman, Dana, an artist who had been at Art School with Jon and was later to do the illustrations for my first book for children, *The Doll's House*. At that time Dana was in thrall to Merlin; I was enthralled, too, and almost every performance went to the ballet with Merlin, ostensibly to help carry and hold her paraphernalia but really to be near the magic.

Fa had come to the end of his halcyon time in Tezpur and he and Mam came back to England, this time for good as Fa had retired reluctantly, tearing himself away from everything he loved. "I can shoot, fish and sail here," he had said, not realising how much in Britain they cost. They had decided to settle in the West Country and while they were looking for a house—they could never agree on this—rented one at Tigley Cross, near Totnes in Devon. They had brought Rose with them, Jon came from Eastbourne to join them and, when the London season ended, I arrived with Jane and Chini so that, except for Nancy who was running the dancing school for me in Calcutta, we were all together again, "For a short while," Mam mourned. Jon and Rose were getting ready for their weddings.

Roland Oakley had adored Jon from the first time he saw her at a children's dance in Eastbourne—his mother and Mam had been at school together. He was a dear and attractive person in spite of his real ugliness; he, too, loved books and art and was an outstanding dancer which appealed to me but he was always Jon's. She had met him again in Calcutta when, for a short while after Nigel's death, she had come there to try to earn her living by commercial art, staying with me in the School and going round the offices of every sort of firm to show her work but soon, "I would rather starve," said Jon. She did get orders, "out of pity," she said, which was not quite true; paradoxically, her drawing had grown stronger, lost the slight whimsiness of the chinoiserie paintings and showed clearly what she had always had, an unusual eye for colour and composition.

Reading her diaries I have come across an entry I had not seen before: it was written soon after Nigel died:

I shall see the sun again and feel different and soon there will be left only a shadow in my mind. That is the worst part of it, that it gets better and we are tricked into being happy again for a little while. It is a continual betrayal; of what use is the strongest love against death!

I can hear the Doctor saying to me, "Now you must try and reorganise your life," and can feel again the cold despair and rebellion that came over me as he said it. Since then I have never made the least attempt to organise my life, everything has just happened to me. No-one else has ever realised this.

It explains much about Jon. How irresistible Roland's love and protection must have been; she "let it happen".

In a way Rose, too, had let it happen. She had accepted C.D. Why not? He offered her every enticement: a quite palatial home of her own, servants, clothes—clothes mean a great deal to Rose; her own car, travel—C.D. went skiing in Yugoslavia and in France.

She could indulge her passion for animals, especially horses—a passion he shared—he gave her a race-horse, Benares —but C.D. was far older than she; a cold, reserved man, she warm and impetuous, and we felt she was uncertain, how uncertain we were soon to know.

As a wedding present Fa had given her a course of lessons from a famous Belgian riding master—I shall call him Monsieur Charles—who taught dressage and haute école at Mill Hill; she went up and down by train from Devon. Rose must have been outstandingly good because, one evening when she came home, she announced that Monsieur Charles had offered to take her in with him; she had accepted and would not go out to India or marry C.D.

Everyone was flabbergasted.

"Go in with a frog!" Fa raged.

"Fa, he's Belgian, not French."

"No difference," said Fa.

I tried to defend Rose. "She's not going to ride in a circus," which became the legend handed down about Rose: she was going to ride in a circus. I wish she had, in haute école which has always fascinated us. Sitting side-saddle, in a tailored habit, top hat with a little veil, a silver-handled whip, silver spurs on her boots, she would have looked superb; there was one horse of Monsieur Charles she especially loved but, circus or not, to Fa, then, any professional to do with riding was beyond the social pale and he stopped the lessons at once.

Mam had been intrigued. "Is Monsieur Charles good-looking?" and I half hoped Rose would run away but she was never a fighter. "Rose, don't marry C.D.," I wanted to say, perhaps Mam did say—she never liked C.D.—but, "It is arranged," said

Rose. Rose not only accepts but seldom gives an inkling of what she is feeling, which is worrying. "That girl's a good-looking oyster!" said Fa in despair.

The plan was for Jon to travel out with me and Jane that October; Rose to follow later.

In this book it must seem we go back and forth to India like shuttlecocks, which we did. I who was there the shortest time made twelve sea-voyages, several by air; Jon perhaps thirty not counting going by sea via Madagascar, the Cape and New York; Nancy, who stayed longest and knows more about India than any of us, has lost count.

We were to sail on the *Orion* of the Orient Line from Southampton as far as Ceylon where we would stay a few days in Colombo with the Simons. Jay was stationed there now and he and Jimmie had a daughter, too, Gemma, one year older than Jane and also red-headed. We would then catch another boat for Calcutta.

Doctor Percy and Florence came down to Tigley Cross to say goodbye and to collect Chini; with their usual generosity they had offered to keep him until I came back which I hoped would not be too long.

Fa was driving us to Southampton. It was arranged we should all leave together as Doctor Percy had to get back to his practice and, after luncheon, I went upstairs to get Jane changed and ready and fasten our cases. Chini was lying on the bed watching me, his eyes wide with apprehension; pekingese are even more alert to what is happening than most dogs —he had refused to touch his food that morning and his tail had drooped all day. This was the second pekingese I had had to leave and I could not help remembering what had happened to Piers. "I'm coming back, Chini, I promise." The eyes were still wide.

I carried Jane downstairs, then came back to fetch him. He was gone, only a little dint on the bed showing where he had been.

We searched the house and garden. Rose and the houseboy, who was "let" with the house, went into the fields. Fa drove up and down the road and into the village. We telephoned the police. I called, listened, called. At last, "We have to go," said Fa. "We'll miss the ship."

Chini was never heard of again. Had he slipped out, got onto the road, been picked up by a car and stolen? Been run over and put in the car by someone who did not want to confess? I had nightmares of his having gone down a rabbit hole and not been able to get out, of being caught by a paw in a trap and dying, shrieking with pain, then becoming limp with hunger and thirst. There is no torture worse than not knowing. What must it be like when a child disappears, your husband, your wife? Chini was only a little dog but it still torments.

"Do you have to go back to India?" Merlin had asked me that autumn. "You shouldn't."

Should or should not? There had been no choice because, at the core of all those months was the warm little glow of Jane, and Jane belonged to Laurence as much as to me.

Nancy and I were the lucky ones. Neither Jon nor Rose had children.

Nancy was the last of us to marry, in

that quiet church on Dartmoor; Dick, later Sir Ridgeby, was another Foster, which, though he and Laurence were not related, led to difficulties. "I mean the Mrs. Foster who was a Miss Godden," people used to say.

Dick was an outstanding man; coming from comparatively obscure people—his father was a seedsman in a modest way, his mother a teacher—he had made his way himself from Reading School to Reading University and a scholarship to Cambridge. For a time he was in the Imperial College of Agriculture in Trinidad but was picked out by Imperial Chemical Industries who sent him to India where he ended up as Chairman of ICI India, President of the Chamber of Commerce and with a knighthood. He was also extraordinarily handsome, tall, black-haired, eagle-nosed, and had an intriguing scar on his cheek which might have been got in a student duel in Heidelberg—one of the legends about him; in fact, as a small boy, he had climbed up a tent at a flower show and fallen into a glass frame and was badly cut.

Nancy and Dick were to have two sons;

Simon, the elder, inherited his father's brilliance in business, the younger Richard, the Godden artistry but in films. Simon might have been my son, I had so much to do with bringing him up.

They, though, were to come later; Jane was at present the only grandchild and had her first birthday in Calcutta. Laurence was devoted to her; we seemed a happy family, and to make it complete Sol and Wing came to us. After Chini I had said I would never have another pekingese, but a young woman we knew was suddenly widowed and had to go back to England and leave her two pekingese behind, an old one, Sol, and his son, Wing. I shall not forget the day she left them with me; both pekingese went to the end of the lawn and sat with their backs to the house, their heads turned resolutely away to the wall. They did not die, as, in Chinese history, bereft pekingese died of broken hearts; they lived, perhaps because I did not attempt to cajole them but respected their grief.

Laurence and I had this in common, our love of animals. As a little boy he had had a hulak monkey; hulaks have enormously long arms and Laurence's mother Florence told me how the monkey and the little boy used to walk together, sit together—they were inseparable—with the monkey's arm wound twice round Laurence's neck. At first he was not sure about the pekingese. "Lap dogs," he said, as do most people who do not know them, but he was soon won over, especially by Wing.

Sol was a mandarin, golden-coated, but his son, Wing! Pekingese do not breed well in India, as I was to learn, but never have I seen such a disgrace to the race as Wing. To begin with he was liver-coloured —an unacceptable colour—smooth-coated, not a trace of feathering and had a ruff of such peculiar coarseness that it stuck out like a collar of quills. His tail was a tuft, his legs bowed almost to a half-hoop—I am sure he had "crab toes"; his nose was brown—unthinkable—and his face had the hideousness of a cheerful kylin, but even in a thousand years there could never have been another Wing. He did not know of course how hideous he was nor, soon, did I.

It was partly Wing's cleverness, his spirit of fun; I have not known another dog who would play hide-and-seek with humans; he used to wait for Laurence to come back from the office, hiding under a chair behind the door, ready to spring out on him the moment it opened, then dash away to hide all over the house; Laurence had to hide too.

It was partly, too, Wing's philosophy; when he first came he was mortally afraid of water and would never swim in the "tanks" or pools on the Maidan as, in the hot weather, the other pekingese did, but for a short leave we went to the Coromandel coast where the high surf-rollers pound along the beach; bathers there have to wear the local fishermen's pointed wicker helmets to break the waves and prevent themselves from being stunned.

We are walking on the sands by moonlight and Wing is catching crabs and follows them too far downshore; suddenly a roller catches him and sweeps him far out into the Indian Ocean. We think he is gone forever but the next wave brings him back, rolling him stunned, bruised, breathless and sodden at our feet.

He was never afraid of water again.

Our household staff was augmented too. With Sol and Wing had come Khokil, their sweeper; I think he would have gone anywhere to be with them because he shared my passion for pekingese and his pride was enormous when I bought a little white bitch, Moon Daisy. On feast days Khokil gave each dog a chupatti, a soft biscuit like a waffle, that he bought in the bazaar. Every dog he looked after, every puppy, remembered and adored him.

Khokil was a Rajput, the warrior race, tall, well made with big features and a huge moustache, more like a general than a sweeper. He wore good clothes, a spotless flowing dhoti, a khaki shirt and a black silk hat, and had manners and courtesy but was, of course, an Untouchable whose duty was to keep the house floors clean, attend to the bathrooms but not touch basins or baths and, particularly, look after and cook for the dogs. Over the years he became a real friend—and there was Old Ayah.

It turned out to be fortunate that I had been vouchsafed those few summer weeks of ballet; though the royalties on *Chinese Puzzle* had not yet reached that nadir of threepence, it was clear I could not, at the moment, earn a living by writing but earn I must and, willy-nilly, had to take over the School again from Nancy freeing her to go to England for her marriage. I was worried on two counts: first, Jane—Calcutta is an unhealthy place for small children—and secondly because I knew, in every nerve and instinct, that there was one thing vital I had to do, hold to the writing—difficult, almost impossible at that time, to do, but if you wait for a favourable time you will never do anything. *The Lady and the Unicorn* was written sitting at my desk on the School's verandah, which was also my office and the waiting room, mothers, nurses and ayahs all round me, classes going on next door.

*The Lady and the Unicorn* is a sad book —perhaps poignant is a better word because it is the story of Rosa, a young Eurasian girl—she could have been one of the cabaret girls I had come to know so well—who, when they fall in love with an Englishman, are almost inexorably doomed to unhappiness. I have a tenderness for this book; it belongs to a poignant time.

After being with Peter Davies, Merlin Severn and people of their kin, I was more of a misfit in Laurence's Calcutta than ever and began, for the book, a different life nobody saw or knew about. I haunted old Calcutta: its once-great houses like Hastings House, where a mysterious coach and four, or the sound of it, pulls up at midnight under the portico, doors are opened and there are voices, laughter, the rustle of silk and taffeta, footsteps in light boots, until it drives away: I spent hours in the old Park Street cemeteries which go back to East India Company days, walking among the headstones, many of them of people too young to die, young ensigns, young wives, many many children. I walked where most Europeans went in cars, if they went at all, into narrow reeking lanes and alleyways, one of a throng of people, forced into the gutter by cars, tongas and buffalo carts, dodging rickshaws and bicycles, goats, hens, pai-dogs, sacred bulls: stepping over babies, pools of cess, garbage and all the time looking into rooms where perhaps a whole family lived, furnished by a bed with a tattered mosquito net, a table covered in oil cloth, a meatsafe for a larder, clothes hung on a string and all kept in Eurasian fashion, immaculately clean.

It was a world away from the society round of golf, tennis, riding, cocktail parties, dancing at the Four Hundred Club, racing at Tollygunj or the Turf Club's members' stand on the race-course for Gold Cup Day: the Viceroy's Ball at Belvedere: children's parties . . . all of which I went to and often enjoyed, but never told where I had really been.

"What have you been doing?" Laurence used to ask when I came in late.

"Nothing."

"It must have been something," but what it was he could not know. Laurence never read any of my books, nor did I want him to, or my children because I know how extremely hard it is for anyone in an author's family to read their work; there is an innate shrinking, simply because they are too close. There are, of course, rare exceptions but those are bibliophiles and ironically a time came when my grandchildren had to read some of the books because they were "set" for examinations, but we have never discussed them.

This double life of mine was made possible by two people, Ears and Old Ayah.

When I had arrived that autumn with Jane, it was to find that Ears had already sent to Sikkim for his aunt—he was sure no-one but his own family could be trusted with Laurence's baby. Old Ayah was as sturdy as he, but darker-skinned; she wore immaculate white skirts, a tight white bodice with silver buttons, some handsome jewellery, and a red wool tartan headcloth. From the first moment she took full charge of Jane, to Jane's content—I think she owes part of her serenity to her years with Old Ayah, who was wise and calm. After she left us she became a Buddhist nun. How I should have loved to have taken Old Ayah with me to England but, in

259

those days, if you took a woman servant "across the black water" you had to sign a contract that you would bring her back "in good condition" and I was not at all sure I was coming back.

Things were getting steadily darker, the news from Europe more menacing, disturbing even Calcutta where its own miasma of greed and evil seemed to be growing. In January 1938 my dear German doctor committed suicide; it was not only shock and grief for him that seemed to raze me; I needed him—there was to be another child.

Paula Janaki was born on 2 September 1938 in Cornwall where Fa and Mam had found a house, so that I had them as a refuge. The house was Darrynane, down a steep hill below the village of St. Breward on the Bodmin moors. "You will love Darrynane," I wrote to Jon. After the rented houses we had come to think of as our destiny in England, it seemed unbelievably gracious.

It is set on the side of a hill, looking far

down the valley and is built mostly of lathe and plaster like an Indian hill house, which is why Mam loves it and Fa hates it. [They could never agree on homes.] The garden is wild and beautiful; there is a waterfall, quite a big one, and the drive is bordered by blue hydrangeas growing taller than one's head. The rhododendrons, red, pale pink and white, and the azaleas are so vivid they throw coloured reflections on the room walls. There is one big sitting/dining room with a log fire where we sit for sherry in the evenings. They have a cook, and a house parlourmaid and a gardener, Neal, who is already Mam's ally and slave. He comes at seven in the morning and leaves his pasty on the kitchen window sill for Dorothy (the cook) to find and warm for his dinner.

This time, the doctor—not Doctor Percy —told me, "Well, you have had a funny little scrap," and a scrap Paula was—so tiny the villagers thought she was a changeling; very premature, at three months old she only weighed five pounds and the doctors told me not to set my heart on her; of course it was set already.

To keep her uncertain wick of life alive, Paula had to be watched around the clock and I had to maintain a nursery establishment in the small Lodge that belonged to Darrynane. There was Nurse, professionally trained. I am grateful to Nurse; only a professional, meticulous in care, could have brought Paula through those months —but I could not like her. She would do no nursery work and I had to keep Alice, the village nursery maid originally engaged to help with Jane, but now to wait on Nurse, who would not even sit down at table with her. Nurse and Alice did the days, I had to do the nights. My days being spent writing.

To Jon:
You would laugh if you could see us. One of Doctor Percy's rich patients has given me a Rolls-Royce of a perambulator, opulently white which pleases Nurse and every afternoon she, in uniform, parades up and down the village street with Alice, in uniform too, pushing the carriage—poor Alice! You

know how hilly St. Breward is. Nurse holds Jane's hand. Jane is in a tailored coat with a velvet collar—from the same source as the pram—white socks, white gloves, while I in ancient slacks, jersey and tousled hair, work in the donkey hut, the only place available—Fa has installed a stove and a table—and wonder how in heaven on earth I am going to pay for all this.

I need not have worried. On the voyage home, not feeling able to cope with shipboard life—second-class on the *Orion* again—when Jane went to bed at half-past six, I went to bed as well. A kind steward brought me dinner and, as she slept in the lower bunk, I, sitting up in the top one so that my head almost touched the ceiling, wrote in cheap little Indian exercise books, filling one after the other, until ten or eleven at night. Bombay to Tilbury then took eighteen days and when we landed at Tilbury I had almost the full draft of a book.

The book was *Black Narcissus.*

# 9

## Black Narcissus

"FA, I'm writing a book about nuns."
"Don't," said Fa. "No-one will
read it."

"Six printings in one week": "Steadily
climbing the Best-Seller Charts":
"Third in the Charts": "Top of the
Charts"—

As a matter of fact *Black Narcissus* did not
make the top of the charts but,

"The most unusual and delightful book
of the summer", "I have bought a dozen
copies for those friends I most cherish."
"Don't miss it."

Written in 1938, now, in 1987, *Black
Narcissus* has never been out of print.
 Long, long before this when I was, I
think, eighteen years old and we were in

Shillong, we went on a picnic to nearby Cherrapunji, a deserted cantonment on a plateau, high above the surrounding gorges. I wandered away from the others and going down a steep little path came upon a grave; it was marked only by a small headstone in the shape of a cross with a name, "Sister . . ." and two dates; she had died when she was only twenty-three.

No-one could tell me anything about her; no other graves were near, no sign of any mission, but the villagers had made her grave a shrine; it was daubed with whitewash and there were offerings: a saucer of rice, an egg—in India eggs are thought particularly valuable—a string of marigolds.

I never saw that grave again, for all I know it may have disappeared but, twelve years later in that bunk on board the *Orion* I began: "The Sisters left Darjeeling in the last week in October. They had come to settle in the General's palace at Mopu which was now to be known as the Convent of St. Faith . . ."

All imaginative writing starts the same way, from some note of sight or sound, heard, read or seen—once, for me, it was a painting—that does not pass away, leaving only a memory but which lodges in the mind like a seed. Why one thing more than another I do not know, nobody knows but, like a seed, it germinates, occasionally at once but, usually, years later. When it does quicken, it begins, like a grit in an oyster, to use another metaphor, to secrete things round it— "secretes" because this should be an intensely secretive time. This—can it be called a process?—goes on until the grit grows into a whole. The result, of course, is seldom a pearl but it is a whole book, novel, short story, children's book or poem.

I finished *Black Narcissus* in August 1938 a month before Paula was born. She coincided with the Munich crisis when Mr. Chamberlain flew back from his confrontation with Hitler and, as he came down the steps from the aeroplane, flourished a piece of paper, proclaiming it was "Peace, with honour". I wonder how many people believed him; if they did they were quickly disillusioned. I, like thousands of others of my age, had signed the

Peace Pledge: "In no circumstances will I fight for King or Country." We soon knew we would have to break that pledge, and, in those nights of watching over Paula, walking up and down the room with her, trying to hush that weak wailing, get her to sleep for at least a short while, I thought of my dear doctor's suicide in Calcutta, of what was happening to Jews like him as the evil of Nazidom spread over the world, and it seemed it was not one to bring children into; the broken nights turned into such real insomnia that I seriously thought of hiring a caravan to take Jane, Paula and myself up to some remote place on the moor and ending everything by setting fire to it.

I am ashamed to remember this now yet am glad, in a way, that I knew that abyss as it has helped me to understand other people's hopelessness.

To Jon:          New Year's Eve 1938.

It seems, thank goodness, this depression isn't only me—I mean in my mind—if I've still got a mind. Dr. Bailey says I have some terrific-long-name nervous affliction of the heart and has given me masses of pills that are probably worth their weight in gold! It explains all these bumping and palpitations and sleeplessness; now that Paula is better over sleeping I ought to be able to sleep too. He says I must have no mental strain or worry! I can only say, "Ha. Ha." I cannot though deal with Laurence over money any more; he makes me feel like Dolly in *Anna Karenina*, always nagging, always fretting.

It seems when I am on the brink of despair—as I have been several times—something has always happened to rescue me; only once, though, something as wonderful as *Black Narcissus*.

Spencer Curtis Brown had had the book typed for me. I was not able to go to London and see him or the Davies brothers—they must have thought I only came to England to have babies! This time it was Nancy, on a short leave, who went to them for me. Curtis Brown was then in Henrietta Street, close to Covent Garden;

Nancy had a little oriental-looking hat and, with her slightly tilted eyes, looked almost Chinese; the vegetable lorry drivers used to call out to her, "Hello, Chu Chin Chow."

The initial reception of the book was kind but not enthusiastic though Peter Davies did say it was a beautiful piece of work and increased my royalty, doubling the advance to fifty pounds. Spencer said it seemed "a most satisfactory book" but in the same letter told me there was a chance of my getting an American publisher for *The Lady and the Unicorn*, on condition that he need not publish *Black Narcissus*; he feels, wrote Spencer, it would be a much less attractive book to the American public—obviously that publisher shared Fa's view. "No-one will read it," and so it seemed that, with this book, there was not a great deal to look forward to, either in money or notice. In that dark winter, sealed off, as it seemed with Paula, I almost forgot about it . . .

*Black Narcissus* was published in January 1939. By some oversight nobody told me—probably Spencer and Peter were too dismayed by what was happening in Europe; the lull after Munich was more than uneasy but it was at least a lull and as Paula was better, in February Fa suggested I should go with Mam to London for a few days. "To have a change, do some theatres, spend some of that fifty pounds," and, "*I'll* look after Paula," said Fa.

As with Nancy, who had been almost as delicate, Fa had taken notice of Paula from a baby; he would carry her with extraordinary tenderness and often he could still her crying. "I'll look after her." He had, of course, Nurse and Alice to help him, Dorothy, the cook and a maid—Fa did not make as much as a cup of tea for himself, though now and again he was moved to concoct one of his two specialities, either that quite elaborate dish, a stuffed marrow or a potato salad, particularly the last. "No-one else can make it taste!" he said; his was made with chives and, not the usual mayonnaise, but a French dressing. For these gourmanderies, he had to be left completely alone in the kitchen and used almost every pan, bowl, spoon, knife and fork, which he did not consider washing up.

Before we left, I had a letter from Peter Davies telling me that there had been, "quite a little movement in sales" and that "taking it all round . . . it [*Black Narcissus*] has had a good press". I then had not seen cuttings and, as I meant to devote myself to Mam and we had our plans, there seemed no particular reason to break into them and see either the Davies brothers or Spencer, especially as I had not settled on an idea for another book but, the day before we were due to go back to Cornwall, I was travelling along Charing Cross Road on a bus, which was held up for a moment or two opposite Foyle's twin bookshops which were divided by a narrow street, Sutton Row. There, stretched between them, hung a banner: "BLACK NARCISSUS by RUMER GODDEN". I was nearly run over as I flung myself off the bus; I went into Foyle's, and stood there dazed.

Foyle's is a tall bookshop. It has, I think, four floors and each is made to look smaller by the shelves and stands of books, more books set out on tables and perhaps there were not really as many people milling round as there seemed to my amazed eyes; most of the people were round a table in the centre of the shop which was piled high with *Black Narcissus* in its striped green and grey jacket, stamped with a stylised *Black Narcissus* on the spine. My *Black Narcissus*! People were queuing as two salesmen tried to deal with them.

I stood and watched trying to believe this was really happening. It did not occur to me that I could have made myself known but, back at the hotel, I telephoned Spencer who was as irascible as only Spencer could be. "Where the hell have you been? We've been trying and trying to get you. Come here, first thing tomorrow morning."

I could not come. Nurse was going on holiday. "Damn Nurse," said Spencer, which I could not do. When we reached Darrynane there were telephone messages, two telegrams and a pile of letters. "Oh, yes," said Fa. "A lot of people have been bothering but I thought it could all wait until you were home."

To Jon: March 1939.

Spencer has written asking for photographs and biographical details. He says, "They'll want to know all sorts of things; if you are kind to cats and a judge of light French wines." He tells me Humbert Wolfe is going to review *Black Narcissus*. Oh Jon!

Jon and Roland's marriage seemed, at any rate on the surface, to be a success; they had moved to an exquisite small house outside Calcutta, near the Country Club of Tollygunj. Roland, though, spoiled Jon even more than had Fa and Mam so that she could be a termagant; it was only the war and, later, her own work—she was to turn from painting to writing—that gave her any sense of perspective and, of course, the sensibility she never lost.

Calcutta.
(perhaps 1938 or 1939?)

I like my house, the animals, the anchor I have made, its colours and its beauty; the food we eat, the liking we have for drink, the making of salads, new and exciting, the making of lemony-rum cocktails, planning the menus. [She had a superb cook; Roland was a gourmet.] All this is good and I like it. Now I have a horse, Mirabelle, and can see the feeds being mixed and watch the syce cleaning the saddle, here at my door. Now my clothes are right and my hair is at last right, close and smooth to my head. [She had an ayah, Jetti, solely to look after her and her clothes.] When I have been out I love to come back to this cool shut-away house and the green garden . . . [but it was not all well].

Yes, all the externals of my life are pleasing and good and at last I have a shell round me that is light and easy and well coloured if not perfect, but inside the shell there is nothing, no heart except perhaps a feeling for R [Roland] but there is nothing to build a life on. If only I could write and have a core of hard work, an inner life—which is the only real life—how much more perfect the shell would be. If only I could say, all this is *added* to my real self, my real life that nothing can spoil or take away from me, then life would be worth-while, but I can't say this—not yet.

From England, *Black Narcissus* spread to the Continent, and to America, where my publisher, not the doubting one but Little Brown of Boston, had the idea of bringing out, each week of that summer, a publicity postcard from an established and notable author—some I had revered for years: Margaret Kennedy of *The Constant Nymph*, Maurice Collis, Tennyson Jesse, A. A. Milne, America's Alexander Woolcott.

To Jon:
Alexander Woolcott is the critic who wrote about "the dozen copies bought for the friends I most cherish". Every post seems to bring cuttings or paragraphs from newspapers.

In that summer of 1939, in spite of the threat of war, nothing seemed to go wrong. Laurence came on leave but now I had not, willy-nilly, to be bound to him, or he to me, and there was enough money for him to go from golf course to golf course, playing where and as much as he liked. He was not often in Cornwall and, when we went to the Fosters, taking Jane, I escaped to London.

To Jon:                                London.
                                19 June 1939.

I have achieved a room in Queens Gate Terrace on the fourth floor of a very nice house run by Austrians. It is clean and quiet, rather expensive but it's such bliss to be there where I can work in quiet. I am planning to be out half the day collecting colour for *Cygnet* [a tentative book to be set in the ballet, which, never written, became the prototype of others] and for the rest work in my room at *Gypsy Gypsy* [a novel] which grows daily more highly coloured and impossible but fascinates me.

Later:

Dana has got me a ticket for the Victoria and Albert Museum reading room. It is a bit risky as it is meant for studying art and makes me feel a cheat as every day

I have to take out books—presumably I am studying the French Impressionists and put them up around me, while in the middle I am writing *Gypsy*, and how beautiful they are: Degas, who of course takes me straight away from *Gypsy* to the ballet: Monet, Manet, Renoir: only to look at them makes me want to stop writing and sink into their beauty. I shall be caught out, though, as some of the books are in Italian and German—I can only just cope with French.

I was caught out; an elderly man near me whispered something I could not understand, at which he looked pained and surprised; he was German and the book I appeared to be working on was in German! All the same I found it bliss.

The reading room is so spacious and scholarly—do you realise, Jon, we have, neither of us, been in a scholarly place before? At one o'clock I come down and buy my lunch at the canteen—a roll with butter, cheese and tomato or ham costs 4d., a cup of coffee 2d.—I take them into the courtyard where it seems always to be sunny. If I get stiff from sitting I go into the park and Kensington Gardens and wander along the Row or by the Serpentine where I can watch the horses and ducks as I think out a scene or some lines of dialogue.

This has always been my habit—writing in my head while I am walking.

Jon herself had at last started to write, first an attempt at a novel about an alsatian bitch which was eventually to become her successful *Told in Winter* and also short stories, so that our letters of this time and, I suppose every time after this, are about writing though mixed, of course, as our lives were, with everyday things: accounts of her house, East Lodge in Tollygunj: "I love the sound of your house," I wrote to her, "full of flowers, birds, fish and pekingese and would love to see it." The birds were in a huge aviary in the garden; the fish, tropical with fantails and fan gills of glinting colours, were in glass tanks on the verandah, with floors of white coral, sand and shells and water plants growing above them; besides her own pekingese she was keeping Sol and Wing. Roland loved them as much as she did. "How lucky you are to have Roland. Someone always ready to help whom you can talk to and rely on."

In my letters I wrote of Darrynane, Fa, Mam and particularly of the children. Jon had a deep bond with Jane.

Jane is delicious these days, not so much pretty as what Nannies call "taking" and tremendously friendly—everyone from our neighbouring Duchess to the chimney sweep are Jane's "special friends". Paula is coming on slowly but is still something of a snowdrop.

Jon and I sent each other everything we wrote, this until almost the day of her death.

Darrynane.

"Miss Passanah" [a short story] came this morning and it is exquisite, Jon, not quite balanced yet but right in every detail. I find it hard to criticise at all but think you have perhaps underwritten the point of the story—i.e. the paradox of human nature shown in her overwhelming pity for the animals in contrast to her cruelty to the coolies and the child, Lily, which should be the strongest, whereas the bit about the slaughter cart haunts me still and please, please, at the very end, let Miss Passanah go to sleep with the child's sobs going on unheeded. That crying *must* go on . . . Anyway it's a beautifully done piece of work that was difficult and delicate. When you have thought over all this will you let me show it and the others to Curtis Brown?

"Miss Passanah" was sold to *Story Magazine* in America.

Jon was, and always had been, more talented than I but, though she was to have critical acclaim—her first novel to be published in Britain was a Book Society Choice—she did not have the same measure of what is called "success". Yet she rejoiced if anything good came my way and not once was in any way envious. She wanted me to tell her everything.

*Black Narcissus* sold 16,650 copies in America last week and over 5000 here and has been sold to Tauchnitz, Norway and Holland. I now get 20% royalties in America.

And myself in the midst of all this? A writer's life is, necessarily, such a lonely one, so uncertain that we flourish on praise and I was now on firm ground, acknowledged in the literary world and confirmed in the belief I had cherished so long in secret, that I was born to be a writer. This almost did away with two miseries that have beset me—and, I know, have diminished me all my life—jealousy and fear. I hope I was a nicer person. Some people are improved with success, as long as it does not become a habit; with writers there is little chance of that, there is always that next book to write.

"What are you going to do now?" Spencer Curtis Brown had asked me. "Write *White Carnation* or *Purple Petunia*?" He did not know, nor did Peter Davies, that I was already working on *Gypsy Gypsy*.

I am *obsessed* with *Gypsy* and what a mess it's in! As I go on, I clearly see I shall have to take out nearly all I've written. I must do it again, and send it to you to sort out for me—only this will take *months*!

One of the bonuses of that year was that I came really to know Spencer Curtis Brown, that strange unpredictable man.

The first time I met him outside the office was when he and his wife, Jean, asked me to drinks at their house in Belgrave Street. Their daughter, Phoebe, was about eight years old and prettily handed round little "eats"; what Jean and Spencer did not know was that, after perhaps half-an-hour, as Phoebe presented her bowl of, say, nuts, she whispered to each guest, "Wouldn't you like to go home now? You see, if you did, they might read me a story before I go to bed."

*Black Narcissus* had not been published a month before the dramatic rights were sold. The producer, the papers reported, was in a great hurry to get this best-selling novel. The script is to be ready by October 1 and the New York Opening is scheduled for early November.

This, of course, did not happen—with plays and films it seldom does; to begin with, the script when it came was farcical and, "Why don't you write it?" said Spencer.

"I? I've never written a play."

"Then write one now."

I came up to London to do this, and every evening, for nearly a month, Spencer came to help me, going over the day's work with me then taking me out to dinner, to talk and sometimes to dance. He was unfailing.

Some of his authors have written about Spencer as if he were a cruel monster, as he could be, and sometimes a violent one, but there were two Spencers and, for a long time, the only one I knew was gentle, even tender.

During the war I was to be exiled in Kashmir and often doubted that I should ever again be a writer and, every two or three months, Spencer would send me a cable, not about anything in particular, simply to let me know he was there. It was a life-line and when I was able to come back to England, he and Jean did wonders to help and hearten me; yet now, I often wince when I think of him.

I knew that this happy and exhilarating time of *Black Narcissus* could not last— of all that it had meant to me in ecstasy, excitement and growth it is impossible to tell.

Laurence and I had decided that Jane, Paula and I should not go back to India with him; to begin with, there was nowhere for us to go—my beloved house had had to be given up as naturally Mr. Mehta would not renew the lease—and in an effort to economise, Laurence said he would join a chummerie, while I could stay cheaply at Darrynane—I had kept the full financial prospects of *Black Narcissus* to myself which made me feel mean but I was learning wisdom. I might, I thought, bring Jane out later on, but Laurence left in August and war was declared before he reached Calcutta.

To Jon:

What is remarkable, is the sort of patience with which everyone is facing the menace of this time; there seems to be none of the scrambling, nervous sort of courage that people showed in the crisis last September, only a patient steadfastness.

The Phoney War, as we called it, lasted through the winter when life seemed much as usual; the evacuees, most of them, went back to their homes, the panic over gas-masks subsided.

I was either in London working on the play of *Black Narcissus* with Spencer, or else at Darrynane and came back for Christmas which, considering we were at war, was a strangely happy Christmas; I had been able to send Laurence a cheque, repay Percy and Florence for at least some of their generosity and buy presents for everybody. One present, though a special one, fell flat; thinking to give Mam a tremendous surprise I had gone to the bank and got a hundred pound note—the first I had ever seen—put it in an envelope and hung it on the tree for her. I had expected a stunned surprise but Mam had not seen a hundred pound note either and, thinking it was for five pounds—both notes were on thin white paper—said quite calmly, "Thank you dear," and put the envelope away.

Spring came, April, May, more and more ominous.

To Jon: April 1940.

There's no use in talking about the war—we all know what we're feeling but I would like to say this to you: it most definitely does not mean that writing is to be abandoned. For a while it may peter out but in my view it will be needed more than ever, and in the worst times, if we can manage even to get through to each other, it will keep something alive that is vital to us, and I think, too, vital to the world. Naturally I don't mean our work is vital to the world, but that the spirit of which we have a touch is vital. We are artists and artists are, in a way, like priests; in the "Story of a Country Priest" the young man is told, "You have God's Word in you—and, remember, the time will come when you must give it back to God." It is something like this I mean.

It was getting closer; Fa had begun to say "You must think of the children."

As Jane and Paula grew older they loved me to tell them stories about themselves and the stories always began the same way: "Once upon a time there were two little girls, one with hair like marmalade and one with hair like honey."

Jane remained a redhead, her eyes the colour of aquamarines; she was a plump, solemn little girl with an originality and strength of character that astonished me.

At five o'clock every day, Nurse brought the children up from the Lodge to the house for an hour's play while Alice had her tea in peace—as I have said Nurse would not eat with Alice. From having been bewitched by Nurse, Jane had come to dislike her, chiefly from the way she treated Alice of the friendly happy face, pink cheeks, brown bobbed hair, almost round blue eyes that gave her the look of a child, and her Cornish speech with all the genders mixed up, which Jane faithfully copied. "Where be my socks?" she would ask.

"Really Jane!" said Nurse.

"Yes, where she be?" asked Jane.

One late afternoon when Fa, Mam and I had all been out we came back, just before six, to find the children with Nurse in the drawing room, Jane by herself in the corner with her bricks. She seemed rather subdued and white and after Nurse had gone, she came to me and said, "I've hurt myself," and showed me a great burn on her arm. It was burnt right through till it was raw. It appeared that when they first came up to the drawing room, she had begun to play on the granite kerb of the fireplace. "Jane, if you play there you'll hurt yourself," Nurse said and, sure enough as she said it, Jane slipped. Nurse ran and picked her up. "You have hurt yourself!"

"No, I haven't," said Jane and walked away. She had endured that burn for over an hour without saying a word. I do not think many four-year-olds are as stoical as that.

She believed Jon could do anything. "Jane says," I wrote to Jon, "Will you draw her a picture of a daddy hen playing golf," and Jon obliged. Jane herself had such a talent for painting that it was clair-sentient; at three, four and five years old she was formidable—a strange word to use of a little child but she knew exactly what she wanted to do and how to do it. When she painted cars or carts or perambulators, she always put the wheels on top and would not change them. It puzzled me at first until I realised that is how a small child would see them.

Michael Cardew, the potter, his wife Mariel and their three small sons had come to live at Wenford Bridge, down the hill from Darrynane, where he set up his pottery and at first scandalised the village. St. Breward was conventional, interbred, and chapel-ridden, as I had found out when I started a dancing class for the children and was stopped from using the Hall because the class was for that wicked thing, dancing. At first the Cardews were quite unconscious of how outrageous they were thought and how incomprehensible. Their house was bare of carpets or curtains, armchairs or sofas; there were plain stone flag floors, oak furniture—the nearest to accepted comfort was a wooden settle—but they had hundreds of books and Michael's pottery and her paintings. The boys went barefoot, they all wore brightly coloured clothes—for the baby they had an old perambulator which they painted green with a pattern of sunflowers. The village was shocked and when they found out that Michael was a conscientious objector some ugly things happened. It is good to record that Michael ended as the pride of St. Breward, not only for his fame as a potter—I have one beautiful bowl—but for his championship of the Cornish language, while Mariel became its best-loved person to whom everyone went in times of trouble; she was even asked to lay out the dead, accounted a great privilege.

In the evenings, when I was at home, I used to work in Darrynane kitchen. If I had stayed in the Lodge I would have had to spend the evenings with Nurse; Alice went home when she had put Jane to bed. Darrynane was built on such a slope that the kitchen was on a lower level than the rest of the house—a wonderfully comfortable place with the warmth of the Aga, a sturdy wooden kitchen table on which to write—I have always preferred a table to a desk—and, too, the windows seemed set into the garden so that the flowers looked in. There was a lift to the dining room above, worked by pulley ropes, and when Fa and Mam had their bridge parties, at the appropriate time Mam would open the lift, call down and I would send up tea and coffee, sandwiches and cakes.

Sometimes though I would drive down to Wenford Bridge and see Mariel. In those quiet evenings there was time to think, think more deeply. Mariel and I were reading Ouspensky and Gurdjieff and discussed them endlessly. Then a curious thing happened.

Michael, then, was not well known and I suppose did not charge a great deal, especially if the order was one that interested him. He was an agnostic but was piqued—in the sense of being intrigued—when a convent asked him to design and make a set of table pottery for them—bowls, small for soup or puddings, large for serving, and platters, all they needed, but for them a serious business, a whole new set they would use day in, day out, and a serious expenditure. They little dreamed what they were investing in; a Michael Cardew bowl of the right period can now be worth ten thousand pounds.

I remember the design: plain, deep cream with a cross on the side of each piece in red brown, not defined but flowing—Michael tried endless experiments. He fired the kilns himself—in those days they had to be stoked which meant three or four days of intense work, anxiety and sleeplessness and usually, no matter how carefully the kiln was packed, there was a percentage of loss, it could be as much as a quarter with vases, bowls, dishes, plates imperfectly fired.

The Mother Superior wrote and asked Michael to telephone as soon as he had fired the kiln. "We shall go into prayer." Michael may have thought it nonsense but he obeyed—you do not easily gainsay a Mother Superior—and when the kiln had cooled and he unpacked it, every bowl and platter was perfect.

Coincidence or the power of prayer? I

had no idea then which but I gave up reading Ouspensky.

In the days of their difficulties, Mariel had started a playschool to which Jane went—to her lasting good. Mariel let the children paint on large sheets of brown paper spread on the floor—the paints were in saucers—no niggling little paint boxes—the brushes large so that the painting could be bold and Mariel never interfered. Jane painted a picture larger than herself, "The Raggle-Taggle Gypsies"; it had a caravan and gypsies round a fire where a kettle hung on a tripod. Mariel sent it to a children's exhibition the British Council was holding and the man in charge telephoned her. "You say this child is only four but that caravan has perspective!" and the picture was hung. Sadly the talent faded. In Kashmir, when she was six, Jane for a short while went as a day child to Srinagar's convent school. The kindergarten children were told to paint a Madonna and Child; Jane's was "Mary with Jesus Inside Her", a baby illuminated with rays inside Mary's stomach. The nuns said it was irreverent; perhaps they did not know that St. Ann, Mary's legendary mother, is the patron saint of cupboard makers and carpenters, because she had Mary in her cupboard. "Shocking!" and the kindergarten nun tore the picture up. "I'll never paint again," said Jane. She did, later, but it had faded to only a craft.

Paula was a wisp of a child with flaxen hair and the Hingley bluest of blue eyes. She was still tiny but she had a body as graceful as an elf's and as wiry; she walked and even ran before she was a year old and in that autumn I was able to dispense with Nurse.

Paula was, too, one of those uncanny children who seem not to need much sleep; I had been one myself and remember the misery of being forced to lie still in the dark and not put on the light, so that I let Paula be as, in the next generation, we let my grand-daughter Emma, though it is eerie to see, at one o'clock in the morning, a small figure tripping downstairs and going quite happily to write or draw at her desk. That winter of 1939/40 Paula and I saw the New Year in together:

Everyone else in the Lodge and house,

probably in the village is asleep; there are no church bells ringing, no festivities and, of course, no lights [it was the black-out] but there is a feeling of newness, of immensity and, though I try to shut it out, of fear; Paula can't talk [she was only fifteen months old], but she is a comfort, as in her fluffy pink dressing gown she sits on my bed, a shawl round her toes and listens as I talk, the fair hair like baby down on her head, her eyes intensely blue and impish. We drink to the New Year in cocoa.

Before she was two years old we were in India.

This book is, I suppose, a calendar of books but I only mention *Gypsy Gypsy* because the most difficult feat of a writer's career is to write the next book after a success. Perhaps it is a mistake even to try —because there is a great difference between a book written when you are looking for something to write, searching for a theme, and one that seems to arise of itself, demanding to be written. It is better to wait and I should have waited because that eventually came—was vouchsafed, as it were—with my fifth novel, *Breakfast with the Nikolides* but, at least, with *Gypsy Gypsy* I had broken away. I do not really remember what happened to it, so it was with surprise that I have come across a further letter from Peter Davies written in January 1940.

My ears are long and I heard you were in London. My arms are long and I knew *Gypsy Gypsy* was lying in Henrietta Street. My heart told my feet to get busy, my feet went to Henrietta Street, my arms went out, my hands grabbed and my eyes and my brain drank in the story last night and this morning I have to write at once and tell you I am enchanted with it . . . You have, very rightly, had exceptional praise for your descriptions of India and the Himalayas and I am absolutely certain you will now get praise for your description of Normandy . . .

Spencer was more acute. "You know where you got that from?" he asked when he had read *Gypsy Gypsy*. I had not known but it was true; my *Gypsy Gypsy*, though its theme was completely different, was strongly influenced by D. H. Lawrence's *The Virgin and the Gypsy*.

| *D.H.L.'s Gypsy* | *R.G.'s Gypsy* |
| --- | --- |
| His pose was loose, his gaze insolent in its indifference. He had a thick black moustache under his thin straight nose and a big silk handkerchief tied round his neck. . . . The curious dark, suave purity of all his body . . . a purity like a living sneer. . . . He managed to insinuate such a subtle suggestion of submission into his male bearing that she began to hesitate. | He had on a hat that was only a shape in the darkness and a dark scarf around his throat, and in his ears he wore small gold rings. . . . his face was smooth and ripe . . . a lion's face that disarms the attention from its fierceness of heart. He was like an animal as he examined her from head to foot, puzzled and a little wary. . . . There was a dark unconscious coldness about him, something feline . . . she was afraid. |
| The man was gone, without looking round, gone like a dream | On the doorstep lay a |

which was only a dream. dark bundle with a flash of red. It was the gypsy's clothes and his scarf and on top of it was his hat, soaked to a smooth goose brown; its feather was hung with a drop of rain; they watched as it slid down.

Which shows what the unconscious can do.

I suppose *Gypsy Gypsy* had a measure of success. It seems it was a Book Society Recommendation, was published on both sides of the Atlantic, had foreign sales, paperbacks, dramatisation, but I had gone into a mélée of war and such trouble that, despite my brave letter to Jon, for the first time in my life books and writing did not seem to matter.

As for *Black Narcissus*; if it had been a bird, it was as if it had been shot in mid-flight. I did not know then that it would survive.

# 10

## Thus Far and No Further

I HAD meant to fly out to Calcutta in the autumn taking Jane while Paula, who, as everyone told me, was still too delicate for India, stayed at Darrynane with Fa and Mam and Alice to look after her but, by May, everything had changed alarmingly and, "If you are to go at all, you must go now", said Fa, "and, of course, take Paula." He did not need to say, "Out of danger"; it seemed almost sure that Britain would be invaded.

The October flight I had booked on had been cancelled but Jay Simon managed to get me two cabins on the Peninsular and Oriental liner, *Strathallan*, sailing the first week in June. I wound up my affairs in London while Mam and Fa packed what they could and brought the children to Southampton. I cannot bear, even now, to think of our parting; we knew that it was more than possible we might not see one another again.

He and Mam would not be quite alone. Rose's marriage had broken up and she had come home.

Rose, like Jon, was destined for sadness; on the voyage home she had met Gordon Armstrong, a young flight officer in the RAF who was all that C.D. was not, young, extremely good-looking, warm and affectionate. There seemed every chance of happiness except that they could not marry. Rose's divorce was delayed because of the war and she trained to go into the Mechanical Transport Corps, passing with honour; her first assignment was to drive an American General whom sometimes she brought to Darrynane; all the same, that morning at Southampton I felt I was running away but, "Your place is with Laurence," said Fa and so Jane, Paula, their new Swiss nurse, Giovanna, and I embarked.

Giovanna had entered our lives. I had thought, that spring, things were safe and well enough with our small family, that we had the position and money to justify my engaging a nurse or nursery governess to take out to India. I had wanted to take Alice but her mother would not let her go. "It's they submarines," she said in which she was right; besides Alice was only eighteen, young for Calcutta, and she left to make munitions in Bodmin.

Giovanna had arrived that April. The train journey from London took six hours then and, meeting her at Camelford, I found a tall dark girl, dressed in an old-fashioned grey gaberdine—it had belonged to her mother—and an incongruously smart red hat she had bought with her own money. She would have been handsome— Giovanna has a naturally glowingly healthy olive complexion—but now her face was livid, grey-green. Her only luggage was a covered basket and a mandolin and she was almost speechless with tiredness, hunger and apprehension.

The apprehension grew worse. To get to St. Breward we had to drive in darkness over Bodmin moor where the wind howled and rain beat on the car; it was a wild wet night, even for Cornwall. I could see the whites of Giovanna's eyes rolling in terror and when I spoke to her the only answer

ATTDN21

was a faint "Si" that sounded like a hiss of dismay. Arrived at the Lodge and shown her bedroom, Giovanna flung the mandolin on the bed, fell on her knees and began to pray in wild Italian, "O Madonna Santa! Aiutami"—"Help me, Madonna Santa!" It was not a promising beginning. Next morning she gave me notice and has stayed now, almost as my daughter, forty-six years, coming and going.

Giovanna is Swiss-Italian. Her father was the station master at Locarno where he had built a house on the shores of the lake, choosing the side that got the least sun because it was cheaper. She could not remember her mother but had a step-mother who, not wanting her at home, sent her to be brought up in an orphanage by nuns so cruel and strict that Giovanna's eyes flash as she tells about them. At fifteen she went out to work as a mixture of tweeny, slave and machine for families in Switzerland, her father taking every penny of her money until she ran away and became a barmaid in a hotel in Zurich. Yes, my children's nurse had been a barmaid. The hotel sent her to England to learn English where she was to work as a parlour-maid in London but "lacked the polish", the Agency said. I can quite imagine it; Giovanna is totally uninhibited. The Agency had noticed her love of children and sent her to me. "She *is* a little unusual, still we think you should try her," but, "I must leave. I cannot stay in this strange place"—"Questo paese é alla fine del mondo"—"Forgive me, I cannot stay." At that time I agreed with her.

The next morning she met the children. Jane had picked a nosegay of flowers for her, and Paula presented an egg she had found when feeding the chickens with Mam; she was carrying it with enormous care. To our surprise Giovanna cracked it and poured it raw down her own throat, "Good! Good! Buono! Sehr gut!" and, "You must do that," she said to wide-eyed Paula. "You, ma petite reine." She seemed to speak Italian, German, French without knowing which was which. Then the pony, Basket, came nuzzling for titbits; I had bought Basket so that, with panniers each side, I could take the children up on the moor. We took Giovanna. It was a still, sunny day; primroses and violets were out, the gorse beginning, larks singing and, "I love the nature," said Giovanna as I have heard her say a thousand times. She had been so over-wrought and now looked so tired and thin—her large bones made her look thinner—so much in need of food and rest and obviously with little money that I was moved to say, "Of course you must leave when you like but as you are here and the weather is kind, I think you should stay a week or so and get rested and well before you try for another post." Bless the day I said that. There was nothing devious about it; Giovanna seemed quite unsuitable for taking out to India which Fa endorsed vehemently but Mam said, "I like that girl."

Giovanna is as lovable, appreciative and attractive, as she is wilful and fanatical; she works quite naturally from morning to night, full of zest and innate happiness and is very fond of food. If any morsel or even quite a large helping is left in the dish, she will say the Italian rhyme:

"Piuttosto che roba vanza
Crepa Panza . . ." and finish the food.

She is also superstitious; if she sees a spider in the morning—bad luck—she puts a tumbler over it so that she can see it again in the evening—good luck. "And was I not right about the spider?" says Giovanna and tells me, "When I was looking for a post, the Agency sent me five letters and one fell on the floor, the face down so that I did not know which one it was. I go to pick it up—it was evening time—and a so small lucky spider was sitting on it. I think, that is the one for me, and it was yours."

To the children she quickly became the sun, moon and stars and was the best nanny I have come across though quite unorthodox. She made the children independent and capable; from two years old Paula had to dress herself, tie her own shoes, and like Jane, even in India where there were servants, clear her breakfast, lunch and tea things away. I can see the three of them now, sitting round a washtub each washing out their "smalls". In the early morning Giovanna had them outside for a run and taught them to yodel. "Good for the breath!" I never knew her punish a child, except to banish it into another room or take away privileges, or saw her lose her temper yet discipline was strict. "You will sit up straight at table," and for some reason I could not fathom, when not eating, keep the left hand palm down on the table. All this came later; in May of 1940 it was not possible to get her back to Switzerland; I felt I could not leave her friendless, except for Fa and Mam, in a country at war and while she was still new we made that long fraught sea journey together.

The "Strath" Peninsular and Oriental liners were so fast that we did not go in convoy but the voyage still took seven weeks. We called at Las Palmas, then went out into the Atlantic coming down into the South Atlantic to go round the Cape, week after week when every day seemed stretched to eternity. I could, of course, not write—not even letters—I did though keep a sporadic diary.

June.

At Las Palmas no-one is allowed ashore but sellers of linen and baskets and fruit come down on the quay. Giovanna barters two packets of cigarettes for a pair of tea-table cloths worked with hand-drawn thread and lace. Cigarettes, it seems, are like gold.

The amazing part is that, in this time of crisis, the normal round of passenger-ship life goes on; there are still the attentive stewards in their striped jackets—white in the dining room: still stewardesses in starched aprons: long chairs are still arranged on the deck with rugs and cushions, the traditional hot Bovril and water biscuits—Bath Olivers —are brought round at eleven for the British "elevenses". There are deck games for which a tournament is arranged and, as usual, eager, sport-impelled passengers trying to recruit, even compel you, to join in, the difference being we are nearly all women. Another difference is that there cannot be the daily sweepstake on the ship's run: we are not allowed to know how fast or slow she goes or where she goes.

There was, later on, the usual children's fancy-dress party when I knew we had

crossed the Equator as Neptune arrived—
Jane was sure, out of the sea—with a net
full of toys.

The bugle still blows for lunch and
dinner. For these the same rules apply:
Giovanna, as an employee, has to have
her meals with the children in the
daytime and go to the second-class for
dinner.

She, too, had to dress and I had given her
a dinner dress, deep red that suited her
splendid darkness—she looked absurd in
uniform which she insisted on wearing—I
think it made her feel like a proper nanny.
The red dress showed a little of her neck
and left her arms bare; her dinner time
was before mine and, going to fetch her, I
found her shrinking in front of the
looking-glass.

"Ah no! Ah no! Madre mia! I cannot go
out like this. My father he would kill
me."

"Your father isn't here. Come."

"Ah no!"

At last I have to say cruelly "Well, if

you don't come now you will have to go to dinner alone. I shan't be there to take you."

As it is I have to put her in charge of the chief steward but I notice she is not too bashful to look at the menu!

It was more than two hours before Giovanna came back. She had thought—out of politeness—she had to eat through the whole menu, alternative dishes and all, until the head steward rescued her. "No no, Signorina, you take this or that." "You mean I can *choose?*" asked Giovanna. "Am supposed to choose? Oh! Mamma mia!" She was covered with confusion and, poor girl, was sick as well as seasick all next day.

The normality was owing to the Captain. I have not admired any man more than I did that Captain though I only spoke to him twice. He kept aloof; there were none of the customary invitations to cocktail parties in the Captain's cabin, no Captain's table in the dining room at which the elite would have been asked to sit, nor were any of the officers allowed to mingle with the passengers, which was wise; there were more than eight hundred women passengers on board with perhaps ten male passengers among them; most of them had children, even teenagers, with them and almost all were separated from their husbands, many in anguished anxiety, some hysterical and some who threw any restraint overboard and, even if they had small children, were always in the bar. There must have been the same element in the crew, not the seamen but among the stewards; as the weeks went on you could not go up on the boat deck at night, as I loved to do, without one of them coming up behind you and whispering.

It was impossible for nerves not to be tense; fourteen times a day the radio blared out the news which grew more and more disastrous—I have never been able to listen to the news since—but it was the normality that held us together, made most of us behave while we knew, all of us, that nothing was normal. Everywhere we went, even for a few minutes, we had to carry our life-belts and bundles; the bundles held a blanket, a water bottle and rations. When we put the children to bed they had to be fully dressed, their coats and shoes laid ready at the end of the bunk. The worst discipline of all was that we had to learn—and how difficult it was to learn—that when the siren sounded the alarm as it did sometimes twice in twenty-four hours, no matter where we were, or where our children were, we were not to rush and find them—if we tried a stern stewardess or senior steward blocked our way—we were to go straight to our life-boat station; every child, the Captain told us—and, as the voyage went on we found it was true—had a member of the crew or a steward assigned to it and always each one was delivered as soon as we arrived on deck or sooner; strangely enough, Paula, who screamed if any stranger touched her, did not protest even once.

The worst part is not knowing if the alarm is real. We stand in "our stations" on the dark wet slippery deck, life-belts on, our bundles at our feet. Paula clings to my neck like a limpet. I know she is too small for any life-belt. My right-hand holds Jane; her face is whiter than any child's ought to be, her forehead strained with bewilderment. Giovanna clutches my left arm; she is too appalled for her usual prayers and, mute, I can feel her trembling. The deck tilts alarmingly—this must be real—and she gives a little gasp. The sea seems extraordinarily noisy, rising up against the ship and falling into a void of darkness, laced with angry white. There is a whistling creaking of ropes as the life-boats come down, gusts of wind bringing sounds of men swearing, and the orders barked by the Third Officer who is standing near us—he looks no older than some of the teenage boy passengers. There is the crying of babies, then the sea blots everything out. What is it going to be like down there? "It will only be a few minutes, darling," says a brave mother beside me. "Then we shall be with God."

"I don't want to be with God," quavers the child. Nor do any of us and, "Why did I bring them?" I cry silently. "How protect them against those waves? Why, oh why, did we come?"

I had not travelled in such luxury before;

the City Line's best ships were steamers compared to this, and in the Orient liners I had only been in the second class. The "Straths" were truly great ships in strength, speed, beauty of design, in every detail, and comfort; they were only to be surpassed by the late "Queens", the *Queen Mary* and *Queen Elizabeth I*. It is a thrill to feel the engines start and the ship come to life with a pulsing that is in every part you touch, under your hand in the banisters that lead down the staircases —too wide to be called companionways— or in the deckrail as you lean to look over the side; feel it pulsing in the deck under your feet and all through your body as you lie in your bunk.

The staterooms on the *Strathallan* were panelled and furnished like a stately home. On Sunday morning the ballroom was used for Church Parade taken by the Captain; any of the crew who were free could attend and were drawn up in rows among the passengers. Though I, then, kept away from church, I took Jane, it seemed part of the steadiness the Captain engendered and when we sang:

"O hear us when we cry to Thee
For those in peril on the sea . . ."

we meant what we sang.

"That is the worst child on this ship and
that is the next worst." The voice was
clear and clarion; Bim looked at me and I
at Bim; in fairness we had to agree. Hers
was the "worst", three-year-old Adam, or
"Original Sin" as we called him because
no-one ever knew what he would do next;
he was immensely strong and pugnacious,
with a bellow like an outraged bull. Paula
was the next worst. Doctor Bailey had
been right when he told me she was still
too delicate to take out to India; always
quick to feel tension she began to have
screaming fits and tantrums which were
frightening for her and for us. Meal times
were an impossible ordeal; most children
threaten to throw things, Paula really
threw—that first month I had a bill for
thirty-four pounds for broken china. Over
and over again, I would be called to the
nursery dining room and find her white
and shaken in her high chair, food and
broken china scattered round. She had

eaten nothing while Giovanna, crimson with shame, her head bowed, had taken refuge in her lunch or breakfast.

Bim had other struggles with Adam; she had to net him in his bunk or he would have wandered over the ship at night: he would fight too, almost every boy, small or big, he met.

I would not, I think, have come through that voyage more or less unscathed if it had not been for Bim. She was unconquerable, the only way to describe her, a quality inherited by her children—she had three—even Adam, as he grew older and became tempered had the same quality. They all stood out—and stood firm. She had been a Lawrence and no two men have done more for India and the prestige of Britain than the Lawrence brothers, John and Henry, especially during, and after, the mutiny of 1857. Sir Henry died in the siege of Lucknow while John, later Lord Lawrence, succeeded Lord Canning as India's second Viceroy. Bim was of the same calibre and all through those weeks she stayed calm and helpful with a beautifully ironical twist of humour.

Italy has declared war and I am sent for by the Purser.

"Your children's nurse is Italian."

"She isn't. She is Swiss."

"Swiss?"

"Yes. Look at her passport. She is Swiss-Italian."

"That's Italian. I am sorry to inform you that as an enemy alien . . ." Giovanna an enemy alien! "She must be interned."

"Don't be ridiculous!" I want to say, but instead ask to see the Captain. To my astonishment he takes a stern view of it.

I protest. "A simple convent-bred girl."

"So she says, but I never cease to be surprised, and you admit you have not known her very long."

"But she is interned already. How more strictly can one be interned than in a ship?"

"There are such things as radio."

"Giovanna does not know what radio is."

316

"How do you know? She is attractive, young and a woman. I have over four hundred men serving in this ship, officers and crew." A great many were Indian or Goanese from whom Giovanna would have shrunk: but that left still some two hundred, "Many of whom are young themselves, homesick and so especially susceptible," says the unyielding Captain.

Giovanna was not interned but when we reached Cape Town she was not allowed ashore. "Tempi," said Giovanna, shrugged and told the mothers—the ones she liked, Giovanna has strong feelings—"You go and have nice change. I look after the children for you." "Due, al venti, non importa. Two children, twenty children, it is all the same."

Approaching Cape Town.

One night, before Cape Town, I come down to dinner so early that the saloon is empty except for our own steward who does not come to pull out my chair with his usual welcome and I see that he is crying.

He is young, not more than twenty-five, curly headed, with usually, a smiling face but now it is pale, red-eyed, tear-stained. "John?" He starts. "I'm sorry"—and a word jerked out by P and O training—"Madam." He cannot tell me everything then, others, stewards, and diners come in but I wait for him on deck that night, Bim with me.

John had been married only a year and his wife was expecting their first baby. He was to have gone on leave after the last voyage but the ship came into Southampton only to turn around as swiftly as possible and go straight out again, bound for Australia. All shore leave was cancelled, no telephone calls or letters were allowed, and there would be none, not even telegrams, until the ship reached Australia, "If then," said John and could have added, "If at all." None of us, including the crew and their families, knew what ports we could call at, except now, Cape Town, and presumably some time in the future Bombay—"and I

318

won't be allowed ashore at either of them," said John in despair.

They lived in the East End of London, near the Docks, most vulnerable, most likely to be bombed and, "I don't know if they're all right. I don't know if they're *alive*," said John and, "She must have had the baby by now and I don't *know*." He broke down again.

Bim and I concocted a scheme. We, passengers, were able to go ashore at Cape Town and, through a South African friend, we sent a long complicated cable to Bim's husband, Chang, in Bombay—Bim and Chang: their names seem the epitome of the Thirties and Forties but they were far more than that; I am sure their help is still as unquestioning today. Chang was to cable John's wife, she to cable back and he would come down on the quay when we docked at Bombay—we knew he would not be allowed on board. If all was well he was to wave a white handkerchief—if there were trouble, red—when we would go to the Captain. If it were a boy, something blue, pink for a girl.

Another three weeks had to pass but it was a white handkerchief and a pink scarf.

319

John was on the gun, one of its crew, and in return he used to give me a secret sign to tell me if the alarms were precautionary or real.

24 July.

Everyday I go and stand for a little in the bow of the ship.

I am sorry for anyone who has not made a long sea voyage when you can have the freedom of the ship—surprisingly enough, at this time, nobody stopped me. To go forward and lean high over the rail is joy, watching the prow cleaving the waves, sending a high one each side, and feeling the power of the great ship, the clean salt wind in your face and even, at that height, spray.

Sometimes there were dolphins leaping and playing in the twin waves of the bow, snouts coming up, silver grey flanks turning, cleft tails lifted in somersaults of ecstasy and, ahead, the sea, sometimes laced with patches of foam, meeting the horizon all the way round as in

Narayangunj, like a great bowl turned upside-down, which gave a feeling of a loneliness as immense as the sea. Sometimes there was another ship, so small in the distance it looked like a toy but then we, too, were a toy under that sky.

To stand in the bow at night is even more magical especially when there are stars and phosphorescence shining luminous on the waves.

In the South Atlantic and the Indian Ocean it was hot, and grew hotter and, while Giovanna went to dinner, I would keep the children, mine and others, on deck and tell them about the stars, showing them the Southern Cross. Some of the mothers—"les putains" severe Giovanna called them—had their children in bed by six o'clock, regardless of the heat; it was the wild desire to get into the bar and blot the stress and tension out, but "Poverinas!" cried Giovanna and persuaded the "strumpets" to let their children come too. It was a refreshment sitting there with boys and girls of all ages gathered round in their pyjamas—all of us looking up from the sea to study the sky.

"Look at the stars! look, look up at the skies!" I used to quote. "O look at all the fire-folk sitting in the air!"* "Fire-folk," they used to echo and, "That's the Southern Cross, the star that ships were once steered by. There's Orion with his belt and sword; the plume in his hat is the Pleiades, and there's Sirius the brightest star in the whole sky— Sirius means sparkling. That's the moth-soft Milky Way."

When Giovanna came back and it was my turn to go, she would take my place, often with her mandolin and the children would gather closer.

July or August.

We find ourselves in Mombasa where we stay for an uneasy week; there are two cruisers and other battleships in the

* From Gerard Manley Hopkins's sonnet "The Starlight Night".

harbour and the Italian planes come over every night, attacked fiercely by ack-ack fire. It is our first taste of gunfire.

We take on a hundred and sixty Indian refugees from Kenya to be put off at Bombay. They are in a pitiable state and, poor souls, are battened down on E Deck of the First Class and told to stay there, though the children swarm up in the lifts and companionways; it seems cruel to repel them but they are unspeakably dirty, covered in sores, their noses and eyes running. The stewards threaten to go on strike because of the filth they have to deal with, a filth that surprises me because most Indians even in adverse circumstances are fanatically clean!

It was not only filth but disease; as we voyaged slowly across the Indian Ocean and Arabian Sea to Bombay, first Jane, then Paula developed chicken-pox, then ringworm; the mixture of spots and rings in that heat was almost unbearable. What was worse, some of our children incubated what only showed far later; at first it was thought to be beri-beri but was far more deadly. Paula was amongst them.

August. Coming into Bombay.

I have a bill from the ship's Doctor so inordinate that I am taken aback.

I suppose looking at it from a distance, he had to treat all those Indian refugees and many of the passengers for nothing, and I was travelling first class, had a nurse for my children—the only one on board—and, also, word of *Black Narcissus* had crept in; at the time, though, the extortion was so palpable I was outraged and went for advice.

When you ask anyone to advise you it is as well to look carefully at the one you go to and ask yourself if he, or she, is the kind of person you would wish to be. In my case it was much so. She was the grandmother of an Austrian Jewish family —I was told they were international bankers—travelling out to Australia for the safety of the children; there were four with a young mother and a still younger aunt, daughters of the grandmother. They were obviously rich and exceedingly good-looking—there was an enchanting baby boy, the jewel of the family, the rest were girls—but none was as elegant, as beautifully poised, as the grandmother. She was what could be called "gowned" not dressed, in quiet perfection and exquisitely groomed; her hair truly silver, her eyes curiously young and alert. Invariably polite, she kept herself aloof and never, for a moment, betrayed a hint of what must have been the anguish she was feeling with three sons serving in France and no news of them. Now and then she and I had talked about books, particularly poetry, and I went to her in my indignation as her daughter, whose children had also been smitten, had had a like bill. "I won't pay it."

"I should if I were you."

"It's a cheat."

"I know it is but, my dear," and she put her hand on mine, "never, never quarrel about a professional bill. That will only bring you a great deal of trouble and expense. Pay it and do not use, or even think about, that person again. Dismiss him."

I can see her face as she said those two words—I should not have cared to be the person dismissed; it was valuable advice which I have followed with advantage ever since.

I had planned to go straight from the ship to the train, booked for Calcutta, but when the Bombay Health Authorities came on board they refused to let us travel and Jane, in spite of my pleas, was whipped away into hospital. "She has suspected smallpox," said the Health Inspector. Nothing I or the Ship's Doctor could say would move him.

It was then that I really knew the strength and friendship of Bim. To begin with she took me, Paula, who for once had escaped fairly lightly, and Giovanna straight to her house—fortunately it was spacious—but she had not seen Chang, nor he her and the children, for two years and they could not have wanted visitors. Then she swept me off to the hospital, where we found a cowed and terrified Jane in a bed between a child with scarlet fever and a woman with typhoid. Bim used her usual majesty—and Chang's position—

and, in half-an-hour, Jane was released and Bim had taken her, too, into her home.

"But Bim, think of Adam and the others."

"Chicken-pox won't kill them," said Bim.

"We must go to an hotel."

"No hotel would take you," which was true. "Don't fuss," said Bim.

She not only kept us but entertained us royally, taking me to the Yacht Club, out into the country, organising picnics for the children, sending Giovanna to a dance, until, at last, permission came for us to travel, and then it was in a special carriage attached to the back of the train and marked with a large red cross. Jane and Paula had to wear white cotton pyjamas tied at the ankle, wrist and neck, and a cap—fortunately their hair did not have to be shaved. We were not allowed to set foot on the platform to Giovanna's chagrin— Indian stations with their pedlars are fascinating; no one came near us except an orderly bringing us food, though with Bim's help I had brought our own.

The journey took days in the broiling

August heat of the Indian plain and it could not have been an attractive or endearing family that Laurence met at Howrah but he gave us such a welcome that I thought, This has been worthwhile.

Though of course the war overshadowed everything, for our particular small family everything that year seemed to be going well. The children had recovered though Paula was still nervous and difficult. Giovanna had settled and was happy; we ran a playschool for Jane and her friends, Jon had found us the lower half of a house in Alipore with a garden and I was able to furnish it, even buying a grand piano, a Steinway which arrived on the heads of eight coolies who had carried it miles across Calcutta and up the long Alipore road, walking with the rhythm in which they had been trained, giving an absolutely even tread which did not jar the instrument and keeping the rhythm until the big piano was set down safely in our drawing room.

We had Ears, and Mrs. Ears to help Giovanna, other servants, a car and a driver. Khokil of the magnificent

noustaches was back, as were the peking-
se, Sol, Wing and Moon Daisy.

Alipore.
November 1940.

Everywhere I go, sit, stand for a
moment there is a pekingese; as I write
they lie in whiting shapes around me,
head to tail; except for Wing, of course,
their coats are beautiful; Sol's runs from
cream, through gold to raven, his face
is almost tortoiseshell. Moon is purest
white.

That autumn I mated her to an imported
white dog, Snow Prince, owned by a large
Armenian lady who was more than proud
of her Prince and barely condescended to
mate him to Moon, "Not what I should
call a good pekingese," but, as Moon was
the only white bitch in Calcutta, "There
isn't a choice," she lamented. It was for
pick of litter. "If the puppies are good
enough," and, "Must be white. Colours
creep in, you know, unless you are expert
in breeding," which she clearly thought I
was not.

There were four puppies; first-born, an uncommonly large bitch puppy, then two more bitches all white and, finally, the smallest puppy I have ever seen, a male and I knew that I held in my hand that extremely rare pekingese, a miniature male white. "Shabash!" said Khokil in a reverent whisper.

All four grew to be strong healthy puppies, the eldest looking like a snowball but light-boned, and a little long in the back—a fault of Moon's which I had hoped Snow Prince would correct; the other two bitches were pretty too but the little male was near perfect, already heavy as a tiny faggot with the required flat face set with huge dark eyes.

"Pick of litter" must be chosen when the puppies are three weeks old. The Armenian lady was coming and "Khokil," I said, "It's no use setting your heart on that puppy. The Memsahib will take him."

Khokil said nothing but his moustache bristled. I knew Khokil and, when the day was fixed, "Khokil," I said again, "after have brushed that puppy and put him in the pen"—they had a pale blue pen—"you re not to give him anything. You are not to touch him," and as Khokil did not answer, "Do you hear me, Khokil?"

"I hear," said Khokil.

The lady came and I took her on the verandah where the puppies were playing, and I must say they were a ravishing sight, but as we came nearer I stopped; only three were playing, the three bitches; in the corner of the pen lay a small miserable object not white and fluffy but smooth and dark cream. I looked at Khokil—Khokil looked at the sky.

The Armenian lady had instantly picked the large puppy out of the pen. "That isn't the one," I felt bound to say. "I don't know what has happened to the tiny one, but he is a male, a miniature, rare . . . I think you should come back another day and see him . . ."

"So! Is that what you are telling me?" Her voice was high. "That I don't know what a peke should be when I see it! Trying to foist off a runt like that on me, who has judged at shows, let me tell you, won prizes. No, I am not the fool you think. You will please reserve this bitch pup for me. You can keep your runt."

"Khokil," I said when she had gone.
*"Khokil."*

He still looked at the sky.

"What did you give the puppy?"

"Nothing."

"What did you do to him?"

"I? Nothing."

"Then?"

"Was it my fault", asked Khokil, "if the puppy crawled into a saucer of black coffee?"

These were light moments which grew fewer. Jon was now head of St. John's Ambulance in Calcutta which had an acute shortage of nurses. We members, with our minimal training, were sent into the hospitals not as auxiliaries but nurses—we could only pray we did not do too much damage. I worked in an Indian hospital down in the docks two afternoons a week and in a slum clinic for babies; both were appalling but as yet the need was not as serious as it was to become when, as the Japanese invaded Burma with horrific casualties, Jon and Nancy hardly took off their uniforms.

Nancy was near us with Dick and the

baby Simon. Rose was in England waiting for her divorce and was now driving for the Red Cross. The St. John's work took me back into the deeps of Indian life and soon I was writing again.

Alipore.
January 1941.

When I come out on the verandah to write at the table it is not quite day break but the shapes of the trees and their leaves, the flower beds on the lawn are clearly visible. We are having the usual after-Christmas few days of light rain and the drops make a quiet pattering as in a lane in England but then, over the sleeping houses and roads the Muezzin calls from the Mosque's "high minaret", "Allah akbar Ashha a, La illah illa llah, Allah abbar, la llah illa llah."

Almost every day now, I am out here, awake and writing when the Muezzin calls.

The book was *Breakfast with the Nikolides* which, of all my novels, though I know it is faulty, comes nearest to our "truthful writing" and nearest to the India I love so deeply. Set in a juxtaposition of Narayangunj and the Agricultural College near Dacca where I had worked on the jute seed with Fa, some of those small intimate glimpses of Indian life I had seen on my lonely rides came back.

A young woman makes a small white image on a stand. It is like the clay images of the gods sold in the bazaar at festival times; this one is made of rice flour, a goddess with four arms; she is a "sri" which means "grace": one of the attributes of Lakshmi, Goddess of Good Fortune . . .

The girl—she is not much more than a girl—finishes the figure and now makes the rest of her rice flour more liquid and begins to decorate the stand and the floor in front of it with patterns; with nothing to guide it the pattern comes quickly, the liquid flowing through her fingers.

"How does your hand know where to go? How do you know the pattern?" I want to ask and she would have answered, "I know it. My mother knew it and her mother. Even my mother's mother's mother . . ."

This is alpona, an art handed down through generations; it should be done with the hand hardly lifting, or the fingers stopping the flow, until the pattern, in loops or curves or straight lines, is finished.

When we were filming *The River* the Indian dancer, Radha Sri Ram, who took a chief part, taught me to do alpona, often on the floor of the Studio in the long intervals of waiting while a scene was set. I could only do the simplest pattern and even then dots had to be set to guide me.

On those long-ago rides, perhaps I saw an old man wrapped only in a cotton cloth, sitting on the edge of a field and knew he was "watching his crops grow".

In the spring his small field will be filled with tender green; soon the rice will be knee high, chased with wind patterns; women will come to harvest it, plucking it out of the water by handfuls, their saris tucked up around their hips. The earth will then be ploughed—a hand plough with an ox, or pulled by a man, and weed fires will smoke in the evening.

In a stucco house a man in white clothes tends a small earthenware lamp, shaped like a leaf in which a wick burns in oil, throwing light on his brown face. Every lit doorway shows a still life: a block of wood hollowed out, with a handful of spices and a pestle to grind them with: chillis, bright red in the lamplight spread on the floor: behind them on the wall is a wicker scoop for separating the husks from the rice. Here a mother sits and oils her baby; all it wears is a string around its waist with a silver charm; its big eyes seem made bigger by kohl. Here two men squat comfortably on their heels sharing a water pipe.

Scene after scene came; I seemed to know exactly how to write them; the people's voices were in my head. How strange, in the midst of war I was able to write that book held in such peace and I finished it before the bubble burst.

Laurence had seemed more settled and responsible than I had known him; he had been promoted and given the right of signing the firm's name, and seemed extraordinarily busy. The firm had a fleet of little green cars with the front passenger door taken off so that the broker could leap out, go into an office to see his client and be back in the car without wasting a minute; only Laurence's driver knew where he went or had been. For the last months he had not been out as much to parties or to the Clubs and was unusually loving, especially to the children. Then, one evening in that June, he came back from the office and abruptly told me he was leaving in four days for the Army. "Requisitioned?" I asked. He did not answer.

Jane and I saw him off at the station for Bangalore, the officers' training centre, and came back to the house. There were babus and banias—merchants—sitting along the drive and on the portico steps—a distressed Ears had managed to keep them outside. They all had bills, some writs.

That night Donald, one of the firm's directors, came to see me. "Do you know much about Laurence's affairs?"

"Everything," I said proudly.

"I don't think you do," said Donald.

Laurence, like many other young men before him, like my own Godden grand-father, had gambled on the Stock Exchange and, when he lost, to try and retrieve himself had gambled still more; ironically his very having been entrusted to sign the firm's name gave him the power to do this, added to which, wanting him truly to be head of the house, I had left our expenses to him, making over money when he asked for it, but nothing had been paid. Sometimes I still cannot believe it; Laurence had stood by while I sold the furniture, knowing that he had already sold it twice over to different people. He had sold the car. When I went to the bank to try and cash the children's policies they had already been cashed; our joint account was empty and, "Here is a list of his debts," said Donald, "as far as we know," and he asked, "What are you going to do?"

I said, "Pay them."

Of all the silly things I have done in my life I expect that was the silliest; it took almost all the *Black Narcissus* money I had saved. In those two words I threw away what would have been some security for myself and the children but Fa did not say "Don't" when I told him. Instead, "There was nothing else you could do," said Fa, which was how it felt to me.

"Perhaps you were wise," Roland told me. "The war may go on a long time and at least you will be taken care of," an aspect that had not occurred to me; the policy among firms in Calcutta, if any member of their staff were called up, was to keep his position open for him, give his wife half his salary and pay his children's school fees. It was not until the debts were paid—as far as I could, I could not pay the money-lenders—that Donald told me Laurence was dismissed. There would be no half salary, no school fees for us. To Jon I was to write,

> The worst sting is that he went without a word of warning, knowing he could not be brought back. He must have been terribly afraid of me.

Jinglam,
Rungli-Rungliot Tea Estate,
Darjeeling.
August 1941.

> They say if a worm has been cut in half and you put the two ends into quiet earth in a flowerpot and do not disturb them, they will grow into as good a worm or better. Will that happen to me here?

A worm is, of course, an exaggeration and in my case I could not lie down or bury myself; though my one desire was to get away from Calcutta as quickly as possible, there was too much to be done; you cannot dispose of a house, servants, duties, in a day and, besides Jane and Paula, I had the responsibility of Giovanna, a young woman without real friends or family in a foreign country. Of the servants, Ears, Mrs. Ears and Khokil had been with us so long that I could not, as with the other servants, give them a month's notice and there were four pekingese, but I needed a respite, time to think.

By providence, before Laurence left, we had decided I was to take the children and Giovanna out of the heat to the hills and Roland had lent me Jinglam, an "out" bungalow on one of his firm's tea-gardens; the assistants on almost every tea-garden had gone to the war, the managers were managing alone and many of the bungalows were vacant. It had all been arranged, our fares mercifully been paid. I had even sent a few things in advance, in particular the children's desks, a few pictures and vases—Giovanna could arrange flowers as no-one else could and taught Jane; there were, especially precious, three little bowls of Cantonese pink enamel in three sizes with which the children loved to play the story of the "Three Bears" and in particular my first extravagance in what perhaps I love best, a Persian carpet. It was a Tabriz hunting carpet, "hunting" because horses, deer, hares and dogs were woven into its pattern. These few things were saved as they had already gone. We lost everything else.

Rungli-Rungliot means in Paharia "thus far and no further".

Once upon a time, perhaps when Noah lived and perhaps this flood was Noah's flood too, in another time when the earth was filled with violence, the waters of the Teesta river in North Bengal, India, began to rise in the valleys of the Himalayas, whose ranges are higher and more terrible than the Andes. The water rose higher and higher, past the foothills and the lower hills, past the villages of Riyang and Teesta Bazaar, until it reached to the spurs nearly at the top of the mountains and the people began to be seriously afraid that their retreat would be cut off by the sky. Only the spines of the ridges showed in the water, spines of monsters and dragons petrified, with their colours hidden in the Teesta that today, after the rains, is that same milky blue. The prayer flags were snatched and carried to the ridge, horns blew and the drums sounded, while behind and inaccessible, the line of snows that not even a flood could reach, reared themselves into the sky.

Down below them the consternation continued and the water spread and rose and spread.

In a temple at the top of one of these ridges, a Lama was saying his prayers. The people went in and disturbed him, but they disturbed him quietly; the horns stopped blowing, the drums were not beaten, and the people stood still as their headman went to him.

"Well, what is it?" said the Lama.

"The water—the water is coming up." It was. The people were standing in it; it was lapping the temple steps.

"Tell it to go down," said the Lama.

"*Tell* it?"

"Yes. Give it a positive order."

"But—it won't pay any attention."

"Won't it?" said the Lama. "Then I must tell it myself."

And he came out from his prayers and put out his hand.

I think of him as looking Chinese in

a stiff robe, with a Chinese absorbed and peaceful face. He looked at the spines of the hills and the water swirling round them and the jumbled colours of the people and their frightened faces and silent horns and agitated flags; he looked up at the sky and the unmoving snows and back at the water, and he put out his hand and said, "Rungli-Rungliot. Thus far and no further."

The flood immediately stopped; the water went down and the Lama went back to his prayers.

The words that he said stayed there in the place as its name.

Rungli-Rungliot is a real place on the spur of the Himalayas, facing south above the plains and the gorge of the little Runglee river that they say was left behind by accident when the Teesta water fell. Rungli-Rungliot is now a post and telegraph office and a police out-post; it serves eight tea estates.

It was the postal address for Jinglam, Roland's "out" bungalow, where we stayed for eight months, unique in beauty, humour and joy. This was surprising as I had no expectation of anything, certainly not of joy, but all the time we were there we seemed to be living under the protection of that little yellow hand and, like the worm in the pot, I was made whole again.

It had, of course, to end.

February 1942.

I wake to a violent day. After the stillness there is a violent cold wind sweeping across the garden and sweeping the mist into black clouds. Down the path after breakfast comes a green-khaki figure, slowly slowly creeping, with an umbrella that it is too windy for him to hold. I know him. He is the Rungli-Rungliot telegraph peon.

I know, too, what it is before I open the envelope. We have to leave.

had to make swift arrangements. Khokil was to take Sol and Wing and go to Jon in Calcutta; Moon and Candytuft came with us. Ears and his family decided to go back to Sikkim. "You are sure Sahib will not need a bearer?"

345

"Quite sure, Ears. He is in the army," and I explain about batmen.

Mrs. Ears tells Jane and Paula how she Ears and the children will walk to Sikkim getting colder and colder, far away from anyone, more wild. "We shall sleep in the jungle and we shall have only a lantern."

Jane comes to tell me trembling with pity.

"Tell Ayah I envy her," I say. "Sikkim is one of the most beautiful places in the world."

At Jinglam, high above the terraces of tea, there was a ridge where I used to go to pace; I could look down on the little enclave of the bungalow, its servants quarters and garden and away to the snows, the great peaks of the Himalayas, Everest, Kanchenjunga, Kabru, Siniolchu, Simbhoo; even on the ridge, you do not realise how high you have to look; most are over twenty thousand feet, some nearer thirty, all eternally white with snow. My especial peak is Kanchenjunga, the unassailable, which no-one has yet climbed. Sometimes they were hidden in cloud, sometimes clear and glittering; only a drift of snow like a veil would blow and

346

isperse. Otherwise they were unmoved, mmutable. I would look, look and be estored.

ïven in those difficult days writing, for ne, was not finished—quite.

I feel divided like this valley; part of me is steadily here, the part that orders lunch and makes marmalade and remembers the chickens and Paula's manners, and hears the reading lesson, but this is done under mist, almost subconscious; it is suddenly broken through sharply, and then I feel poignantly. Small things break it: when Candytuft looks at me and obediently spits out the goat berry as I order him to: a remark of the children's: a letter; but most of it is mist. Next there are folds and folds of uneasy hills, all the war news and worries in my mind; they loom so large they block out the snows.

The snows are my own, my secret snows. I know they are there; they are only hidden by the hills, behind the clouds. It is only that they are hidden,

lost in the cloud; only that I have no
seen them for days.

When we had gone, Jon put together the
pages of a diary I had kept at Jinglam
edited them and sent them to London
and Curtis Brown. In 1943 they were
published as a wartime edition, poor paper
and paper cover, and called *Rungli
Rungliot*; they have been published twice
again as *Thus Far and No Further*.
In the foreword I wrote:

There are only a few things in this book

Jinglam—I called it Chinglam—and its
hills and valleys.
Work.
Flowers.
Children.
Servants.
Animals.
There is nothing else because there was
nothing else.

It has brought me more letters than
anything else I have written.

# 11

## An Abandoned Family

Entrance into Kashmir.
March 1942.

Surely it is as Russia must once have been, coming across frozen marshlands into this land of winter, such winter, strangling the country with ice, snow, frost, sleet and mist. The flat land shows pools of black ice through which the dried desolate stalks of crops make a frozen stubble. The road runs straight, through avenues of tall bare poplar trees; along it peasants shuffle in rags, thin shawls and straw sandals and the light tongas move as silently as sleighs, except for the horses' bells.

We pass through villages of wooden houses, high above shut walled gardens of skeleton fruit trees. Each village has a mosque with a painted dome that might have been an Orthodox church, and the men in the shops, in their fur hats, baggy trousers and shawls look Russian in the Eastern sense, imbued with the Oriental, the Persian and Turk as in Russia's old name, Scythia of the almost animal peasant, of prosperous merchants with fat bellies and flashing fine white teeth and women, uniformly ugly or uniformly beautiful, all in the same way except for the healthy carnation pink in the faces of some, wan blue shadows on the others.

WE came to Kashmir as an "abandoned family" which is not as tragic as it seems, meaning in wartime simply an army wife and her family whose husband, normally based in India, was serving overseas. The army was responsible for us and we were told, as there was no possibility of repatriation, to choose one place in India to which we would be taken and where we had to stay for the duration under the protection of a Provost Marshall. I chose Kashmir because of the better climate—though I had not realised how frozen the winters would be—because there were possible schools there and because, in the high north-west corner of India, it seemed comparatively safe.

We arrived, far too early in the year, after another long train journey across India and a ten-hour drive up the gorges from Rawalpindi; now you can fly from Calcutta to Srinagar in a day.

We arrived in Srinagar itself at last daylight, driving past handsome carved fronts of rich men's houses rising out of the rottenness of the lanes around them; beside the Jhelum river is the huge palace of the Maharaja, built of white stone in that city of wood, with fluted pillars, columns and long glassed windows; on the few occasions the Maharaja visits his State, the people float roses down the river to greet him. Now the palace is shuttered, empty, while over the bridges, in the slush and muddy snow, a stream of jostling life goes along the narrow railed foot paths either side and, in between, cars and tongas, slow-moving ekka carts drawn by oxen and pack ponies churn up black mud and snow. Snow is heaped up against the shops, open-fronted booths in some, flares or petrol lamps are beginning to be lit, showing the shopmen sitting warm in shawls and carpets in the midst of the multitudinous wares they sell: piles of fruit, grain, nuts, spices, steaming bowls of food, fritters, chupattis: shoes, galoshes, fur hats, embroidered felt rugs called "numdahs": and everywhere the air steams with a thousand different breaths. All the populace seem to have large noses, red or blue with cold, and men, women and children look pregnant because of the kangris—firepots they carry under their robes—a kangri is an earthenware pot in a wicker holder with a wicker shield, the pot filled with live charcoal.

The women's cotton robes are filthy but the colours are blended by the very filth, dull blue and muted green, a prune colour or purple; they wear white veils and not one silver earring but bunches of them hanging either side of the face. "Ah, well," says Giovanna. "We should feel at home in this land of big noses, you and I." I feel far from at home.

I had been in Kashmir as a child and remembered its beauty. The old water-city of Srinagar—it has been called the Venice of the East—is beautiful with its bridges over the Jhelum, its tall wooden houses with carved balconies over-hanging the rivers or canals, its tiny lanes with steps leading down to the water; the filth, though, is indescribable and the disease. Once, standing on one of these flights of steps, waiting for my shikara—a light paddled boat—to fetch me, a girl came down beside me to fill her water pitcher; her face was plastered with leaves; a leaf fell off and I saw she had, unmistakably, smallpox.

New Srinagar is hideous, with villas and straight dull roads; most visitors stay in houseboats, moored along the Bunde, the river-bank of the Jhelum, or out on the Dāl Lake so that they seldom see the ugliness but we, I found, were quartered in a hotel, one room for me, one for Giovanna and the children, a hotel filled with officers' wives and their children. The wives spent most of their time waiting for officers to come up on leave, or going to the Club; true they knitted khaki "comforters" for the troops and rolled bandages for the Red Cross, but it was a life of eternal gossip and chit-chat. They were, I am sure now, suffering terrible anxieties for their men-folk and their families in Britain; they, too, had been turned out of their homes and were trying to cope in the way they knew best and, I am sure too, if I could have brought myself to confide in them they would have been immeasurably kind. I shrank from pity; they were all "abandoned families", but we were more abandoned than most— they could not imagine how abandoned. At least the husbands they worried over were steady—and had sure salaries. I could not have gone to the Club even had I wanted because I could not have paid the dues. Laurence was only a subaltern, so that there was an infinitesimal marriage allowance for me.

I had forced myself to come down from Jinglam to see the directors of his firm; one of them had taken up cudgels for me and told the others they could not leave a woman and children without any means in a country like India. At last they agreed to allow me two hundred rupees a month, slightly over twelve pounds for the three of us and that for only one year, "Until you can get work." What work? What could I do with two small children—for Giovanna I knew must find another post; writing, though I still believed what I had written to Jon about its necessity, was at a low ebb. I had to take the money though I should have liked to have thrown it in their faces.

To add to the difficulties the hotel was so insanitary that, one after another, we all got dysentery, and a child developed typhoid. I trembled for Paula and, sure enough, the disease which had lain latent since board ship declared itself and she was so ill that we had to move into a houseboat to isolate ourselves.

In the houseboat, Hoopoo.
April 1942.

How many times in how many remote places have I sat alone and listened to the rain? Even when there was peace I was solitary and separated, now in this horribleness I am still more alone. I hate this cruel land that is killing Paula.

There was a bump beside my window; a shikara had come alongside. I knew who it was, the carpet, wood-carving and fine shawl merchant, Ghulam Rasool.

As soon as we had come to the houseboat, he had called on me. "Not to sell," he assured me. "To show you what is precious," which he did, at precious prices. He was reputed to be the worst rogue in Srinagar, something he gloried in, calling himself "Subhana the Worst". I called him "Profit David"—because he talked endlessly of scriptures, especially the Quran.

He says he likes to talk to me; he feels he can open his heart. "In the Koran," says Ghulam Rasool, "it tells, 'Man shall not eat of pig. Man shall not drink wine but these in great extremity he may do but, though it is to save his life, Man shall not lie.' How is it then," asks Ghulam Rasool, "that we tell lies all the time?"

"Do you tell lies, Ghulam Rasool?"

"Indeed I do, Lady Sahib." He calls all of us, his feminine customers, "Lady Sahib" to flatter our egos. "Of course I do. I could not carry on my business else and I shall cheat you for one anna because I shall not be able to resist it."

When Profit David laughs, he shows his teeth that are disarmingly small and pearly like a child's; his skin is olive and rose showing the sleekness of the well fed and well tended. He wears a mammoth turban and a series of superb paschmina wool shawls, finely embroidered. He has a silken beard and his eyes are brown, usually merry.

That April afternoon he was out of his shikara and in the houseboat sitting room before I could hide my tears. His bigness seemed to fill the room with warmth. He did not speak but put on my desk a little figure, perhaps eight inches high, of a woman so exquisitely carved that she seemed to breathe. She was carved in coral, the colours flushing from cream to pink to apricot; one hand held a lotus and its bud; the other rested on the head of a bird like a phoenix looking up at her and her face was delicate, alive, gentle, humorous.

357

"She is Kwan-Yin, Chinese Goddess of Mercy," said Ghulam Rasool.

"But . . . Ghulam Rasool," I said when I was able to speak, "she must be worth a fortune."

"She is."

"I haven't any money. I should never be able to buy her."

"And I shall never sell her," he said. "She is my heart and she is to stay here with you until the Baba is better."

Slowly, steadily, Paula did get better.

When at last spring came, I had our house-boat moved away from the city to a mooring in the Dāl Lake and, "There is a quality here in the beauty that steals you," I was able to write. "How glad I am that, even in stress and trouble, I can be 'stolen'."

The Vale of Kashmir is set, the poets say, like a pearl between the mountains, a pearl of water and flowers. The water comes from the glaciers on the far snow peaks of the Pir Panjal mountains and runs through high alps and valleys where gentian and primulas and edelweiss grow, through forests, down rapids till it falls to the Vale floor and flows into its lakes, rivers and waterways.

In the spring, the lakes are fringed with willows where kingfishers live; the foothills are reflected in the water, in green, pink blue and white from the orchards and ricefields, mulberry gardens and fields of flax. In the villages, the roofs of the tall houses are turfed with scarlet tulips and yellow mustard growing on them; they stand in groves of chenar, walnut or fruit trees, scattered on islands or along the shore with narrow hump-backed bridges and built-up roads between them.

There is an endless traffic of boats, wood-boats, grain and cargo boats; a traffic of shikaras that are so light they skim the water, paddled with heart-shaped paddles; some are bare with only a child gathering weed, or a fisherman standing with a spear poised, watching for fish. Some are taxi shikaras, paddled by three or four men and have embroidered canopies, curtains and cushions and waggish names to attract tourists: "Whoopee", "Here I am, Where are you?" "Dream Boat". There are merchant shikaras, like Ghulam Rasool's;

the confectioners carry their cakes in bright red chests that are reflected in the water, but best of all I liked the flower boats and found it hard to resist them laden as they were to the gunwales with fresh flowers, narcissi, anemones, wild hyacinths, lilac. I liked the people, boatmen, farmers, shepherd boys, the ponymen, all Mohammedan, and the Hindu pandits with their decorative wives, immaculately clean and well dressed in contrast to the poor hard-worked Mohammedan women in their dirty pherans, a short magyar cut robe of quilted cotton.

The owner of our houseboat was a Brahmini Pandit, a tiny nervous man with a big nose perpetually twitching in apprehension; he was always, too, cracking some seed with his teeth to help his digestion. He reminded me of a mouse—if a man can be like a mouse—always watchful but exquisitely courteous; he was, too, a little wistful and an idealist. He liked me because, with a husband away in the army, he could compare me to the Goddess Savitri, "A most devout lady. Her husband was warrior too and, like you, separated by cruelty of war. She prayed and prayed they would be reunited and they were."

"Pandit Sahib, I don't pray."

"I know you do," he insisted. "I *know* you do." Perhaps I did.

He invited us to go with him to the Moghul garden of Nishat where Vaisaki, the Hindu New Year, was being celebrated.

Vaisaki in Nishat.

As we walk along the road below the garden to the Temple, we pass scores of picnic boats tied under the willows, their prows knocking the shore and we can see inside them; they are swept and tidy for the day, carpets laid down in each compartment, piles of quilts and pillows stacked against the matting walls: a hookah put ready, bunches of lilacs hanging from the roof: in the stern, the cooks, hired for the day, are cooking the feast. Otherwise the boats are empty, the people are gone to the temple or are in the garden.

The Pandit took me into the temple where the men were immersing their little boys in the water. I went alone into the women's court; they had their own pool and were standing naked on the steps, the chenar trees making a shadow leaf pattern on their soft ivory-yellow bodies—Kashmir women are pale-skinned.

Outside, Brahmin priests sat on the grass waiting to make the tika mark in vermilion and sandalwood on each forehead to show that the ritual washing had been observed. They sold too the sacred lights that are set to float on the water, tiny earthenware lamps shaped like Aladdin's and filled with sheep grease.

Thinking about religion brings me to the thought of the Catholic Church; it seems to me to be one of the solutions —maybe the only solution. It is universal, it has a common tongue. It was founded by Christ, not man. This does not mean I want to become a Catholic now, does not because, to become one, I would have to shut my eyes to many things—or see beyond them and

362

at the moment I cannot see. There is though, this: I sense that no-one can appreciate the Catholic Church until they are part of it.

The Bhagvad Gita says, "On all sides all paths lead to Me." That I believe but, at the moment, I have no path.

Money was running short. I dared not take Paula back to the hotel, even though the army paid for it and the houseboat cost far more than the firm's pitiful allowance—already half the year had gone and Fa wrote to tell me that only a few hundred pounds were left in my writing account. In the same letter, he offered me a power of attorney over the small capital he had kept in India, but I knew how little he and Mam had to live on and vowed I would not touch it.

I admit though I panicked, trying by any and every means to earn money. All these months I had known I had to do something for Giovanna. As long ago as Jinglam she had come to me with a letter from Switzerland.

"My step-sister, she is married. To the

Postmaster! And my friend Teresa, she is married too, and my cousin Tilde. I was like eldest sister to those. I was the *eldest* sister."

What had hurt her most cruelly was that her father had given her step-sister the dot Giovanna's mother had left for her, "Linen, all made by the hand with *lace*," and this was the father for whom she had embroidered a monogram on a fine handkerchief with her own hair for his Christmas present.

"He thinks I old maid!"

"Giovanna, listen to me," I had said. "You must be a sensible girl and leave us."

Giovanna's eyes are the colour brown of stones in water and have flecks of green in them like infinitesimal leaves. At once they were full of tears.

"I do not want to go. I feel me here not homesick. I am not discontent and the children"—the tears fell. "After so long we have affection . . ."

Now she had to go; by providence an English school, the Garden School, had been opened in Srinagar by a redoubtable little woman called Mary Groves. It was for children who, because of the war, had been uprooted and brought out from Britain and Mary took Giovanna as Under Matron, working especially with the younger children, to her delight. She was well paid and I knew Mary would look after her and understand her; she would be near us and could come when, and as, she liked; it was a great relief. I myself taught every morning in the kindergarten —our playschool in Calcutta and Mariel Cardew's in Cornwall stood me in good stead—and, by Mary's kindness, I was able to take Jane and Paula with me. In the afternoons I taught dancing in the Garden School and the Convent which meant I had to leave the children with only an ayah. It worried me—it was really Jane who looked after Paula. In the evening after they were in bed there was a good deal to do getting the kindergarten work ready for next day; I had the houseboat to run and had to do for the children all that Giovanna had done. Desperately, perhaps idiotically, I tried to write as well.

ATTDN25

**To Jon:** Houseboat Hoopoo,
Dāl Lake.
June 1942.

Laurence has been commissioned and is
in the 11th Sikhs and is delighted as he
likes the regiment. They are still in
Rawalpindi but "on call" ready to go
overseas at any moment so that we can't
join him even if I wanted to. He is
repentant and says he wants to come up
on leave and "sort things out". I don't
believe they can be.

He came and we managed to get away on
a week's trek so as to be alone together,
going over the Harnag Pass, some fourteen
thousand feet while, in one of the Garden
School's "breaks", Giovanna looked after
the children.

Doctor Percy had sent us the money; I
told him nothing of our difficulties and am
sure Laurence had not but I think he and
Florence sensed that there was trouble.
They gave us this week of peace and
beauty—what was the use, I thought, of
nagging? Laurence was probably going
overseas; he might even be killed as many

of our friends had already been. I gave myself up to him and enjoyed it; another bonus was that I met Jobara.

Jobara, our ponyman, had been passed on to me by the Head Mission Doctor who had retired. "Here is a Kashmiri you can really trust," he had told me and Jobara fulfilled that trust over and over again, not only as my friend but all the family's. He had lived in Sonamarg his entire life, through all its snow-blocked winters and knew every mountain and pass, valley and route—he had never been nearer civilisation than Srinagar. He owned, perhaps, a hundred ponies, riding and pack, was headman of the village and, too, head chowkidar or caretaker of all the district's Forestry bungalows, rough small chalets built of logs—several times he lent one to me—and every time we went up to the valley he himself took charge of us.

I am thankful to say that Laurence paid him. Nothing of course was sorted out. Laurence did not go overseas, the Regiment stayed in Rawalpindi but, although he was so close, for the rest of the summer he seemed to vanish.

Giovanna has a great effect on Mohammedan men; to them her height, well-rounded plumpness—her legs are magnificent—her glowing skin, dark hair, brilliant eyes and, especially, her strong features, have an instant appeal, especially it seems to carpet sellers—she had suitors amongst them in Calcutta, and now, in Kashmir, Mohidin, said to be the richest merchant in Srinagar except perhaps for Profit David, comes to me wanting to marry Giovanna. It seems she is still my responsibility.

"But, Mr. Mohidin, you have three wives already."

"No matter. I will put them away," and he waves them away with his hand.

"Miss Beltrammetti"—Giovanna's surname means "beautiful little tram" —"Miss Beltrammetti is Christian. You are a Moslem."

"No matter. No matter. She can convert."

"I don't think she will."

"She must—if you use your influence."

"I cannot do that. In Europe, girls like to choose their own husbands and I think they should."

"*Madam!*" He is astonished. "That is very bad thing. You must use your influence," and he says, "You shall come to my shop and choose for yourself any one of my Persian carpets. They are like jewels, Madam," and I am sure they are.

"Some are priceless," says Mohidin and, seeing my face, adds with craft, "You shall choose *three*."

Giovanna does not know what peril she is in!

No-one has loved Kashmir more than the Moghul Emperors, especially Jehanghir and his queen, the matchless Nur Jehan, Light of the World. There are three Moghul gardens on or near the shores of the Dâl Lake: Nasim, which is only a grove of chenar trees—the chenar leaf is painted, carved and embroidered in all Kashmir's myriad crafts. Shalimar is the most famous, and Nishat the most beautiful and both, in the true pattern of Moghul gardens, are terraced, with wide terraces having a centre water channel of marble with pools and fountains. The water runs from terrace to terrace down slants of fretted marble cunningly carved to make the water-music that so soothed the Emperors' nerves; each slant has a small marble dais about it so that they could sit and listen. Above the lake, on the mountain, is another little garden, the gem of Chashma Shahi, the smallest Moghul garden in India. All have lawns under fruit trees, Persian lilacs and mounds and tangles of roses.

Our family has a fondness for breakfast picnics and on almost every Sunday of that summer we would go across the lake—the houseboat had its own shikara so that it cost nothing—for a breakfast picnic in one of the Moghul gardens; it was on Sundays that the water for the channels and fountains was turned on and, if we were early, it would still be running slowly enough for us to hear the water music; the patterns on the stone slats are all different:

| one had deep honeycombs | another rickracks; some are horizontal | some vertical in soft waves |

It is this that makes the rhythms.

While the three children played and

Giovanna, who was often with us, wandered, talking to people—no matter that she spoke no Kashmiri or Urdu, they no English, they still seemed able to talk—I used to sit on one of the small dais and, like the Emperors, let the worries be soothed away.

I am interrupted by Giovanna calling me and find her sitting in a circle of women; as they are wearing burkhas—garments like a tent, hiding them from head to foot with only a small lattice for their eyes—I know they are not peasants. Their children are gathered round them, the girls in trousers and tunics, with a little embroidered cap, the boys in the muslin equivalent of jodhpurs, a shirt and embroidered waistcoat; they too have caps. The women are murmuring in excitement and, "I do not know what they want," says Giovanna.

One of them lifts her bracelets towards me—she has opened her burkha and I can see her face pleading, "By your kindness, can we look at that?" and she points to Jane's doll.

It is a chubby baby girl doll with

golden hair, eyes that move from side to side and when she is bent forward, she makes a cry "Mama"—Ma, the name for mother the world over; even lambs say "Ma". The women make exclamations but Mignonette is Jane's greatest treasure and she is reluctant to hand the doll over. I am not going to force her but, "Sois gentil, Jane," pleads Giovanna and soon the women are passing Mignonette from hand to hand with soft noises of wonder; the girls crowd round while the boys hide their laughs behind their hands.

I ask about the children. One young woman holds a baby, "Boy or girl?" I ask.

"*Son!*"

"Shabash," I say and the woman beside her, not to be outdone, stands up. "And what is this?" she cries and under her burkha shows a tiny curled-up baby asleep.

"Son?"

"Ah, ha! Ha! What else?"

"Shabash!"

Presently they all stand up, salaam and walk away, their velvet trousers showing beneath their burkhas, their little embroidered shoes, with upturned tips, deep in daisies.

On those early mornings no-one but the Kashmiris were about. Our boat houseboy Ramzana always brought a small brazier and when the coals were hot I cooked scrambled eggs; we had tea from a samovar and the gardeners brought us fruit, laid down on leaves.

It was on one of those mornings that, crossing the lake, I looked up and saw above Nishat, high on the mountain, a little house standing alone in a fuzz of green trees.

I cannot be coherent about that year, it was all too hasty and bewildering. The war was worsening in Calcutta, Nancy and Jon were in turmoil and, in July, Nancy brought Simon to me for safety and so that, amateur as she was, she could do almost full-time nursing at the Military Hospital. Simon was three years old—we called him Chamba, meaning the smallest in the house—and was one of the most fetching small boys I have seen, flaxen-haired like Paula but with brown eyes; he was Calcutta delicate, which was to add to my problems, but from the first day he flourished.

The Vale in summer grew so hot that, with Nancy's help over money, we were able to go up and camp in the mountains chiefly for the sake of Chamba. We did not go to Gulmarg, Srinagar's accepted hill station, for which I was grateful. We chose Sonamarg, which means "meadow of gold", and it was sheeted with flowers, pine forests rising above it to snow mountains, with trees undercarpeted with columbines and wild strawberries. It was then known only to a few climbers, or people trekking through on their way to fish or shoot, as Fa had done. Missionaries, old hands, came there every year in search of peace and to get away from the crowded squalor in which most of them worked; they, like us, made semipermanent camps on sites rented from the State and stayed two or three months.

A motor road was being made to Sonamarg but that summer it had only reached as far as Kangan where Jobara met us with riding and pack ponies for a two-day march, spending the night in a dāk—or post house—on the way.

I owe my life to Jobara. In that September Nancy and I went on a long and arduous ride, leaving the children with him; it was too long for me—and in the night I had a miscarriage. I had not known another child was on the way. I haemorrhaged all night and all next day; the bleeding would not stop. Nancy was as frantic as she was helpless but Jobara had heard, in the mountain people's mysterious "bush telegraph", that a mission doctor was on her way up to holiday in Sonamarg. He told Nancy and rode full bent to fetch her.

Doctor Maidie Sherborne and her nurse companion, Vera Studd, must have been two of the most intrepid women in India; their hospital was at Tonk on the border of Afghanistan. When the troubles became serious—though there were perpetual troubles—the authorities told the Doctor she and Miss Studd must leave, to which she retorted they would not think of leaving, this was tribal country and, "the tribesmen will never hurt us". It was still insisted upon that she must have an armed escort but this brought a request from the tribesmen: when she went on her tours into their rocky fastnesses would she be sure to wear her doctor's white coat so that they could be sure and not shoot her, "only the escort". After that she went alone.

When Jobara found her she did a forced march and reached our camp that evening; both she and Miss Studd were exhausted and told Nancy that Doctor Maidie must rest before she operated—she could not trust her hands.

Nancy was exhausted too and it was Jobara who stayed with me that night. "Feel her feet every now and then," Doctor Maidie told Jobara. "If they get too cold, call me."

I could sense Jobara, quiet and strong, beside me through what became a memorable night. I seemed to be on a tide ebbing from the shore into a pearly incandescent distance—I suppose my life was ebbing; it was drawing me away with no fright, only utter peace and a bliss such as I had never known. I did not want to come back but, now and then, felt Jobara's hands, warm and steady as he felt my feet and heard his voice, "Memsahib—Mem." For courtesy's sake I had to open my eyes and saw the familiar tent—it was lined with yellow— and the lantern burning. "Let me go," I wanted to say, but could not speak. Towards dawn Jobara called Doctor Maidie.

The coming back was not pleasant. Doctor Maidie had nothing with her—the missionaries had had to learn that if they brought a doctor's bag with them they would have no holiday, no rest at all, which they needed vitally. All she had now was a kitchen knife and a pair of nail scissors. I can remember dear Miss Studd, who was strictly teetotal, giving me swig after swig of brandy.

I am afraid I ruined that part of their holiday for them. They stayed with me until I could be moved on a litter and then Doctor Maidie came with us on the first day's march back to Srinagar but it was Jobara who brought me the rest of the way. Torrential rain came down, turning the track into such slipperiness of deep mud that the litter had to be abandoned but Jobara held me sitting sideways on the steadiest of his ponies. I remember Nancy, soaked and streaming with rain, riding up and down our caravan with Chamba on her saddle bow.

I did not tell Laurence.

The 11th Sikhs had not moved from Rawalpindi and, still weak but convalescent, I took the opportunity of a seat in a car and went down to see him. "You must know where you stand," wrote Jon. I soon knew.

To Jon:          End of September 1942.

Laurence is utterly content with army life, and obviously doesn't want the content disturbed by us. He has, too, found a boon companion in a young officer's wife; her husband is overseas. I don't think it is serious but we talked of a divorce. He blithely agreed on condition that I gave him complete financial freedom from the children which hurt!

I came back to Srinagar and a horrid realisation that I should have thought of before. Hill boarding schools in India do not have the usual three terms but, with only long weekends and ten days' break in June they have one long term that lasts from March until October when the weather is cool enough for the children to go back to their homes in the plains. All the schools then close so that in Srinagar, for nearly five months, there would be no teaching, kindergarten or dancing. There was, too, an almost complete exodus among the Europeans; Mary Groves had found Giovanna a holiday post with two motherless children who lived with their father in Delhi—a good opportunity for her, but for us? We could not go away because of the fares and how was I to find work in that long winter?

I could, I thought, teach English to emancipated Hindu or Mohammedan ladies but, even were this successful, lessons would not bring in much. What else could I do? Soon I would not be able to pay the houseboat rent. I quailed at the thought of going back to the hotel and grew frantic, every day more nerve-ridden, tired and cross.

It settled itself in a way I had not thought of. All three children became ill with virulent influenza and I had no choice but to stop work—fortunately it was the last two weeks of term. As they began to convalesce I was ill myself and not only with influenza.

In their mercy—and through Mary Groves—the missionaries at the Mission Hospital took us in. The hospital was for Kashmiris but it had a wing meant for visiting mission doctors; by providence, it was empty and the Head Doctor lent it to me. "You can pay us when you can," he said and, "You must stay in bed," said the Senior Sister to me. "You have paratyphoid and pneumonia. You are not very well."

I thought that was something of an understatement but my case was trivial compared to most in their charge; the only diseases there was room to isolate in the Mission Hospital were leprosy and smallpox and the people came in every extremity.

I will never countenance a word against missionaries, knowing at first hand the depth of their selflessness, courage, endurance and kindness. In that hospital of more than a hundred patients there were only two nurses but they found time to come to me morning and evening; for the rest I had to manage.

For two weeks, the last of the Garden School term, Mary our good angel sent—at considerable inconvenience to herself—Giovanna to look after the children, but it could only be for two weeks; after that Giovanna had to go to Delhi. The last night she came and knelt by my bed weeping. I had a wild hope—I think she had too—that she would not leave us but we both knew it was impossible. I could not pay her, or even keep her, she was pledged to take her two small charges to Delhi, but it was a desolate parting. After she had gone I could hear Paula and often Chamba crying, Jane's patient little voice and the scoldings and grumblings of the old crone of an Ayah who was the only one I had been able to find.

It is uncommon for a Kashmiri woman to be a servant, most are too ignorant, too coarsened with manual work. Ayah was one of the few but she could not mend or sew, not as much as put on a button. She wore a soiled white pheran and a great deal of silver jewellery and tried her utmost to instil better habits in me: that underclothes should not be changed all winter, or windows opened; stoves kept roaring— never mind the cost of wood; fruit gives cold and honey is bad for children who should be given quantities of pure white sugar. She liked to keep the children by the stove while she told them stories but Ayah's stories were gruesome. "Winter has Three Sisters," she used to tell. "Thirty days Death, then Twenty and then Ten and it is the Third Sister who, though the shortest, takes the most deaths because, by then, people are weak," said Ayah, "and your Mummy very weak." Even Jane burst out crying and I thought of our own old Ayah in Calcutta and how Jane had loved her; of her cleanliness, sense and wit, but old Ayah was in her Buddhist nunnery. Ears and Mrs. Ears would have come but, even if I could have sent for them, I would not have wanted them to see us now. They were the sort of servants, I would never, I thought, have again.

To Jon:
You ask why I didn't ask you to come —as I knew you would of course have done at once. Jon, you were doing war

work and that was far more important than us. Somehow I knew I would weather it though at times I couldn't see how.

The wing of the hospital was dark and gloomy, added to which it overlooked a Mohammedan graveyard and, as the weather grew wet and cold, sometimes with flakes of snow, all day long there was the sound of burials. Poor people in Kashmir are not buried in coffins—that would be too expensive—they are tipped out into their graves; even if a baby is wrapped in a towel, the towel is taken away—"Who would waste a good towel?" asked Ayah. As I lay in bed I could hear the Maulvi's voice chanting: "There is no god except one God, Allah. He is the only One. He alone is worthy of praise. There is no god except . . ." The people, though, took some things into their own hands; when spring came they would plant irises on the graves—in Kashmir the iris is the symbol of money, so that in the next world the dead would not be quite dependent on this one God. In my delirium, Giovanna told me, I had gabbled about irises.

When she had gone I said to the Senior Nurse. "Sister, I must get up, I *must.*"

"Have you looked at yourself?" asked Sister and brought me my hand looking-glass. My face and skin were sulphur yellow.

"Oh no! No!"

"Yes," said Sister, "jaundice," and she said, "Dearie, your best chance is to lie still."

Saint Francis de Sales, most balanced and sane of saints, once wrote that most people when they are in trouble behave like a bird caught under a net, fluttering wildly as it struggles to free itself, only getting more and more enmeshed; if it would only be still, it would see that the net has holes in it through one of which it could escape. I had not heard of Saint Francis de Sales then but, as I lay helpless, I began to see I had been exactly like that bird, struggling, struggling, and for what? Only getting to spend. Forced to lie still, I began to see more clearly, and saw what might be a hole of escape. Suppose, instead of living to get money to spend, we lived by not spending? Somewhere away, where it

384

would be so quiet and simple that a little would go a long way?

There was a lane outside the hospital through which the country people made their way into the city and when I was allowed up I watched them. The country women and children had more pink in the olive of their cheeks, they were fatter and the men were sturdy and big under their rags.

"Ayah," I ask, "how much would a peasant like that one need to live?" The peasant was an old man, in straw sandals driving a pack pony.

"Country people are fools," says Ayah. "They do not know cinemas. They do not know shops. What do they need? Suppose he has a house, and a field that has rice in it and a patch to plant with sāg"—sāg is Kashmiri spinach—"He has some fruit trees and a walnut tree. He will have a few hens, a pony and a goat. He has a fishing spear for fish. He burns his wood for charcoal. He sells his nuts for salt and tea dust, maybe a new firepot or tobacco for his hookah. If he needs some clothes he can

385

work a few days for someone else or hire out his pony. How much money does he need? None," said Ayah in great scorn.

I do not quite believe Ayah but it is near truth. If we went to live like peasants in the country we should be rich, rich by being poor.

It was then that I remembered the house I had seen from the lake, that speck among the faint far green of trees, the small house alone on the mountain.

# 12

## Winter Pass

I DID not tell anyone where I was going or what I meant to do.

As soon as I could walk I hired a tonga and, taking only Sultan, the young houseboy the Mission had found for me, drove along the lake to Bren, the nearest village to Nishat. Before we came to it, a track led off the road onto the mountain-side and I could see the house standing above us. The track did not go far; we had to leave the tonga and walk up a steep mountain path. I stopped several times to lean on Sultan.

The air seemed more clear than any I had breathed for a long time. The only sounds were the splash of a stream as it ran down the mountain, an occasional high bird call like an eagle's and, faint from the lake, the sound of paddles and a splash from the casting of a fishing net.

The path went up to a knoll where a

gap in a baked-earth wall served as a front gate; inside the wall spread a garden of terraces and fruit trees which led to a rough lawn and there, set so perfectly that it seemed to nestle into the side of the mountain, was the house. It was built of pink-grey stone with a wooden verandah and a roof of wooden shingles. Beside it the stream fell from terrace to terrace and in front, rising almost as high as a gabled window in the roof, was a magnolia, one of the slender kind that would have white flowers and purple buds. I stood and looked. If Sultan had been Hindu instead of Moslem he would have known I was taking "darshan" except that I knew at once I would not, simply, look and go away.

I have always loved houses and have written books round them. Fa's and Mam's house in Cornwall was, in part, China Court: my grandmother's in London, though not as large, was the house in *Fugue in Time*. I have had several cherished houses; always, by circumstance not by desire, I have had to leave them but never have I loved a house as I loved Dove House.

It was a rarely beautiful little house; in spring, all round it were flowering trees, peach, apricot, cherry, almond, acacia; in summer it was hung with vines and honeysuckle and scented white roses, while along its terraced orchards white iris grew wild. In the courtyard the stream splashed to a small waterfall and, high above, the mountain cut off the sky; the lake below was divided in two by a built-up road and a bridge, like a brooch, pinning them together; the far horizon was broken by the range of the Pir Panjal snows.

It had not crossed my mind that the house might not be empty and empty it was. A Kashmiri caretaker came, unwillingly unlocked it and I walked in. There were four rooms, two up and two down, each with a slit room behind it; they were separated by a narrow hall and a wood staircase and, on the first floor behind the gable, was the smallest by-room, looking across the lake, its window almost brushed by the tip of the magnolia tree. At once, "My writing room," I said.

The whole house was dilapidated but the wood was sound, the earth floors dirty but not damp. There was no glass in the windows, only brown paper, no electricity, no means of heating, no water except the stream and, as I discovered later, a spring on the mountain; except for a two-roomed hut in the courtyard, meant for a kitchen and servants' room, no other house was near. No road went to Dove House, only that steep rocky path. "Every possible drawback," everyone was to say.

I took it for five years.

In India, a woman, any woman, Western or Indian, does not live alone unless she has a label: school inspector, missionary or, if Indian, holy woman or guru, and, "If you do this," said the Provost Marshall, "you will be out of my jurisdiction." As Kashmir was not British India but an independent State, the Provost Marshall was appointed by the army to watch over and protect any army personnel, visiting or living there, particularly the wives and children of men serving in other parts of India or overseas and, "If you get into trouble," he told me, "I cannot help you. You will be on your own." The missionaries were more blunt.

"You have lost your mind," and Sister said what I was to remember afterwards, "It's not right to take your children to that remote place." I wonder now how I dared but it seemed then I had no alternative except to go back to the stultifying and disease-ridden hotel; rents, even for a small house in Srinagar, were two to three hundred rupees a month, houseboats much the same and, "I would have given you the house for nothing," my new landlord told me, "except that under Kashmiri law it would become yours and I must, for respect of my father, keep it for mine."

He was a well-born Mohammedan Kashmiri with the title of Khan—we called him Khan Sahib. His father, who had built the house, had been a poet—I could have guessed that. "His idea was to come here," said the Khan, "and write his poems in peace," which was why he had called it Dove House. "I think dove is the symbol of peace? But he died and it has been empty ever since," and the Khan wept a little. "He wanted so much for it to be lived in but what am I to do? I have to live in the city for my work. Madam, I have twenty mouths to feed and not one of them my own. I cannot take care of it," and he rented it to me for five rupees a month—in those days seven shillings and sixpence—for the house, garden and the land under the trees; he kept the fruit.

A Vakil (lawyer) drew up the contract written in Urdu with a huge State stamp. It not only had to be signed, finger prints were taken as well. I thought that ignominious. "One should trust people."

"Never," said the Vakil. "Never."

I had to give the Khan the right to make charcoal on the land, promise not to pick almonds—the most valuable crop—and not to burn for firing any of the wood of which the house was made. "But I *wouldn't*," I protested.

"If you were very cold you might," said the Vakil. "Tenants have been known to take the shingles off the roof and I think you will be very cold," said the Vakil.

I had of course to put the house in order and cabled Fa to send me three of my remaining few hundred pounds. "I can spend three, no more," I told him. Three hundred pounds to clean the house, mend the roof, the floors and the broken banisters of the staircase which had been used for firewood as the Vakil had warned; to make a bathroom of the slit behind one of the upstairs rooms, put glass in as many of the windows as I could, distemper the walls, and buy almost all of the furniture, kitchen things, crockery, rugs—the hunting carpet had long ago been sold to Jon. It was a challenge and I revelled in every minute of it.

I cajoled the Pandit to come and see Dove House. He had begged me not to leave the houseboat when we had to go to the Mission Hospital, even offering to put the rent down, an astonishing faceabout for him, and it had hurt him further that I had taken a house, not come back to his boat. "Pandit Sahib, it is a twentieth of the price." At once he understood and, curious to see this astonishing bargain, offered me a lift as he was on his way to see his family goldsmith. "Each time I return to Jammu, I am taking costly gifts to my family," he said in pain.

The distemper I want on my walls are the colours of the Pandit's and the goldsmith's turbans and I ask if I can take a snippet of each to try and match them which causes much amusement. The Pandit buys a silver dish in the shape of a chenar leaf—"For politely offering pān"—paste for betel-leaf chewing—it costs him six rupees. I have never met anyone so afraid of spending money, and he plainly does not understand why, if I want a bargain, I do not go back to the hotel, "Where it is free," he says, *"Free!"*

"Never!"

"But in a house, all your requirements you must provide yourself."

"Our requirements are very simple, Pandit Sahib."

"There are things you must have—all European ladies have. Toothpaste."

"We shall use willow twigs, frayed at the end as you do."

"Toilet paper!"

"We could use leaves," but it does not do to tease the Pandit.

When he sees Dove House even he is mollified. "It will be nice when it is swept," he says.

To Jon:                    Mission Hospital.
                           December 1942.

Laurence came for two days—I have a feeling Giovanna wrote to him when she had to leave me. I was so glad to see someone of our own family that I could not say anything but am dismayed at what the missionaries must have thought; here am I living rent-free and Laurence arrived in a large coupé Plymouth, having driven himself up from Rawalpindi and wearing a splendid new camel-hair overcoat; they did not know both the coat and car were lent and he had twenty-seven gallons of petrol, free.

Still it was bliss being driven to and from Bren in cushioned warmth after jogging in freezing tongas through rain and sleet. I think he was rather appalled at my appearance, still more appalled at Dove House but relieved it was so inexpensive. He is now a Staff Captain so should find it easier to manage—when didn't he? But I mustn't be ungrateful; he brought me two little pale pink and crystal flasks of Elizabeth Arden's Flower Mist and Hand Lotion, hardly suitable but irresistible to my spirits. He was charming, helpful and amenable but I am sure still the same Laurence. He didn't want to talk about the divorce but I have agreed to wait a year before doing anything drastic.

As it turned out I waited four.

Some things are a pleasure to buy. I went to the pottery shops and chose deep blue cups and saucers, plates, dishes and bowls in the cheap Kashmiri pottery that is made in strong native colours, blue, yellow, green or brown. I bought Kashmiri numdahs, pale fawn with white edges, and, for curtains, hand-printed khuddha —Indian cotton cloth—with small designs in yellow and black of stylised flowers on cream; they would be lined with pink to match the three-bears Cantonese enamel bowls.

The furniture could not have been more

simple. The beds were Indian charpoys, a wooden frame on wooden legs with string across them; we had no blankets, only country cotton quilts. There was a small dressing chest of unstained wood made cheaply by the carpenters and a single cupboard built into the bedroom wall. I could not afford to warm the down-stairs rooms so that in winter we lived in the two rooms upstairs and all four of us slept in one bedroom. In winter, too, the kitchen was moved into one of the slit rooms downstairs; a kitchen in-side the house is uncommon in India—but the chula—a clay cooking stove—helped to warm it. For other warmth, each room had an iron stove standing on legs with a pipe that went out of the window.

In the sitting room was a small walnut-wood dining table, with four chairs, made by the carpenters too, and a few wicker-work easy chairs that I cushioned with quilted khuddha; there were stools for the children. On the landing was one small shelf of books, all we had and, in the writing room, some shelves for papers and a handsome walnut-wood desk and chair that Jon had given me. Downstairs, in one room were the children's desks, where I hoped to make a playroom and, in the kitchen, a wooden table, a wire-meshed safe for food, and shelves for pots and pans, which were the handleless Indian kind called dechis made of indigenous brass; I liked to see them scoured and shining. For light I still had the oil lamps I had bought for very little in the Thieves Bazaar in Calcutta to take to Jinglam and also, my one extravagance, a papier-mâché lamp, golden, painted with kingfishers in deep rich colours. There had been, almost unbelievably, six pounds left over from the three hundred. I should have kept it for emergencies but I spent it entirely on the lamp, ninety-six rupees. "What is the difference in it to cost all that?" Sister had asked me when I had showed it to her. She too had bought papier-mâché in the bazaar, a box that had cost three rupees. I did not want to spoil it for her but, "Tell me," she insisted. "That box is made of newspaper and painted with cheap Japanese colours," I told her. "Look how crude and shiny they are. Papier-mâché should never shine but glow. That box will crack in a few months while this," I touched the lamp—it was pleasure to touch its sheen—"this is made of hand-made paper from a village that has made it for generations. It is pulped and moulded by hand and painted with colours ground from semi-precious stones; the blue is lapis lazuli, the pink, cornelian, the gold, real gold leaf. Its painting is so fine it takes two weeks to do one lamp, the pattern is traditional and, after it is painted, it is lacquered with a lacquer of amber and oil. It will last longer than I shall."

Now it gives its glow to the whole sitting room.

We moved into Dove House on New Year's Day 1943 in snow.

To Jon:

The Vakil was right, we are cold but we'll get used to it and the house looks so fresh and gay with its colours, pale walls and rugs: it smells of new wood and mountain snow, a little of wood-smoke but I put apple chips in the stove to keep the smoke fragrant. The rooms are bare and not, I have to admit, what people call comfortable but, Jon, as we had our first tea, all of us sitting round the new table—it is waxed into pale gold—using our blue cups and saucers, eating milk, honey and new bread, I felt such a tide of relief and release.

The bread was kulchas, Kashmiri bread like a doughnut sprinkled with sesame seed—at first it scandalised Jane that we should eat it; the tea was mint tea from wild mint I had dried, real tea being prohibitively expensive as were all imported things.

Already the children have some colour in their cheeks, even Paula—Chamba is positively rosy. They have space to play in, good fresh air and, more than anything else, a home.

They were beginning to chatter and laugh and after tea, for the first time for weeks, I read them a story. As they sat on stools round the stove even Jane seemed reassured. "I *was* right," I told myself. "I *am* justified."

In the early morning Ayah, who had moved her bed into the kitchen for warmth, went outside to relieve herself as Indian servants do. As she tried to open the door she felt something heavy pressing against it; she pushed harder and the door opened; it was a snow-leopard.

"If there is a leopard we must be very very careful of the dogs." Jane had a new worry —it was always Jane who worried and this time she was right; dog flesh to a leopard is like caviare or foie gras to a gourmet and we hardly dared let the pekingese out of our sight; Sol and Wing had died, both tragic deaths, but we still had Moon Daisy and Candytuft.

Candytuft was so small that as a puppy he could sit on my hand but he was sturdy; he came on treks with us, often twenty-mile marches on which he would sometimes sit on a pack pony; he lost half his tail in the camp fire and a piece of his ear in a fight with an upstart terrier. When he had been born in Calcutta people came, even from far away, to look at him and his three sisters because they believe that a white animal is a chosen soul on its path up the Ladder of Existence, so fine a soul that it might, one day, become the Buddha.

I had meant to keep Ayah until I was a little stronger but she left next day; now I was the only woman at Dove House among what seemed to be a horde of men—kindly men. For a housewarming they brought presents: the Khan Sahib, as our landlord, a bowl of red honey: Lussoo, the dirzee who had made the curtains and quilted the chairs, gave me fruit and nuts: the care-taker/gardener Nabir Das brought eggs and a goose: the Pandit sent honey cakes: Ghulam Rasool nuts and toys of turquoise and brass for the children, doll's-house-size chairs and tables—a tiny rickshaw. Ramzana of the houseboat sent walnuts and a good-luck card.

The Khan Sahib found us our servants. "Never," he said, "never engage anyone, deal with anyone, except through me," which was good advice; he was held in great respect in the village.

It must seem odd to people in Europe or America for someone with as little money as I had then to have a servant at all but there are customs in India that even an independent woman would not be wise to break; in Calcutta we had kept eleven servants, even in Jinglam, five; now, not counting Nabir Das who was paid by the Khan, I had one servant, a cook-bearer, Madhu, and a sullen sweeper boy who came for an hour in the morning and evening. Sultan had had to go though he pleaded and wept; poor Sultan, he had one "chit" or reference, a cruel one which he displayed with innocent pride: "I can recommend Sultan Mahomed as a perfectly useless servant."

Our bathroom was a partitioned-off space under the eaves of the bedroom; a door had been cut to a back stair, not much more than a ladder, which allowed Habib, the sweeper boy, to come up with his basket and take out the pots of cess, carry them down and empty them.

This led to endless altercation. What

could be simpler, to Habib, even Madhu, than to empty the pots at the foot of the ladder? "In the *courtyard!* Close to the house! Think of the smell!" "What smell?" their faces plainly said. To their mystification I had caused a deep pit to be dug in the furthest-away place on our land and there Habib had to carry the pots and, after emptying them, had incomprehensibly to sprinkle on earth and lime from the piles I had put beside the pit. Every day there was a battle and it was not until I fined Madhu that I had any success.

"Going to Kashmir is like putting your head into an exquisitely beautiful hornet's nest," Ghulam Rasool had cautioned me. "You will be stung." Every day somebody tried to cheat me over money or work and I had to learn to be hard. "It is the only thing they understand," the Khan Sahib told me. When the village women began pillaging my vegetable garden, I took away their tools which was cruel as the tools were their livelihood. "They will make great outcry but they will give in," said the Khan, "because they understand," and they did. Madhu and Habib did not understand about the cess pit but they understood the fines.

Who was it who said, "Compared to cleanliness, godliness was child's play in that house?" It was true of Dove House. In summer it was simple, the children swam in the lake but, when it was colder, we bathed in front of the bedroom stove; a zinc tub was put close to the stove, a dust sheet spread and the water was heated in the kitchen in two old kerosene tins with a stout stick bored through for a handle. I could not ask Madhu to carry more than two full tins up the stairs and we managed with those; first Chamba, then Paula, then Jane went in; finally, when they were dried and in their dressing gowns, I stood, shivering, for a sponge-down in now tepid water. Next night I went first, they sponged. Madhu emptied the bath tub out of the window—soapy water is good for roses.

To him it was all another extraordinary and unnecessary idea because, all over Kashmir in spring, the lakes, rivers and streams resound with screams and cries and splashings as the women give their children the customary once-a-year bath when they will each get a new shirt and pantaloons or a new pheran. The little girls' hair will be undone from innumerable plaits, washed too and combed through for lice. "But those babas", I can almost hear the village women saying it as they look at Jane, Paula and Chamba, "are washed every day in *hot* water. No wonder they are so pale."

An airgraph came telling me of Gordon's death. Rose's divorce had come through undefended but, four months before the decree nisi was granted, Gordon, then in command of a nightfighter squadron, took his plane, a Mosquito—one of the most dangerous of fighter planes—on a night mission, destination unknown, and it never returned.

Rose's world in ruins and it is nothing because the world is largely, and I mean largely, in ruins too.

Dove House.
1 March 1943.

In Kashmir's January, February and

most of March, the sun seldom shines; the whole land seems locked in colourless gloom, grey, white, snow and ice, the mountain dark, its rocks the colour of purple slate but today, this first day of March, for the walk I insist we must have every day, we went along the dyke, the small water canal that runs behind the house all the way to Srinagar as one of its water supplies; though we passed sheep with their wool sodden and a small frozen herd boy huddled under a tree, we came to an orchard and there the almond trees were in full blossom, their branches studded with pink flowers. It was wonderful, in the dark and cold, to see those trees flowering confidently and serenely covered in fragile blossom.

I lifted Paula and Chamba up on the orchard wall to see: Paula stretched out her hands, thin weak little hands as if towards the sun, "Pretty," she said, her face illumined. Next moment she pushed Chamba off the wall.

"You must get a post," the directors of the firm had told me; "Get work," but how could I leave this frail fierce small being?

I picked a spray in bud to take home for our sitting room and on the way back met Nabir Das. "That is badam—almond," he said with a frown.

"It's only one spray."

"You do not know what it is to be poor," said Nabir Das.

As if the almond, first sign of spring, had set it off I have started writing again.

I had been too busy establishing the house and its customs, getting to know the servants and the village really to work, but it had of course been there all the time.

I have become fascinated by Dunne's Theory of Time in which time is all one, not divided into past, present and future —perhaps India's feeling of timelessness is what draws me. Dunne explains it simply: "If you are in a boat on the river and round a bend you cannot see what is behind you, nor, until you have rounded another, what is before you but, were you in an aeroplane, you would see the whole." My story is written from the point of view of the aeroplane and covers three generations of a family living in the same house in London, not told consecutively but mingled together.

Why try and write about a house in London when you are living in Kashmir? but I am obsessed by it. It stems, I suppose, from Randolph Gardens but is bigger, far more grand.

In the play that was eventually made from the book, the setting was the front staircase and the landing between.

The two flights of stairs, one going up, the other going down, give on the first-floor landing that is wide enough to make a sitting room. It has an alcove with a window that looks down on the Place, with a window-seat, and by it a table and chairs and a writing desk. The sound of the traffic in the park road comes in; and every minute and again, the whole vibrates slightly as the trains pass underground. The church clock strikes and the clocks follow after it, the clocks outside and the clocks all over the house, and then settle again to their tickings. Every door that opens can be heard on the landing, and every door that shuts; there are rattlings and scrapings when the range is made up. Everything can be heard on the landing.

The clocks, of course, were important.

The play opened with three different generations of butlers coming one after the other up the stairs bringing the evening post, each in a black coat, his feelings repressed behind his face, each using the same silver salver exactly as I had described in the book.

I had tried it several times before, in fact had abandoned it to write *Breakfast with the Nikolides* which had been published in 1942, making only the slightest impact, except that one critic in America who had been scathing about *Gypsy Gypsy* said "Miss Godden has shown us she can write after all," which was heartening but now, in this book, how could I make the continual shifts from one generation to another blend smoothly into a whole? It eluded me, yet I could not leave the book alone.

It was too cold in my writing room, the desk had had to go into the sitting room and when the children were in bed, I worked. Madhu brought me a firepot like the Kashmiris' and, though I dared not hold it pressed against my stomach as they did, I could warm my hands on it which helped. Soon I found I was writing until eleven o'clock and, as soon as it got warmer, I began again what I had started to do in Calcutta and Jinglam, getting up at half-past four to write before the day began and the children were awake. It sounds drastic but it was far less tiring than trying to work against, as it were, the tide of life and, too, the early morning was a wonderful time; no-one and nothing disturbed me and my mind was as refreshed and clear as the air.

Soon I had even longer; Jane, without being asked or told, got Paula and Chamba up, dressed them and herself and, remembering Giovanna's training, they tidied their night clothes away and aired the beds. I blessed, too, having been brought up in India and in the habit of the siesta;

after lunch we all lay down and I fell as deeply asleep as Chamba.

To Jon:

I worry because I can do so little to help the war effort, knowing what you and Nancy are doing and poor Rose in Europe driving for the Red Cross but suppose, in this stress, there is nothing more worthwhile than looking after children, having Chamba for instance. Mary Groves, too, has asked me when term begins if she can send me any children from the Garden School who fall ill, then need to convalesce—Dove House is so healthy. I welcome this but dread it—children, day in, day out with no relief at all, are draining. I wonder why, when children are so small, their voices are not small to match. Paula's is like a siren. I find it so hard to be "even", which I must be. Mysteriously your own children seem to understand lapses but not other people's! There is a verse in Isaiah: "They shall mount up with wings as eagles: they shall run and not be weary: they shall walk and not faint."

How much easier it is to fly or run than to walk.

As we came out on the verandah to go for our morning walk, the air was warm with sun and pure with snow; suddenly there was the distant roar and tumble of an avalanche. The mountain was hidden in mist, only its crest showed far up in the blue, with dots of rocks and fir trees; the roar echoed behind it and the children were startled.

"What is it?"

A minute or two later there was a second, louder roar. The verandah shook under our feet. The sun penetrating the mist had loosened the heavy falls of snow; it was too far away to hurt us but "*What is it?*" they asked.

"An avalanche."

"We had better not go out," Jane had turned pale. Paula and Chamba took refuge behind her.

"Will it come down here?"

"Will it come down in the night?"

"Will it *eat* us?" asked Paula and I saw the avalanche as they saw it, growling on the frozen mountain behind the mist, growling horribly, a mix I think between a dragon, Ayah's snow leopard and a yeti, the Abominable Snowman.

"I want to go back to Calcutta," said Chamba.

One of the endearing things about Dove House was that the bulbuls, those bold, small birds with impudent crests, white-cheeked with brilliant black eyes, yellow on the undercoat and shadowy grey wings, came round the windows, even tapping on the pane for crumbs. We had golden oriels too, black and white hoopoes with crests like a Red Indian head-dress and a green woodpecker with a crimson head that pecked busily at the magnolia tree outside my study window.

To Jon: May 1943.

All the snow has melted and in one week Kashmir changes colour: last week the colours were pale: pink from the almond and quince trees, pink and white striped from the little wild tulips in the grass, yellow from the mustard flowers, pale blue from the sky, pale green from the willows. Now all this has gone, and on every bank and slope are white and purple iris and a surrounding foam of mauve from the lilacs, Persian and European. These are the colours now: purple, lilac, white and green with, occasionally, scarlet from the roof tulips. Soon there will be blue of Himalayan poppies, fields of them and roses, roses, roses, especially the small pink Damascus roses that grow wild and are used for medicine. In Nishat, the gardeners train roses over frames like topless tables so that the roses make mounds or turrets of flowers. I so hope you will come soon to see them.

It was difficult to believe the lengths to which these people would go for pitifully little; that this was because they had pitifully little, I had not yet understood.

The Khan had advised that we wait until spring to reshingle the roof and, in May, he sent three carpenters to do this. They were all called Abdul, Hed Abdul as he appeared in his bill, Abdul One and Abdul Two who, I think, was Hed Abdul's father, an emaciated old man who did most of the work. Hed Abdul and Abdul One came down every two hours for tea leaving Abdul Two nailing.

The Khan had given me strict orders on how to deal with them; he had estimated the number of nails needed and I had to weigh them; they were so many to the pound—and then, "When the work is done you must go up on the roof and count them," he said.

"*Count* them?"

"Certainly. If you do not, where a shingle needs four nails, they will use one."

"I am too busy, Khan Sahib, to go climbing roofs."

"Then your shingles will fall off."

"Very well," I sighed. "Tell them to bring me a ladder."

Besides the normal busyness, I was trying a difficult part of the book; it was, I thought, beginning to come—and did not pay much attention when Hed Abdul came to me and said they had run out of nails.

"I gave you plenty."

"Memsahib should come up on the roof and see," said Hed Abdul with utmost smoothness. "The nails are all there and still there are more shingles."

The book was nagging. "Go and get some."

"To go to Srinagar will take half a day. May I buy village nails?" I could not see why not and gave him one rupee, eight annas.

"Get them and bring them to me and I will weigh them." Surely, I thought, that should be all right.

All three went to get them and were away a long time, too long—I should have been warned—but presently Hed Abdul came back and showed me what looked like petrified worms with no heads, and I objected. They looked queer.

"They are village nails," said Hed Abdul and soon I heard Abdul Two hammering away again; when I went out, I noticed that he had rags tied round his hands and the rags were bloody. Later that afternoon Hed Abdul appeared and said the last shingle was on; would I like to come up and inspect?

"Very well. Get the ladder," I said wearily.

"Ladder been taken away," and Hed

Abdul offered to pull me up. I should have asked why it had been taken away but, weak, was relieved and said I could not come up.

"Then, with your permission and our pay," said Hed Abdul, "we will go back to Srinagar." I paid them and they rode away on their bicycles with their tools.

Peace settled until the Khan came and, "Where is my new barbed-wire fence?" asked the furious Khan.

I could hardly believe it. "To take the trouble and pain to cut up a fence of barbed wire!" I remembered the blood-stained rags on Abdul Two's hands. "Think of unwinding all those cruel little barbs for one rupee, eight annas."

"It was not only one rupee, eight annas," said the Khan. "They had the nails they stole as well and it is not much trouble to unwind a fence."

Ghulam Rasool came to see the house. "What do you think of it?"

"I think it is bewitchment."

All the same with his foot he pushed my cream numdahs away in contempt. "These

418

for you! Oh no, Lady Sahib. At least let me lend you some Persian rugs."

"They would not fit with this house," but, "I had wished," he went on, "I had hoped to interest you in a Bokhara carpet, wine red. I wish I could."

It would have been only too easy. Profit David was a superb salesman. He had brought two small round tables of walnut wood. "This is brother, this is sister. They must not be separated," and at once I felt that would be sacrilegious. All the same, he sold me sister and, "Why", he asked —he often began with "Why"—"Why do you hire cutlery?"

"Because I can't afford to buy it."

"You pay twelve rupees in hire a month," said Ghulam Rasool. "I will make you a set in silver, Indian silver. You pay me fifteen rupees a month and you will have them for always."

I have them still: the knives are vegetarian knives of silver with dark walnut handles; the spoons—table, soup, dessert, tea—and the forks, large and small, are solid silver, well shaped, and Profit David had had each piece hand-engraved with the Foster crest.

"How do you manage for food, so far from the shops?" people were always asking me and the answer was, "Easily."

No diet could have been simpler, more wholesome and, out in the countryside, less expensive. We had brown bread, some of it Kashmiri, fresh milk, honey: rice from the village ricefields, wheat chupattis —our flour was ground at the small mill beside the stream. Vegetables came from our own garden—Kashmir is so fertile you only have to scratch the ground for things to grow; we had fruit in abundance, cheese that I made from local goat's milk, eggs from the village hens. Now and again we had fish from the lake, sometimes a chicken, no meat—in any case it was mostly goat and ancient mutton, no-one dreamed of killing a lamb for food and in a Hindu-governed State beef was forbidden. Winter was more difficult but we had stores of walnuts which made good dishes and soups, plenty of the local dried apricots, but the only vegetable was sâg which gets monotonous. I grew lettuces on the kitchen window-sill.

Madhu was an excellent vegetarian

cook, unusual in a Mohammedan; he made walnut mince with mushrooms and his "matar panir" was good: he took a cream cheese, spiced it, added herbs and fried it with onions until they were both pale golden. It was served with fresh peas and a tomato sauce. The children loved his apple snow, puréed apple beaten with sugar and white of egg. I made bread and miraculously it rose but when I tried melon and ginger jam it was so hot they cried, and when I bottled mulberries the fruit fermented. The missionaries came for lunch and I made mulberry fool; it tasted delectable but, unused to alcohol, some of them became decidedly drunk. The mulberries must have been well fermented, the rest of them blew the tops off the bottles—the house was filled with explosions like gunshots.

The greatest boon was that we had a spring close above the mountain, a spring famous for its purity; Dove House was the only place I knew in India where there was no necessity to boil the drinking water. It was, in fact, wonderfully healthy; in all the years we were there I spent something less than twenty rupees at the chemist and that was chiefly for things like bandages, plasters, disinfectants.

Every now and then we went to see the honey man who lived in a tall dark house outside the village. On its first floor were his hives built into the wall, square hives of clay with the bees' entry holes outside. When he took the honey he had to break the hive. He had lotus honey which was white: saffron honey, dark gold: red honey: ordinary honey and dirty honey. We always bought dirty honey because it was the cheapest but it meant we had to boil it and strain it ourselves.

Once a month—every other month in winter—we took a tonga to Srinagar to buy stores, as much as I could afford, things like sugar we could not get in the village. The greatest treat was drinking-chocolate. In those years the children never saw a biscuit—except home-made ones—never had ice-cream and few sweets, even in wartime England there were some, though rationed. Now and then we made fudge or toffee and sometimes they were given presents—Giovanna invariably brought chocolate.

A house is not complete without friends. I had, as I have said, kept away from the Srinagar circle that centred round the English Resident or Governor and the Club and, in the hot months, went to Gulmarg, Srinagar's accepted hill station. My friends were not of that circle or any circle.

I was on good terms with Bren's schoolmaster—he taught the boys, not the girls—and the Pir, the Mohammedan religious leader, though they did not come to the house. My visitors were, first, the missionaries; when we had settled, they took to coming out to Dove House on their days off to relax in the garden, picnic under the trees and see the children—the children were a magnet—they came almost too often; to my disgrace, one afternoon when I saw the familiar line of solar topees coming up the path—the missionaries wore topees long after the rest of us had ceased to—I scooped up the children and we fled to the almond orchard and hid in a ditch behind the wall till they had gone.

A young Dutch couple had come to Srinagar, I do not know how or why; he was an artist, she a sculptor of some renown in Holland, a fine botanist as well and with a wonderful warmth and zest for life. Clara was a big woman with dark cropped hair, while Tonteyn was small and wore his blond hair long. "Which is Mr. or Mrs. Hopman?" asked Jane, they both wore trousers which made it even more difficult. Clara had a flaming hot temper; Tonteyn, in all the storms, stayed calm, sweet and steady and was a steady help to me. It was he who had sat up at night with the children when they were ill in the Mission Hospital, he who came out to Dove House and used his authority as a man to help weigh and store our firewood —wood was as valuable as gold.

Like Michael Cardew, Tonteyn was a conscientious objector and so was ostracised by the European community. He would have found it difficult to make a living except that he rapidly learned to speak Kashmiri which few Europeans could; both he and Clara were linguists. He was, too, held in veneration by the Kashmiris, Hindu and Mohammedan, because he was an astrologer. They were the only family I have met who governed their lives by Tarot cards.

"I love your house," Clara said to me when they first came to Dove House. "It is poetical." No wonder I liked her.

Later, of course, people from Calcutta found me out and Srinagar's residents became curious—and I, too, asked some of the British Other Ranks who came up on leave out to spend the day because, unlike the officers, there was little for them to do—but in the early days, it was only my few, perhaps peculiar friends who came.

30 May 1943.

I have my writing room at last with Jon's desk in the window so that as I write I can look at the view but sometimes it is so exquisite I have to turn my desk to the wall.

On these late May evenings, between sunset and dusk when there is only pale and dark, I like to look over the tip of the magnolia tree—in full white flower now—far across the lake to the Pir Panjals. The lake is pale too and still, with only fishing boats out; there is the dark line of the dividing road with the

425

little hump of its brooch bridge. One star, Hesperus, shines but soon lights are lit along the shore, making a necklace. As I stand up to light mine, from the darkening garden comes a gust of sweetness, the scent of flowers.

Tonight I am grateful from my head to the soles of my feet—it is singing in my head and in my steps—for living here, for being allowed to live here.

# 13

## Dove House

I want to stay here the rest of my life. Live here, flying to England only now and then. I want to see these springs as long as I live and have the harsh discipline of the winters to keep me hard and alive; I, the children and perhaps Giovanna and the pekingese; have a pony and a little pony trap, perhaps one day a car; if only I had enough money, not too much, but a settled amount, something I could count on, for this.

IT could not have been anything else but an impossible dream—to begin with it would not have been fair on the children—as it was, instead of the five years in Dove House, we had some twenty months, that first half of a winter, another winter, two summers, one autumn and two springs.

The Kashmiri spring is so brief that it is over before it can be properly seen and soon even the mountain's snow was melted, the streams were running full and the peasants let the water into the rice-fields—they sowed the rice from a basket, scattering it on the water with a thousand tiny splashes.

In May it grew high as did the wheat; poppies came out and there were drifts of white iris but the purple ones and the lilac were over, and soon the quiet was broken by raucous noises: boys frightening the birds from the cherries, jangling tins on strings, clapping wooden clappers, and giving a whistle that sounded like "Pss. Pss."

Later, down on the lake, the lotuses came into bloom covering the water with leaves big enough for Candytuft to sit on and floating their perfect pink cups of flowers. There is a Kashmiri legend about the lotus marriage: the male plant rises up through the water, when the female is in full flower, drags her under and pollinates her in one brief ecstasy and lets her go.

I took the children to another, nearer

Mission Hospital at Rainawari across the lake to have their yearly inoculations against typhoid, yellow fever and cholera.

We went by shikara, not a taxi shikara with a roof and embroidered cushions and curtains, but a village shikara of plain wood—we had to bring our own cushions—and it had only two men to paddle it.

We had to start early and at first there was no-one out on the lake but one boat and the fishermen. The sides of the mountains were dark but the shores of the lake had the sun, pale and hazy except when the rays caught the ricefields and the willows and they became distinct in their green. The lake itself had soft colours of blue and grey, broken by reflections. Our boat was driven over them as one of the men chanted, the song fitting to the paddles; it sounded like. "Yoo-i-pi, Yoo-i-pi-paddle-paddle-paddle-Hull-an-oo. Hull-an-oo-paddle-paddle-paddle." Jane knelt in the prow. Paula had a miniature paddle Nabir Das had made for her. Madhu, who had come with us, held Chamba by the shoulder straps of his dungarees.

When we arrived at the hospital a drove of camels was in the courtyard; a medical

ATTDN29

orderly was injecting them and when Paula and Chamba saw the size of the needles they burst into howls of terror. No wonder. The needles were as long as long knitting needles.

My friends did not approve of one another.

"Those Hopmans!" was the Missionary attitude. "Astrologers!" and they shudder.

"Missionaries!" says Clara and snorts like a dragon. "Cant!"

"It isn't cant," but Clara is sure it is.

"You should not", says the Pandit, "be friends with Ghulam Rasool. He will extort you."

"A Hindu!" says Ghulam Rasool. "They are poor through and through. Look how miserably they eat."

No-one could say that of Ghulam Rasool. Two or three times in those summers he invited us to lunch on his picnic boat. It was delightful to sit on cushions with the matting sides of the boat rolled up to let in the breeze that sent the boat gently rocking. We always had a Persian banquet which, properly, should have thirty-six courses—we were let off with eighteen; it was not, though, gluttonous because they came with three separate servings of rice and only a little of each dish should be put on them: fish in cocoanut: pilaff: mutton balls stuffed with spices: apricots stuffed with mutton: vegetables in crisp batter. The last serving of rice is always honey rice, coloured yellow with saffron, and with it rings of spun sugar, fruits in syrup: thin white toffee topped with edible silver paper. It always ends with cinnamon tea in priceless small porcelain or jade bowls.

I had been afraid there would be difficulty at Dove House about the children's lessons —Jane was rising eight, it was time she really learned. Providentially, it was soon solved. That first summer—and the summer afterwards—the Hopmans took a house down on the lake shore near us. They had two sons, Conrad, the same age as Jane, and Frederick; each had another name, typically idealistlc—Conrad was also Siddartha, one of the names of

Buddha, and Frederick was Aries; to us they were known as Putzi and Dudi.

Putzi was a small dark boy whom they thought backward but Putzi knew the names of all plants, most fungi, the formation of rocks and crystal, the names of the stars. When Mary Groves went on leave she lent me her gramophone and records and it was Putzi who listened to the symphonies but Dudi, whom I could not like, a fat little boy with long golden curls and a high whining voice, was the adored.

We made a plan to share children, taking them day by day in turn, so that both Clara and I could have an uninterrupted time for work. Tonteyn, artist and mathematician and much travelled, taught them arithmetic as it was known then, geography and drawing: they modelled with Clara—a professional sculptor—and out of her rich store of knowledge she taught them nature study, and they swam with her too. I, a pupil of Mona Swann, had them for reading, writing, poetry. Not only this, the second summer the Hopmans were joined by a Frenchwoman, a Parisian Mademoiselle Desprès who had been Montessori's representative for Persia but, because of the war, was exiled from Teheran. She was, too, a pianist and had taught eurythmics for Jaques Dalcroze.

When I had left Calcutta for Jinglam and lost my Steinway, Roland and Jon had given me a miniature upright piano. As the army had paid to move us from Jinglam to Kashmir, the piano had come too. I had lent it to the Convent for my dancing lessons but now it came across the lake on a rice boat and the whole village turned out to see it carried up the hill, not carefully, on trained coolies' heads as in Calcutta, but hauled and lifted, often in danger of being dropped on a rock. We managed to get it up and into the house. Mademoiselle tuned it and taught music and the beginnings of French to Jane and Putzi, eurythmics to all of them and Montessori kindergarten to the little ones. Few schools, I think, could have assembled a team of such calibre.

May 1943.

Mam has made me a member of the PNEU, The Parents National Education Union, which sends material out each

month, not only a good help but a life-
line for me; with every set of lessons
they send literature, poems and extracts,
well chosen, and also a brief study of an
artist, say Michelangelo—with a pack of
reproductions which I value.

Part of the PNEU method, a most valuable
part is "telling back" which not only trains
the memory but makes for concentration;
they claim that students trained this way
never have to take notes at a lecture; they
can remember it. The method is to read
the children a short passage in, say,
history, discuss it, read it again more
slowly then say to one of them, "Now tell
that back to me." It requires effort and
quite often they were unwilling to do it:
one morning I read Putzi and Jane the old
Scots poem:

> Faht's in there?
> Gold and money
> Fahr's my share o't?
> The moosie ran awa' w'it
> Fahr's the moosie?
> In her hoosie
> Fahr's her hoosie? . . .

434

and so on, quite a deal of it, twenty-two lines, so that I read it three times. "Tell it back to me."

Neither Putzi nor Jane could get very far. "You weren't listening," but somebody was. From under the table came a little piping voice which said the poem right through; Paula, at five years old.

The greatest deprivation at Dove House was having so little to read. The post came only twice a week, carried by a postman in high boots and, in winter, a shawl over his turban; cables and telegrams were carefully delivered by registered post which took longer. The newspaper came by post too, three or four copies at a time and I used to put them in order and ration myself to reading one a day. If I wanted to telephone I had to walk along the dyke to an army outpost, supposed to be guarding the water channel, where the Sergeant allowed me to use their aged wind-a-handle telephone; I had to pay three rupees a time which was extortionate —but books were what I missed most. We had only that one shelf-full and I read what we had over and over again. Mam sent what she could and I shared those with Jon who, even with her war work, found time to go to the bookshops now and then for me.

To Jon:

You couldn't have chosen anything better. Jane Austen is exactly what I need and I have only *Pride and Prejudice*. I am reading *Emma* again with utter delight and again marvel that a writer of Jane Austen's generation should have had such a delicious and malicious idea of her own heroine, especially when she is against Jane Fairfax. I have behaved like Emma so often and know those little stabs as you look back on yourself after an evening's behaviour.

Sometimes Jon sent me her own books:

Have you, Jon, a Wordsworth and *Orlando* or *The Waves*? I need them *desperately*.

Thank Roland more than I can say for *Black Lamb and Grey Falcon*! I must try and read it slowly, not devour it. I have been lent the *Pre-Raphaelites* and *The Secret of India* and loved the first but the second leaves me cold, and I have come to the conclusion that, if you want to do Yoga properly—not dabble in it, how I hate dabblers—you would have no time left in which to live and, more and more, it seems to me the most important thing is to live.

Mary Groves gave me T. S. Eliot's *The Idea of Christian Society*: very good for me to read but after a long day of work I found it difficult; an old lady I saw occasionally sent me a novel by Ethel Mannin whom she admired; I firmly put it away and immediately took it out again and wasted a whole evening.

To Jon:
Reading Edith Sitwell's *Notebook*—sent by Mam—I was struck by something I have largely missed before—at least having so few books makes you read more carefully! She—E.S.—says Shakespeare's "Devouring time, blunt thou the lion's paws . . ." is the finest

sonnet in the English language—for width of vision and power. I feel she is right.

I learned, too, the joy of re-reading, something I have done ever since:

Am going through the Old Testament again, leaving out the Rules and begats and lists of Tribes, and also re-reading Thoreau whom, taken with salt, I love.

Nancy and Dick came to fetch Chamba—even with the war close to Calcutta they felt he should be with them. I looked forward to showing him to them; he had come to me as a typical Calcutta child, fetching but weak and pale, prone to painful boils, listless and nervous. Now he was one of the best four-year-olds I have seen—sturdy, full of mischief, rosy, brown-eyed with, my especial pride, curly golden hair. The night before Dick and Nancy arrived, Jane cropped it all off with a pair of nail-scissors. "He did not look like a boy," was her explanation. Probably she had remembered Dick's horror when Chamba had asked for a doll at Christmas;

living with girls it was his great ambition to be a little girl. Why did they have pretty dresses when he had only shorts and shirts?

We felt sad without him and Paula mourned but July brought Jon for two blissful months.

Kind Clara had the children while Jon and I went away for a few days on a donga, or picnic boat. We went to Manasbal, a beautiful lake outside Srinagar, and moored there while I read the book to Jon, a first draft in which, at last, I had managed to reach an end. Jon hated to be read aloud to but submitted. Then, looking at the deep reflections in the lake, reflections of sky, clouds, mountains, trees as if she could not bear to look at me, she said gently but firmly, "It won't do."

In our picnic boat we had kept to simplicity; we had one low table and ate or worked on it, sitting on cushions on the floor. We took two low folding chairs and put them in the prow where we sat in the evenings; our beds were quilts on the floor. That night I lay awake on mine thinking, How? How? The book seemed as far out of reach as the stars. All those months of painstaking, painful work seemed wasted but I knew that Jon was right.

It was during that summer that I came to know the gujars—herdsmen—and particularly the bakriwars, literally "goat people". Nomads with their flocks and herds.

Every year in spring they drove their cattle, sheep and goats up from the plains to summer in the high valley and plateau pastures in the mountains where they had left their huts. In October they came down again and each time passed above Dove House, driving with a peculiar trembling whistle that is their own, something between a hawk's cry and a flute.

They were Mohammedan though the men looked biblical and had biblical names, Jassoof, Ezekiel, Daveed. Their women were prized almost like cattle, desirable as stock and valued for hardihood, endurance and for breeding sons. They used to come to me in camp.

"What do you want?"

"Give me medicine to have a son."

"If I had that medicine," I used to say, "I would have a son myself."

"Oh well," one of them said with philosophy, "if you haven't the medicine have you an old tin?" They always wanted tins. Their babies were often born on the march, an older woman staying with the mother, washing the baby in the ice-streams and then they would catch up with the caravan. No wonder they aged quickly; an old-looking crone might be only thirty-five, but the girls were handsome; their clothes swung as they moved, long tunics and full trousers gathered in at the ankle in black, damson red, crimson, smoke-stained rose and, oddly enough, bordered with rows of pearl buttons. They had small caps, dark blue, a loose black veil over them, and silver jewellery; their heavy anklets clinked as they walked with perhaps a baby in a sling on one hip, iron cooking pots in a string net on their heads and, usually, a sick hurt goat or kid to drive in front of them.

To me they were not simply gypsies, nomads, they were friends. I came to know them through my herbs.

Clara and I had started a herb farm centred on Dove House, she supplying the knowledge, Tonteyn and I organising it and doing the work. Kashmir, with its predictable climate, warm, if not hot, and dry in summer, bitterly cold in winter, and with its abundance of flowers, was a perfect place for it.

We had long drying trestle-tables put up in the courtyard and roofed them with thatch—contrary to what most people think, herbs must never be dried in the sun—and one of the downstairs slit rooms was made into a workroom where we mixed herb teas and simple remedies, packing them for despatch in muslin bags —paper was too scarce—or in small-lidded baskets woven in the village. We made herbal oils, too, steeping flowers in large earthenware vats of oil under glass in the sun for three weeks, changing the flowers each week.

It was enthralling work; every time a load of flowers came in, carried in a cone-shaped basket on the back of a runner, a load of wild violets for cough syrup, or of St. John's Wort for rheumatism oil, all hands were needed, children, servants, grown-ups, to clean and sort, separating flower heads from leaves and spreading them to dry on the trestles.

The Pandit is half-intrigued, half-worried about the herb farm. "Curing people with flowers!" He says "flowers" as if they were weeds. "But you are incurring real expense."

"Not much, Pandit Sahib, and we hope to get it back."

"I hope you will, I hope you will," he says earnestly. "To make sure you must get small image of Ganesh and put him over your door."

Ganesh is the Hindu elephant-headed god who brings good fortune. I have often seen his small image in a niche over the door of shops and banks but, "I haven't an image of Ganesh," I say.

He does not offer to get me one but goes on, "I have heard cures can be made by swallowing gold."

"That sounds expensive, Pandit Sahib."

"Very expensive," he agrees and sighs, but I think he would be entranced by swallowing gold.

We sold our herb teas, oils and powders through a chemist in Srinagar and soon had orders from other parts of India. This

443

made me uneasy because I did not think we knew enough to sell medicines, and should keep to tisanes, dried scented herbs like pot-pourri and moth powder. "Nonsense," said Clara. "It's the medical herbs that are valuable." One day an order came for three bags of our cough tea, made of equal parts of violets, coltsfoot, Achillea millefolium and betonica, which sounds harmless, and I mixed and despatched them. Some ten days later a telegram came for me; it was from Bombay and my heart sank. Had I made them ill? Perhaps killed them? In fear I opened the telegram: an order for ten bags more!

It was the bakriwars who organised the picking of the flowers and sent the runners down. They were skilled and knew every herb—many of our recipes we learned from them. They were, too, particularly skilful with animals. When one of our pack-ponies fell off a path above a gorge and plunged down landing on its back, it was the bakriwars who mended its broken leg; its back was saved by its having a tent pole lashed either side, and a padding of canvas, but it had all our dechis— saucepans—on it and they were crushed flat, a serious loss when we were so far away.

They took the pony and splinted its leg in the way I told of in a short story, *The Black Ram*.

The ram lay with its sides heaving in pain, moisture running from its nose. Ezekiel, squatting down on his ankles, took twine out of the deep pocket of his homespun coat and began to work. He sent a boy for twigs and told Jassoof to hold the ram.

The ram kicked hard with the other leg as Ezekiel pulled its broken leg straight. "Inshallah!" cried Ezekiel and swore at Jassoof for not holding it better. It is animal nature to kick and struggle against forcible pain and the ram struggled wildly but Ezekiel went steadily on till the leg was straight in the splints and the network, woven with twigs and tied with twine, was so firm that even the most energetic ram could not kick it off.

The Elders of the tribes always called on me on their way up or down past Dove

House—each time for a week we could not use any water from the stream or even the spring until it had cleared, but it was a small price to pay. The Elders had tea, a few cakes and much talk, and I would meet them again when we, too, used to go up the valleys further than Sonamarg.

Jon and I had an ambition, to go and see the Sind Valley's fabulous glacier-fed twin lakes, Krishn Sar and Vishan Sar, but it meant going over the Nichnai Pass, 13,387 feet and, "You're not going to take the children up there," one missionary fellow camper said.

I had Jobara and now I asked him, "Can we take the babas up to the lakes?"

Jobara pulled his beard, a small one, thinking, weighing the question, then looked at me—he could read me through and through. "We *can*," he said and, what should have shamed me, "Memsahib wants to see those lakes."

I would not have taken Chamba, he was someone else's child—but Jane and Paula would have chosen to come. It all depended on the weather, of course, and weather at that height was uncertain. It was not far in distance, only some sixteen miles, but the way was rough and steep so that it had to be slow, with no possibility of breaking the march.

The children rode or walked, Jobara and a ponyman jumping them over the stones on the rockiest paths; they wore shorts and singlets, sun hats and had warm cardigans of rough wool. Jane dropped hers, a ponyman had to go back for it but, when retrieved, it was full of holes where it had already been eaten by marmots.

We were all shod like the Kashmiris, with inner laced boots of soft chamois leather, warm and supple and a strong outer sandal that had its tip turned up to protect feet against stones. The pekingese, Moon, Candytuft and Jon's two, Leo and Lu, walked or, when they were tired, sat on the packs of the pack ponies.

Jon wrote in her diary:

You have to cross over the Pass—a tremendous winding pull up, with a glacier at the top, then look down on a green valley with, on each side, bare rocky hills, rock and snow. Marmots, little red-brown animals, like small beavers, come out from the rocks sitting up on their hind legs and making a chattering noise as they look at us.

There were wild ponies, long-maned, the mares with their foals; the only birds were eagles, circling between the mountains and, by the streams, the little cocky white-capped redstarts. It was too high for trees, we had to rely on juniper for fuel but there were millions of flowers, gentian, edelweiss, rose-red and purple primulas, even pushing up through the snow.

We met a Swiss expedition coming down with a great many pack-ponies—we had only six—carrying a great deal of equipment, including oxygen. The Herrs, they were all men, wore mountaineering clothes, gloves and balaclava helmets; they had sun goggles and carried alpenstocks. They stared at this apparition of two women in slacks, short-sleeved shirts—the sun was hot—large straw hats that we had bought in Calcutta's bazaar for eight annas, and with two small children and four pekingese.

The way forward down from the Pass

was even steeper and sometimes led along precipices high above gorges; Jobara would not let children or dogs ride down and with reason—it was here that our pack-pony went over with a sickening thud—but in late afternoon we came to the end of a wide valley and there were the lakes—the first in view, the other hidden above it, but each of them lying clear blue, in the cup of the mountains that closed them in. They are not large but unfathomably deep; the legend says that a man made a rope for ten years and tying a stone to it, let it down in Vishan Sar and failed to reach the bottom; even in August there were icebergs floating on them, gleaming like great glass swans.

Camp was made on the sward facing the lake and there we ran into trouble—it could have been fatal trouble. A blizzard came down and raged for thirty hours. Jobara had our tents tightly laced and battened down with great stones to hold them against the shrieking battering wind and whirling snow. We could only stay quailing in bed, each with a child and two pekingese lying close under the blankets. It was too dark to read, we could not waste our torches and we told stories, sang and tried to sleep. Four times that day, Jobara, his head wound in his shawl, crawled from the servants' tent to ours, bringing a samovar of tea, milk, bread, once even soup—how they got a fire going I do not know but I know if it had not been for the bakriwars we should not have survived; it was they who brought the stones that saved our tents, brought the milk and herded the ponies into their own corral; the poor beasts were mad with fright—if they had not been hobbled they would have run away and Jobara alone could not have managed them—his own ponymen were too cowardly to come out.

"We shouldn't have taken the children," Jon said over and over again and, "You're not fit to have children," I told myself and had agonies of remorse, but next year I took them over the Pass of the Zoji La into Leh or Little Tibet.

September 1943.

The memories of this summer will be stored like a squirrel's nuts; in winter I shall take them out and look at them

450

one by one: the riot of colour in the garden where I have sown zinnias, cottage marigolds, petunias and sweet peas—petunias and sweet peas are wonderfully fragrant when planted together: the song of the hay-makers and the hay itself, full of flowers: the riot of vegetables, tomatoes, egg-plants with their yield hanging glossy and purple: persimmons which we put into muslin bags to ripen: canteloupe melons grown on a ring of lake weed: making cheese and making jam: the sounds of the flocks high up on the mountain: the smell of thyme . . .

I loved the autumn too. When we came down from Sonamarg the trees had already turned—not even in New England with its famed "colours" nor in Switzerland have I seen anything more lovely—and back at Dove House the mornings were sharp, clear with sun but the dew was frosty and a scent of dried dead leaves and hay filled the air. The mountain behind the house seemed many-sided with sun and shadow, its crevices orange with sorrel which, from far down below, looked like lichen; the flocks kept in the sun and the herd boys sang to keep themselves warm. The streams were cold. Across the lake the mountains were already in snow. Soon everyone was gone and it was winter.

January 1944.

I must not expect the postman today— he could never get up the path.

Often the snow was five or six feet deep, deeper on the mountain, we could only get out by walking along the dyke where a path was kept free. I blessed my small accumulation of wood and stores; Nabir Das, accustomed, fought his way up to us with milk, butter and eggs and kulchas, but he was the only one.

Two red king foxes have made a den in the garden. We see them trailing their brushes in the snow. I must keep the pekingese close to the house and on the lead when I take them out last thing at night.

Autumn into winter I worked on the book,

its house and characters growing more and more real, especially the house.

"We existed before you," the family might have said to the house; and the house, in it tickings, its rustlings, its creakings as its beams grow hot, grow cold—as the ashes fall in its grates, as its doorbells ring, as the trains in passing underneath it vibrate in its walls, as footsteps run up and down the stairs—as dusters are shaken, carpets beaten, beds turned down and dishes washed—as windows are opened or shut, blinds drawn up, pulled down—as the tap runs and is silent, as the lavatory is flushed —as the piano is played and books are taken down from the shelf, and brushes picked up and then laid down again on the dressing-table, and flowers are arranged in a vase—as the medicine bottle is shaken; as, with infinite delicate care, the spillikins are lifted in the children's game—as the mice run under the wainscot—the house might steadfastly reply, "I know! I know. All the same, in me you exist."

The book had a name now, *Fugue in Time*; from those gramophone records Mary Groves had lent me I marked how Bach interwove his themes but music and writing, though akin as are all arts, should not really be applied to one another. When the book was published in America it was called *Take Three Tenses* which, though not as subtle, was exactly what I did.

I must have written that book eight times, often in despair, before I found the key: by putting the past into the present, the present into the past it worked—and more remarkably no-one, not even the critics noticed the shifts; the whole had miraculously blended.

There is in London a Wiltshire Square, a Wiltshire Crescent, a Wiltshire Road; Wiltshire Gardens and Wiltshire Place; the house is Number 99, Wiltshire Place. In the house the past is present.

It had begun to race, or would have raced, "If I could have five minutes' peace!" I felt like screaming.

There is a smell of lime-flowers, that

means that it is summer. The crystal in the chandelier gives out a chime: that means that somebody is singing.

I am writing when I hear wails. It is Madhu coming up the path; he is carrying Katji, his youngest little girl.

What I have always dreaded for these children had happened; playing, Katji had upset her firepot and the hot coals had spilled down.

As we laid her on a sheet spread on the table she was inert, her eyes open but senseless with pain and shock. Trembling I cut away the little pheran she wore; she was burnt from her waist to her knees. I fed her with spoonfuls of hot milk and glucose while Madhu heated water. Then we laid her in a lukewarm bath with bicarbonate of soda, all I had, swabbed her dry and covered the burns with strips of gauze, slid her into a pillow case—she was small enough—wrapped a shawl round her and fed her more hot milk and sugar. "Now get a tonga," I told Madhu, "and into hospital as quickly as you can."

"She cannot go to hospital. She is not weaned."

Katji was three years old but I was not surprised.

"Then your wife must go with her."

Madhu shuffled and looked embarrassed. "Memsahib, my wife is young. I could not trust her in the hospital."

"Then you must go too, all of you." I knew the Mission was accustomed to families and as he still looked adamant, "Madhu, Katji may die."

Fond as he was of her, that would not have been a tragedy for Madhu; girl children were not much wanted—there were stories of fishermen taking small daughters out fishing and coming back in their boats alone. I left Katji, Madhu promising not to move her and walked along the dyke to telephone the Mission Doctor. He told me what to do and said he would send out dressings and medicines. "See her every other day," then he added, "but, if you find they have opened the bandages as they inevitably will, refuse to have anything more to do with her. They will hold you responsible were she to die."

Praise be, I am good at bandaging. Katji was brave and when the dressings had to be changed only screwed up her eyes and gave quick little breaths. Baby flesh has a miraculous power of healing and the burns began to heal until, on the tenth day, I noticed the bandages were loose and dirty. "You have opened them."

Madhu could not deny it. "Memsahib, it was my wife."

"Take Katji away."

"Memsahib! Huzoor. Your honour!" but I knew I had to harden my heart because the Doctor was right.

Madhu sent for the village barber who took off the dressings and covered the wounds with ink—after all, for some time we used gentian violet for burns, but Katji got gangrene. She did not die but was crippled for life.

To Jon:

Am re-reading *A Room of One's Own* in which Virginia Woolf talks of Shakespeare's incandescent unimpeded mind. Shakespeare is Shakespeare and he was a man and whether we like it or not that does make a difference; we are impeded in every direction. My mind is a flotsam of figures, sums—I have a perpetual

457

anxiety that makes me constantly check my Pass book—of dusters and meals, lessons, codliver oil, Moon on heat and firewood.

What the war seems determined to teach me is to become an ordinary woman, something, I see now, I have always shirked before—"Miss Godden has a horror of the commonplace," one reviewer wrote. Now I have to do as they do, day in, day out, look after my children, cook for them, try and sew and mend for them—our clothes are getting shabby—it is darning, darning, darning, and I am all thumbs. I have to teach them, play with them, get up in the icy night; look after my house under primitive conditions; look after my servants, teach them too—discipline them, sympathise with them.

No-one could love a house, children or animals more than I do but, it's no use denying it, I am not an ordinary woman.

I know that other women feel frustration, a longing to "express themselves" but with us it isn't that; it is a constant tug of obligation, as in binding yourself by oath, the feeling that we are dishonouring what is God-given; it is significant that the only women poets down the ages who can be called major were single, or, if you count Elizabeth Barrett Browning—which I do not— married with one child.*

Rose, Mam writes, is as silent as ever and Fa is worrying over her future. Poor Fa! If Gordon had lived another month he and Rose would have been married and she would have had a widow's pension. Even if C.D. had offered her alimony she would not have taken it; like me she is penniless except for what she can earn—though, luckily, unlike me she is not liable for debts she had not foreseen.

Possibly mine are the only children who have tobogganed in a Moghul garden. The water channels with their tilted slats made a perfect run and, at the end of each, a dais packed with snow was a stop. The

* I would rank Sappho, Christina Rossetti, Emily Dickinson, and in more modern times, the two of most stature, Edith Sitwell perhaps—and Marianne Moore.

little tailor, Lussoo, had made Jane and Paula trousers, quilted jackets and hoods of the native velvet, it shone sapphire blue in the clear light.

Nishat was frozen—the roof of the pavilion, the steps, the edges and fountains of the water channels, the walls were covered thick and white; each different dais throne was covered and, on each terrace, stretched lawns of white without a stain or footstep. Jane said in a whisper "Walk on the edge. Don't mark it. Don' spoil it."

The gardeners were sitting with their firepots; they too talked in low voices. There was no other sound but a sudden shake or rustle as the snow slid off a tree. Then it was broken with the whoosh of the sleigh, the children's shouts and laughter. Firepots were discarded as all the gardeners ran to see.

February 1944

Clara wants to go to Bombay for a month—after all she has had more Kashmiri winters than I and asks me to have the boys.

Putzi I welcomed but Dudi . . . Children are people and not all people are likeable and I could not abide Dudi; he was like an infant Prinny, the Prince Regent George IV with his fat little belly and, like Prinny, spoiled. At times during that month I used to have to go down to the end of the garden and fight with myself not to beat him *hard*, and managed to grow calm by thinking of the sixty rupees Clara had promised I should have for each of them at the end of the month. "One hundred and twenty rupees," I would murmur. It would mean summer dresses made by Lussoo, the dirzee, for the girls; new sandals for them; perhaps I could buy a *book*!

Clara came back at the end of the month and I was able to hand her a Dudi intact and a happy Putzi. Next morning a coolie came up to Dove House bearing something large and heavy on his head and bringing a note from Clara. She had spent so much in Bombay she was afraid she could not pay me, so sent me this sculpture instead. "In the end it will be better for you," she wrote, "because it will be *most valuable* and when the war is over I shall have it cast for you in bronze. At present it is only in plaster."

It was a large plaster model of a greyhound.

"But Clara, I don't want a plaster greyhound."

"It will *pay* you." Dear Clara, she truly believed she had done me a great favour.

I wrote of Dove House,

> I am really very happy. Happy in my house and garden and the herbs which are doing well, happy because the children flourish, and I do seem to find time for my own work, my secret snows.

There were, of course, bad moments in those years. One winter night I was writing late when I heard a strange scratching. The pekingese, usually good watch-dogs, were too sound asleep to bark, but the scratching went on. I took a lamp and silently went downstairs; a glimpse of light showed in the kitchen. I opened the door quietly and there was a tumble and cursing as two men hurtled out of the far door which was open. They had obviously not thought I should be up as late and they had pulled the kitchen table into the centre of the room, put a wooden crate on it and had been cutting through the earthen ceiling into the store room above where our precious firewood was kept locked in —I carried the key everywhere I went on a kind of chatelaine round my waist. I never knew who the men were but next day the Khan came out and, to my dismay and the children's horror, gave Madhu and Nabir Das a beating.

"Khan Sahib, I am sure they were not the ones . . ."
"They should not have let it happen," said the Khan.

Fa had written offering to buy me a radio "to help the loneliness". This is the wartime air-letter in which I asked instead if I could have a large watch-dog.

21 April 1943.

It is very dear of you all to want to give me a wireless, but there is one crying need: when I am alone here in winter I am often, I admit, rather scared at night as these Kashmiri servants are such cowards and not trustworthy; Jon thinks, and I too, that I should try and get a really big dog to be with us and guard us. These people are terrified of them. Would you mind if I did this instead? Lovely as wireless would be, this is a *pressing* need and though I have tried to get one given me, so far I have not been successful. We had thought of a labrador, a large one, safe with children and a good watch-dog. Jon is here and it is like heaven to have her; she looks frail and thin but is very cheerful. I am trying to persuade her to stay all the hot weather. Paula is very well, and Chamba too and I am better. A lovely, lovely Kashmir spring, I am very busy finishing my new book (rough draft) and with the herbs; collecting and drying and writing the pamphlet. I do hope you are all well.

I bought an alsatian, but found I could not afford to feed her and had to sell her.

More frightening was another night, a warm balmy night of our last summer when I was working in my writing room with the window wide open. It was bright moonlight and, suddenly, I felt someone was looking at me. I raised my head and there, standing on the path, so tall that his head seemed level with the sill, was a sadhu, a holy man, completely naked, his body covered with wood ash which made it gleam blue-black; his hair was hanging in knotted ropes and his eyes were red, from drinking bhang I knew—and also knew its effect. His chest was hung with beads, he carried a little pot in a string mesh and on his forehead was painted the white trident of Shiva—God of Death.

He looked at me and I looked at him and remembered that to Hindus the sex act is holy—if it had happened he would only have been taking what as a holy man was his due, and we were completely unprotected; there was no-one within call and nothing to prevent his coming in. I thought of Jane and Paula lying asleep in the next room and gathered myself together, making myself look back at him, simply look, feeling the cold sweat running down the back of my neck.

It seemed aeons passed. Then he smiled, a curiously sweet smile, raised his hand in greeting and went away down the path with a long loping stride. I watched him out of sight. Shiva is also the God of Resurrection. I felt ashamed to have been frightened and, "I shall never be frightened again," I vowed. "No matter what comes."

# 14

## Fall Down

"WHAT can happen to you," I asked the Pandit when he was timorous about Dove House, "if you stand on your own two feet?"

"You can fall down," said the Pandit.

If we had kept to our simplicity it would never have happened. In any case that last summer things changed; neither Nancy nor Jon could come. The war, as in Europe, was every day growing more acute; the Japanese were within eighty miles of Shillong where Nancy was staying —she had had another son, Richard. Kashmir was too far away for her to travel there with a small baby and no-one was going on leave who could have brought Chamba. Jon, as head of St. John's Ambulance in Calcutta, was doing more than full-time work, helping to run a new hospital for Indian troops, meeting trains of wounded and refugees at the rail stations, overseeing canteens.

Paradoxically, the autumn before, she had succeeded in writing her first novel. The note is in her diary:

14.9.43. Today finished the third draft of my book: In fact it is finished—out. I feel lonely. It is called *The Bird Escaped*. Fourteen years ago today Nigel and I were married.

She typed the book herself and sent it to me. I sent it to Curtis Brown.

*The Bird Escaped* is a macabre and oddly haunting book as its blurb tells:

Ostensibly it is the story of a small ship steaming across the Pacific—with the steward, Prince, the second cook Sebastian, and Jacko the first cook, a great cruel bear of a man with a falcon for a pet; it is the story of a torpedoed ship, a shattering explosion at sea and finally a lone survivor on a lonely Pacific island. It has an atmosphere at once awesome and possessed of some of that terrible fascination as *The Rime of the Ancient Mariner*.

*The Bird Escaped* was never published in England. Looking at it now I can understand this; in spite of its power, though it opened Jon's way as a writer, it does not quite succeed and I had to tell her that I thought Spencer was right in what he wrote to her about it.

Sunday 14 May 1944.

Spencer's letter makes me both sad and glad. I don't think you realise how complimentary it is; that he himself, head of the firm, should write you this long and full letter about the *Bird* is *tremendously* encouraging. I see, too, what he means about the publishers; the really first-rate publishers, having their pick of authors, would say to him exactly what he tells you: "Yes, I should like to have this author on my list but tell her to write me a full-length book for the first one"—*The Bird Escaped* was only a hundred and seventy-nine pages long. A less good publisher would leap at the book because a promising MS seldom comes their way, but it is worth waiting for the best. I think this is what Spencer means.

All the same he, or rather Curtis Brown in New York, placed the book in America. "How exciting about the cable," I wrote, "you must be walking on air," but I do not think Jon ever walked on air; in all her literary span of some eight novels, all of acknowledgedly high standard, she never seemed to realise that she had achieved what other writers would have given their eye-teeth for: steady publication on both sides of the Atlantic: fine reviews—her first novel to be published in England was a Book Society Choice—and several foreign editions. When you remember there are thousands of writers it was an uncommon success but she made little effort to enjoy it, except perhaps with Blanche and Alfred Knopf, her American publishers, who broke down her reserve, and I cannot remember her once returning any literary hospitality. It was, I think, part of her "letting things happen"; sad because she missed what has been, and is, one of the joys of my life, my relationships with the men and women I have met through my work.

In that spring of 1944, though, Jon had little time to write letters and I was even more lonely until I heard that a woman artist had taken a house close to Bren village on the lake. It seemed unbelievable luck.

Olwen was a good artist, especially her black and white paintings of trees—hers were the only landscapes of Kashmir that I have liked. She had lived in India for years, travelled much and, like me, was separated from her husband. She was even more lonely than I and ridden with nerves. Starved for adult talk I thought I had found a boon companion.

When friends from Calcutta, or from other sophisticated places, visited Dove House, they were either horrified at the way we lived, or else fell in love with it and wanted to live there as well—I do not know which response dismayed me more. Now Olwen did both; she suggested she should share the house with me, "Help you with it, and relieve some of the pressure."

When you are hungry enough you will sell anything, even yourself, for food but what I sold was the whole concept and truth of Dove House. Was I blinded or deliberately blind?

To Jon: Olwen does everything so well that I both admire and love her; she would make the garden into a paradise as she is an expert gardener and take that off me. True, as far as writing and books go, she is no use, as her taste hasn't developed, but for music and general things she is stimulating to talk to. There is another thing—it sounds rather like Florence Nightingale or a goody-goody book like *Eric or Little by Little* to say this—but doing a few definite things, looking after Jane and Paula, teaching these four children, making things better for Putzi and, perhaps, helping Olwen to recover herself makes me feel less guilty about not helping in the war. If I have these quite onerous things to do it is obscurely comforting.

Not for long. I had forgotten that Olwen

was steeped in the traditions of the British in India and, to her, our what she would have called "poor white ways", had she been unkind, were unthinkable. She was older than I, forceful, and in a few days had taken over the house; carpets appeared, new furniture, more servants. Olwen had a city bearer, Gaffur, a young man devoted to her but who despised Madhu; other servants were brought from Srinagar, not from the village as the Khan Sahib had advised; a table servant, a full-time sweeper. Madhu could still be cook but it seemed he had to have a "masalchi", washer-up or kitchen boy. In a spirit of independence I sent for the hapless little Sultan who came willingly. "He has been kicked out of every place he has had," Gaffur objected but, "I have never liked any place I have been kicked out of as much as here," said poor humble Sultan.

It could not work. To my dismay I discovered Jane had begun to call my study "The Quarrelling Room" and Jane was my weathercock. I tried to distract her.

"Jane, write me a poem about bulbuls."

"I don't want to," said Jane.

"They are such dear little birds. Try," and Jane wrote:

> Two little bulbuls were sitting
>   on a wall,
> Quarrelling and pecking,
>   quarrelling and pecking,
> Quarrelling,
> Quarrelling,
> Pecking pecking pecking pecking.
> This is more than flesh and
>   blood can stand.
> Now all that is left,
> Is the tail of one bulbul,
> And the beak of the other.

There were continual squabbles, tale-bearing, back-biting. The Khan objected. Nabir Das continually objected and Madhu left, faithful puzzled Madhu; I felt as if I had lost an anchor, which I had. It was turmoil; then, suddenly, peace descended, such peace and dependability as I had not known since Ears; Gaffur had found us a new cook, Salim Ali—which i not his real name.

"You see," said Olwen, "it only needed a

firm hand. Now I can paint in peace and you can write." Oddly enough I could not write and seized the chance when Ghulam Rasool asked me to come to his shop and see the hundred thousand rupee carpet he had bought. He would send his own shikara for me.

Little by little, he, my Profit David, had insinuated possessions into the house, not possessions like Olwen's, clocks, radios, cameras, picnic baskets, but small precious things I loved though I had said I would forswear them. The coral Kwan Yin had had, long ago, to go back to him but, "Why?" asked Ghulam Rasool of my writing room, "Why do you have a silver inkstand and a *brass* paper weight?" He said brass with contempt.

The inkpot had belonged to Fa who gave it to me and I take it wherever I go —it had, fortunately, been sent from Calcutta to Jinglam. It stood on a base of malachite and had two silver holders for my pens. The paperweight was Chinese, a little horse lying down, its hoofs curled under and its tail flowing round. On its back sat a monkey scratching its head as if it were thinking. On the underside there was engraved a cloud. It seemed to me most suitable for a writer's table, but, "Why brass?" asked Ghulam Rasool.

"Because it is brass, Ghulam Rasool."

"Give it to me."

"Ghulam Rasool, I have no money . . ."

"Give it to me."

He brought it back silver and I must say it looked delicious but . . . "I will not cheat you one anna," began Ghulam Rasool and I waited for the worst. "Because I am not going to charge you an anna," said Ghulam Rasool, and he touched the inkstand and little horse on my table. "Now it is perfect. Perfect!" he said.

I am always fascinated by his shop in the Old City below the Third bridge: on the ground floor is a long room with arches opening on the river, the light from the water playing on the walls, and there his workers, embroiderers, papier-mâché painters work; the carvers work in a courtyard shed at the back. On the first floor, a room of the same size holds nothing but Persian carpets piled one on the other or hung on the wall. Cushions and quilts are brought out for us to sit on, a hookah for Ghulam Rasool and, presently, cinnamon tea, sherbet, cakes and sweetmeats are served.

That day, though, Profit David was not his easy self, not talkative—he did not once mention the Quran—nor did he show me the one hundred thousand rupee carpet. "If I do, you would never stain your eyes with anything less," but that was not the real excuse. "Lady Sahib," he suddenly asked, "Pandit Kaul, does he come to see you now?" The Pandit had not been for some time.

"I do not think your friend, the lady, would like it," he had said and sent cakes instead. Jane had been indignant and had written him a letter:

Dear Pandit Sahib,
Thank you for the cakes. We think you are very kind and nice.
Love from
Jane.

"And the Mission Sahibs and Mems?" asked Ghulam Rasool. Olwen had the all too frequent scorn for missionaries but I felt guilty.

"And Khan Sahib?" asked Ghulam Rasool "Khan Sahib likes to arrange everything himself." I, fool that I was, thought the Khan was jealous. "He does not like us having city servants."

"You are not used to city servants, Lady Sahib."

"Ghulam Rasool, I have lived in cities most of my life."

"Not in a Kashmiri city," said Ghulam Rasool. "And you yourself, Lady Sahib, are not looking well."

"I am perfectly well, Ghulam Rasool."

I have not had a more perfect servant than Salim, or a better cook. He seemed able to do anything, arrange anything. There was no more friction; he had the knack of managing everyone, including me, and I began to rely on him.

Salim was light-skinned, big-featured like most Kashmiris; he had quick light-brown eyes that missed nothing—unlike me! I know now there were signs I should have noticed. Salim was unusually well dressed; his achkan, the tunic coat all the men wore, was of fine wool; sometimes he had a silk shirt and his shoes were not Kashmiri but Western. Once coming into the kitchen I saw, on a shelf, framed photographs. "My children," said Salim. Most Indian cooks have children but not their photographs in silver frames, European silver, but I thought no more about it; a strange lassitude seemed to have come over me.

After months of quite gruellingly hard work, I now had comparatively little to do, only looking after the children and my writing. The herb farm was closed; the Government, hearing of its modest success, had stepped in, stopped it, and opened their own but, as they grew pyrethrum for insecticides, it was hardly a herb farm. I no longer saw the herd children who had picked for me, had no commissions for the bakriwars and saw less of Clara.

Now and again I tried to rouse myself. "You don't need to have those children," said Olwen—the children from the Garden School.

"I like to have them. It helps Mary Groves and they need me," but Olwen could not live in a house with what she called a pack of children. "Surely we are happy as we are," she pleaded. We were and we were not. I felt I was being manoeuvred into a category to which I no longer belonged and did not want to belong; it brought separation, and not only from chosen friends; though I had refused to part with Putzi, there was still a separation from the children; to Jane's even deeper indignation there were now parts of the house and garden where they were not allowed to go. "Olwen minds not being able to paint in peace," I tried to explain. "You never mind not being able to write in peace." Jane was not to be appeased.

There was separation from the village too. I had always gone directly to the people but now Salim was the go-between. No accidents like Katji's, no wounds or sores were brought to me for help; the Khan Sahib no longer came.

To Jon:                                 June 1944.

Jon, I hardly know how to tell you. A horrible thing has happened. Honey has died.

When Jon had gone back to Calcutta the autumn before, she had left Honey, her pekingese puppy, with me. "I'm too pressed to look after him properly and he's such a difficult little dog."

Only once or twice have I had a bad-tempered pekingese—Honey was as misnamed as Jon—Winsome—herself; he bit Dudi. "Well, Dudi wouldn't leave him alone," I told the furious Clara. He bit the new sweeper. "Well, he threw stones at Honey." He was devoted to those he knew, especially to me, and never turned on any of the other children but one day I heard cries, more than cries; Candytuft was barking, his high distracted barks mingled with an odd screaming. Honey was on the floor in convulsions of pain, his stomach swollen, his eyes rolled back, foam on his mouth. "Keep away from him, go back," I rapped out to the appalled children. "Keep Candy away," and, "Don't touch him," I told Salim who had come running. I thought Honey had rabies but as I knelt down by him I was not sure. I had no gloves but Olwen brought down a pair of hers—oddly enough she was always calm in a crisis—

and, "I'm going to the Post to telephone and get the vet," she said.

"I go," Salim offered but, "He won't come for you," said Olwen. "Then Memsahib let me help you," Salim said to me.

"Keep away." I was trying to hold Honey still enough for me to feel and see. Again I did not think it was rabies; the stomach was too distended and, though rabies is anguish, this pain seemed too sharp. In a few minutes I had my answer. Honey died and, as I stood up dazed, rabies is not as quick as that, I thought. Then, what?

The vet told me. He came quickly as Olwen had insisted he should. "If you don't I shall report you to the State," she had told him and, "You are quite right, Madam," he said when he had listened to me and examined the little body. "That wasn't rabies. The dog was poisoned."

Never had I been as angry. With all his faults, Honey was too young to die and such an agonising death. "One of you did it," I said to the servants, "So out, all of you. I am sending for the Khan Sahib. Not one of you will stay."

If only I had kept to that, made a clean sweep but, "You don't mean Gaffur," Olwen said at once.

"I do mean Gaffur."

"I won't consent to that." Probably she would have left as well but reason prevailed—reason that always makes you take the wrong decision. "You are being hysterical," said Olwen, calm and measured. "Let's face it, Honey was not a pleasant little dog."

"He was Jon's."

"That doesn't make him more likeable and these people are timid."

"Timid! Cruel cowardly fiends."

"It was probably Habib—or Madhu because you sent them away."

"I didn't send them away and Madhu would never have done it."

"Calm down."

I calmed down, partly because I was beginning to feel too ill really to care.

Dysentery, I thought, usual old dysentery but not quite ordinary dysentery; there was often a strange joy, a feeling of exhilaration, even hallucination when I did not fully know what I was doing. One evening I remember coming to myself and finding I was walking along the dyke path in full evening dress; it was a blue evening dress, midnight blue, wide-sleeved, with sequined stars; Jimmie Simon had given it to me, it was made by Hartnell. I had not worn it since I left Calcutta and now I was wearing it walking along the dyke, over the rough-stoned path where only sheep and goats and herd boys went. Fortunately Olwen and the children were asleep when I came in. The reaction to these times left me weak, sweating and miserable.

For some reason, probably Olwen's influence, I did not go to the missionary doctors but to the Regimental Medical Officer. He was a young man, and not the usual army doctor, being deeply interested in, and curious about, the country. He had obviously heard of Dove House and asked me questions that showed he wanted to come and see it; I still do not know why I was elusive. In the end he prescribed the routine treatment and let me go. I was also taking issuf ghul—rose-seed jelly—the native remedy, but the trouble was no better, in fact, it seemed we were under a spell of illness; the children developed diarrhoea, probably dysentery so that I took them to him as well. Soon Olwen, too, was in bed. I suppose I was so used to illness that I did not take enough notice.

"Is yours dysentery?" I asked Olwen.

"No." She, too, was as accustomed. "I don't know what it is but I feel so ill."

She looked it. Her face and neck and, what puzzled me, her arms and hands, were flushed red and blotchy; she was sweating and restless yet had no fever. "I can't see properly," she said, and her eyes looked strange, the pupils big. "Olwen, you haven't been taking pills, strong pills?"

"Do you think I would be so silly! Besides, I haven't any pills." She was testy. When I felt her pulse it was too fast, next time too slow.

"Olwen, I think I ought to take you to Srinagar into a nursing home . . ."

"Just because I'm ill, you want to get rid of me." She began to cry. I could have cried too. "It's not that . . ." I felt too weak to look after her and, going to the Post telephone, asked the doctor to come.

He spent the afternoon. Salim produced

a marvellous tea, but I could tell the Doctor was puzzled.

I was sitting with the children while they had their lunch—one of the separations was that Olwen would not have meals with them; to her, the proper place for children was in the nursery. They were having dâl and rice—a lentil purée with rice and eggs often given to children in India and a great favourite still with our family, when Jane put down her fork and said, "I can't eat this. It's gritty."

"Gritty? It can't be."

"It is. Look."

I looked, turned the food over and saw grey-white specks. I took a little on my finger and held it towards the light and, as the sun caught it, one of the specks sent out a gleam, then another; the dāl was full of ground glass.

Servants, in India, often crush an electric bulb and put it into bait to kill rats; that, I thought, was what had happened in the kitchen. Salim, gone shopping, had left Sultan to serve our lunches and Sultan was capable of any stupidity. I went into the kitchen and scolded him, made scrambled eggs for all of us but, as the children had eaten some of the dāl, I ordered a tonga and we drove straight to the Doctor.

To my surprise, he was grave and it was not the immediate result he was concerned about.

"Usually they grind the glass too small to do real damage," he said but then, "I don't like this, I don't like the sound of it," and, "You will go back home"—as the RMO he could order me—"Say nothing to anyone but tomorrow send me a sample of everyone's stools and by someone you can trust."

Whom now could I trust? Madhu had left; I could hardly telephone the Khan Sahib on such a delicate matter—in any case the soldiers at the Post would overhear and alert everyone. Tonteyn volunteered.

It was the next afternoon that I heard the sound of boots on our path. Olwen was in bed and I felt so weak that I was lying on a rug in the garden. Clara had taken the children—she was wonderful when a child was unwell—and I was half asleep when I was startled by this brisk unmistakable sound. I thought it was the Khan, who wore riding boots, but, to my amazement, there appeared the Doctor and with him the Provost Marshall.

Standing there, on our lawn in the sunlight, they told me that the specimens, Jane's, Paula's and mine, were full of ground glass; in mine there was charras—Indian hemp or marijuana—which accounted for the hallucinations and euphoria. Olwen's was even more serious, belladonna. "Belladonna?" I must have looked uncomprehendingly stupid because, "Belladonna is deadly nightshade. Poison," the Doctor explained.

"Poison! but that was Honey," I said, stupefied. "Honey, not Olwen."

We were to go at once to Srinagar. "We do not want to arouse any suspicions so this will seem just a routine visit from the Doctor," said the Marshall. "We'll go now and you pack what you need for a day or two."

"But Olwen's in bed." I was still stupid.

"Get her up. I have arranged a nursing

home. A car is waiting and the police will be here within the hour."

As it turned out, an hour was not enough. As the Provost Marshall and Doctor left, Salim came back on his bicycle. He had seen the military cars, in a trice guessed what had happened, and went berserk. In his frenzy he blamed it on Olwen and tried to get at her up the stairs—it was then I knew he was insane. Gaffur valiantly stood on the stairs, trying to fend Salim off with Olwen's shooting stick. Only Sultan and the sweeper were by; they were useless and I ran down the hill to the Hopmans, praying that Tonteyn would be there. He was not, but a young naval officer on leave had come out to see Clara—she had met him in Bombay. He told me afterwards I had appeared as they were having tea and had said, quietly, as if it were everyday, "Please. Salim is trying to murder Olwen. Please come. Come quickly," but my ash-grey face and frantic eyes were far from everyday. With a quick question or two, he raced up the hill, caught Salim and knocked him out, binding his wrists and ankles with Salim's own turban. The police arrived and Salim was taken away.

To Jon:
It is difficult to believe that someone you have known day in, day out, is trying seriously to harm you, but Salim has done this before. The Police Inspector who seems honest, kind and really concerned told me this which I suspect I am not supposed to know. "Salim Ali who did this noxious crime, is homicidal maniac." It seems he specialises in European women on their own, making himself indispensable—as he almost did with me—while gradually breaking their willpower.

The daughter of one of them later wrote to me, telling me that, though it seemed unbelievable, her mother had given him power of attorney over everything she possessed. I could understand his doing this with Olwen but what could he have hoped from an obviously poor army wife like me?
Then I found out. *Rungli-Rungliot* had been published in its small wartime

edition, and had reached Kashmir; a gossip had been put about—the Pandit said by Ghulam Rasool, Ghulam Rasool said by the Pandit—that, though I lived in seeming modesty I, too, was rich, far richer than Olwen, as I owned a tea-garden near Darjeeling.

All this I was to learn. At the moment I was too ill with shock and the effect of the glass and drug to remember anything clearly though some moments are sharp: I can remember the police bivouacked in the courtyard and Sultan trying to propitiate them with all our milk and sugar and butter: I remember I refused to go to Srinagar. As Salim had been taken away —what was the need? I asked. "We'll get better more quickly if we stay here."

"The State won't allow you to stay here," and seeing the shock on my face, "I think I had better send for your husband," said the Provost Marshall. He in his turn was shocked by my vehement, "No." I had not had a word from Laurence, though he must have heard. Poor Provost Marshall! It had been good of him to come when I had renounced his protection, but ungratefully I do not remember his name, or the Doctor's or the Assistant Resident's whom I had to see—the Resident, whom I knew, was unfortunately in Gulmarg—nor can I remember the name of the Police Inspector and only vaguely the sequence of events but, "Not allowed to stay here!" and I said, "We'll go to Sonamarg."

I managed to get word to Jobara and he arranged a double camp, one for Olwen, one for us, and we went there as soon as the police allowed.

Sonamarg had never seemed as quiet and lovely. Our camps, one above the other, had the two big tents standing over built-up floors of wood strewn with pine branches, a durrie over them. The front flap was raised to make a canopy over a table and chairs where we worked and ate, I with the children, Olwen in the camp above. She had sent to the Punjab for a former cook of her own and he sometimes cooked for us but mostly we lived on vegetables and mushrooms—it was an abundant mushroom year—and wild raspberries, the gujars' and bakriwars' milk, cheese and butter and our own home-made bread.

Our beds were in the big tent itself where there was room for the children to play on rainy days. We kept our clothes in suitcases and there was a bathroom behind with an enamelled basin on a stand, a zinc bath and thunder-boxes, as we called commodes. Jobara would not let me have any servants except his son, Amar, who was a ponyboy, not a servant. I was only too glad—and did the rest of the work though we had a sweeper who went from camp to camp.

Slowly, comparative peace of mind and well-being came back, as we stayed until even the bakriwars had left and the valley was glorious in colour.

September 1944.

The thing I shall remember most about these early mornings at Sonamarg is the dew, the chill of it and the intense silver greenness of it on the grass. Because of the chill, Jobara starts the campfire again at dawn and, as the sun comes down the valley, striking the dew, we creep out and sit by the fire as we drink hot cocoa and I make toast on a pronged stick. The air is pure and clear and, as the sun warms it, the chill disappears. We go down to wash in the stream which is clear as crystal and the flowers by the rocks, shining with dew, look as if they are polished. One of the hobbled ponies limps up to the fire: it is little and thin with a soft mole-coloured hairy nose.

The children and I spent long afternoons by the stream that ran wide on the valley floor and, curiously, poetry began almost to write itself in my head: probably from relief. Olwen, too, had begun again to paint. Her landscapes were good, as if she had not been touched. My poems were overdone; "Poems can be too beautiful," Spencer was to say when I showed them to him, but at the time they brought ease.

In the evening, after so long a day, comes a beautiful warm sleepiness, as I sit in front of the fire after supper and the children are in bed. The smell of the burning wood is fragrant; one little fat bird, with rust-coloured breast feathers, sits on a stone by me and makes an occasional soft whistle. I walk a little away last thing, before I say goodnight to Olwen, and look up at the stars, and then back to the camps and their fires, Olwen's and mine. She has a petrol lamp with a white glare, I a lantern that makes a soft glow. Behind and above us, the forest and the mountains—the far ones already streaked with snow—shut off the sky. I can hear Jobara or Amar and Olwen's cook and Gaffur talking softly in the cook tents and feel safe. Last thing in bed I look at the stars again and hear the stream.

The stream led to a crisis. One thing essential in renting a camp site is to have it near a stream, but suddenly ours ceased to flow. An army camp of some forty soldiers had moved in above us for mountain manoeuvre training and their engineers had gone up with concrete blocks, dynamite and tools and turned the stream into their camp. It was consternation; we had paid three months' advance rent for our sites, to move our camp would be costly; I had not the money and was more than worried. Bitter were the complaints sent to the Commandant, who took little notice.

For two days our water had to be fetched from the river; more complaints were sent and on the third day the Commandant came to see me. "I can't send my engineers up again. There is a war on, you know," he said, totally unsympathetic.

"That is no reason to penalise women and children . . ." I broke off.

Where were the children? I realised I had not seen them for some time, in my distress not noticing they were missing. "Could you wait a moment," I said to the Commandant but, "Look!" he said in astonishment because, as suddenly as it had ceased, the stream began to flow.

We were both staring at it when two wet dirty children appeared with a still dirtier Amar, a pony and a spade.

"What the deuce!" said the Commandant.

They came up to us with proud smiles and, "We didn't like you being so worried," Jane said to me, "so we went up the mountain to look. You *have* made a mess," she said to the Commandant. "Never mind. We've settled it."

"What did you do?" I asked.

"Turned the stream back again," said Paula.

The Commandant looked at this small six-year-old as if she were an apparition. "But how?" he asked. "How?"

"We went up higher," said Jane. "Amar dug and Paula and I helped bringing stones. You needn't worry," she told the Commandant, "we left part of the stream for you."

It would have been another healing respite but twice I was called to go down to Srinagar, and had to leave the children, once with an unwilling Olwen, the next time happily with Giovanna, whom beneficent Mary sent to us.

It was true that the State would not let me stay in Dove House but I had to go back there with a police escort—"to vacate" was the instruction.

I have been torn many times by partings but seldom as sorely as this; it was searing to go through my little house and dismantle it under the eyes of the police, leaving the furniture which the Khan wished to have but taking away all traces of us, and paying our few bills. There were no servants left; Sultan, in spite of his pathetic bribes of butter, sugar and milk, had been taken away. I had not the heart to go to the village for any goodbyes; in any case the people would not look at me; I had brought the police to their village, the ultimate disgrace, and it was alone with the escort that I walked down our path for the last time.

The next time I went down was to appear in Court. That startled me. "Why should I?" I asked the Assistant Resident, "I don't want to charge anyone. Nor does the Provost Marshall want me to."

"You were wise," the Provost Marshall had told me, "to get away quietly to Sonamarg"—he who had told me to go to Srinagar. "That has stopped gossip. Try and let it all die down."

It was not possible. "It doesn't rest with you," said the Assistant Resident. "The State is bringing the charge."

"The State? Why?"

"The benevolent State has to be seen to be protective of its foreign visitors and residents and so of course must bring a charge against Salim Ali but . . ." It was then he told me gently that the State would conveniently lose.

"But how can they? There's the medical evidence."

"That can be glossed over, even disappear," and I had a sudden memory of when I was a girl in Narayangunj, of our stately khansamah—butler—whom we called Pooh Bah being brought to trial for adultery. Fa had asked him if he needed help but Pooh Bah was a rich man and, "No need, Sahib," said Pooh Bah. "Fortunately I am able to pay plenty of false witnesses." Salim was a rich man and if he had the State behind him . . .

"But Salim is evil," I said, bewildered.

"There are no evil men in Kashmir," said the Assistant Resident. "Of course they may well have to put Salim into a lunatic asylum, not because he's dangerous, of course, just for his own good, but no-one is going to know that."

"What do you expect?" asked Tonteyn —he and Clara had come at once to the hotel to see me. "The State lives by its tourist trade. The case against Salim won't be proven but, so as not to look too contrived, Sultan will be sentenced though on what count I do not know. Thieving, I expect."

"He didn't thieve."

"I don't think you'll find that makes any difference."

The cross-questioning next day showed me clearly that Tonteyn and the Assistant Resident were right; nothing I said seemed to matter, nothing I did not say. I do not remember much about the Court—if it was a Court—perhaps this preliminary hearing was held somewhere else. I have only an impression of a large high room, full of people, its walls panelled and carved but I do remember the Vakils: the Vakil for the State, Salim's Vakil, Sultan's—those last two, I soon knew, were intent on getting damages from me—each of them in his impeccable achkan and perfectly twisted muslin turban, twisted as themselves, I began to think wearily, as they asked, smooth and sweet as honey, question after question and always seemed to make the answers boomerang back at me. The case was adjourned for further evidence. Salim was released on bail, Sultan, poor scapegoat, kept in prison.

I went to see him—that is graven on my memory. The prison was a small earth-walled building outside the city; when Sultan saw me he burst into tears, fell on his knees and clutched my dress. "Memsahib! Memsahib! You have come to take me away?" and I could not take him away. When I left he rolled on the ground and shrieked. "Perhaps if you had two thousand rupees . . ." suggested the Vakil but I had not two thousand rupees. It was then that Tonteyn said, "You must get out."

Olwen would not believe me. "We're British," she kept on saying. "They wouldn't dare."

"Olwen, this isn't India. It is a State."

"We're British."

As Britons, she was sure we could never be discredited. If I went, I was a coward —running away; she was ashamed of me. If I went, she would not forgive me . . . I think she would have stopped me if she had known.

Sonamarg now had a motor road and

Roland sent the necessary money to Tonteyn—my mail was watched. Tonteyn arranged for a car to come up by night; fortunately it was dry weather and the road was open. Before dawn, I got the children up, hushing them to silence as we dressed. Jobara took our suitcases—we left everything else. I carried Candytuft under my coat to stop him barking, and had Moon on a lead; Jane carried her precious doll Mignonette, Paula some flowers she insisted on taking and we tiptoed out and went down to the road. Jobara came with us—if we were stopped I trusted him to talk us out of it—in Srinagar we changed cars in the Hopmans' garden after a hasty meal and drove full tilt to the Border.

I shall not forget the almost unbearable relief when we passed the Border post—I ached from head to foot with the tension of that drive.

I still feel a traitor to Olwen and know she thought I was one. Though I wrote several times I have never had a word from her, but heard she was kept subpoenaed in Srinagar for six months, with continual appearances in Court only to be shamed by defeat. Salim was acquitted, Sultan got three years. Charges of defamation were brought against her and against me; I cannot go back to Kashmir.

## THE END

# Epilogue

WE spent the night in Rawalpindi —mercifully Laurence was not there, having been transferred to Bombay.

October 1944.

I realise what bumpkins my children have become. They cannot, any more than Jobara, remember seeing a tap in a house and cannot get over the hotel bathroom, turning the taps on and off, off and on. "Hot water," they say marvelling. Paula will not sit on the loo but, fascinated, flushes it over and over again. All three stand round me when I telephone to Jon and tremble with excitement when they hear her voice— only Jane is bold enough to speak to her.

Next morning we took Jobara to the station to show him the first train he had ever seen. He stood on the platform salaaming and weeping as the train drew out. We, all of us, wept too. Later on I was able to send him, by Nancy, what he had always longed for, a gold watch engraved with his and our names and a watch chain to match.

In Calcutta, Jon and Roland, Nancy and Dick were anxiously waiting for us but, "Where is he?" asked Jane as soon as she was on the platform. She had confidently expected Laurence to be there. "Calcutta is where he lives," she had insisted; from her point of view he did—Rawalpindi had no connection with him; Paula hardly remembered who he was.

Jon and Roland took us in for far longer than we had dreamed; though the war was over in May, it was not until July that our repatriation papers came.

We landed in Liverpool and must have looked a disconsolate trio in our dirzee-made clothes, I still thin and pale—I weighed only six stone—while Paula was a thread. Though we were going to Darry-nane—I had told the children much about

505

it—we still felt disconsolate, mingled with apprehension, the same apprehension Jon and I had felt on the quay at Plymouth those twenty-five years ago. I could see it in Jane's face. Paula was too young but she, too, pressed closely to me.

To be trusted can be terrible. I had had everything for them and had lost everything. Even the pekingese had to be left behind—a troop ship does not allow dogs—and there had been another blow of that time: the few things I had packed from Dove House had been sent to Lloyd's warehouse in Bombay for shipment and the warehouse had been sabotaged and burnt. I had packed Ghulam Rasool's silver in our suitcases among our clothes: we had that but not as much as a saucer towards making a new home. We should have to start all over again and I was not feeling brave, except . . . and suddenly I was able to stand straight and say to the children, "Come along."

Two things had happened.

The first was a legacy of Kashmir.

The Pandit had been too timorous to come near us. "I was always afraid this would end in weepings," he wrote. "The goddess Savitri had many persecutors." I do not know if that was meant to console me or not. Ghulam Rasool had written too. 'Honestly all my sympathies are with you. Bible David was always anxious to get trouble as he believed, after it, 'One gets a very good time for a long future.' Lady Sahib, it needs a heart to get worries."

I must have plenty of heart, I thought wryly, but Ghulam Rasool's words were never empty. The second distressing time I had to come down to Srinagar, he had arrived at the hotel. "I want you to come with me."

"What? *Now?*"

"Exactly now. I have a shikara here. Please. It is for your advantage," he added.

"Ghulam Rasool, it's no use trying to sell me anything."

He laughed, showing those disarmingly pearly teeth. "In the Quran it says . . . ."

"I don't mind what the Quran says."

"Then come and see."

It was good to get away from the confusion and worry, to sit once again in the peace of his upper room watching the reflection of the water from the Jhelum moving over the walls; to forget for a brief hour, and look at and talk only of beautiful things.

He showed me rugs he had bought that week from the palace of the Dowager Maharani of Jammu and I suppose I was carried away. There was one, not prohibitive but, "Very very rare," said Ghulam Rasool. "It is an Agra family rug." At its top and bottom, the family's possessions in houses, temples, trees, were woven and joining them was a tree of life in blossom and, at its foot, a phoenix. The colours were deep blue and coral, pale browns and greens, the wool so fine it shone like silk on a cream ground and I bought it for a hundred pounds. We had to arrange that Fa would cable the money, almost my last hundred, to Roland, who would remit it from Calcutta. "I do not think, Lady Sahib, you should bring money into Kashmir just now," Ghulam Rasool had said and then added with what I thought was a sigh of relief, "Now you will be safe."

I knew what he meant. Many Mohammedans invest their money in carpets keeping seven or eight piled on top of one another. In calling him Profit David I had been wiser than I knew; what he had contrived for me was a nest-egg, "Against a very rainy day," he said.

Fa was appalled that I trusted "that fellow". I wish I had trusted him more. That same day he had urged me to buy two more rugs, also from the palace in Jammu and still more after my heart as they were Kirmans, to me the only feminine Persian carpets, as they invariably have roses and flowers and delicate colours. These were a pair—pairs are rare—and were in amber, honeygold and pale blue, again on a cream ground. They would have been worth a small fortune today—as is the Agra rug; fortunately, so far, I have not had to sell it.

The Agra rug was my safeguard, but the value of the second possession I could not calculate then.

Almost as soon as we had arrived in Calcutta an urgent request had come to me from the Women's Voluntary Service; questions had been raised in Parliament as to what British women in India were doing to help the war effort and, in particular, for the troops; the accusation being that they were doing nothing. It could not have been more hurtful; the real trouble was that there was perhaps one woman for every fifteen thousand men. Would I, asked the WVS, tour a province—Bengal was the obvious choice—and write a book refuting this slur. The result was *Bengal Journey* which took me from the Himalayas to the Bay of Bengal, even into the front line. To be as little noticed as possible, I wore every kind of uniform and travelled in every kind of vehicle from Army Dakota planes to bullock carts. Nothing could have been better therapy. It was, of course, voluntary work but I was given a good Ayah to help Jon, who nobly looked after the children and an Army Education Corps sergeant to teach them part-time; on his other days he taught in a prison and told Jon he would rather teach twenty convicts than one Paula! He was Marcus Stone, the writer; next time I met him he was Chief Librarian of Kent.

I would have liked to have had Giovanna. Mary Groves' School was closed for the winter but that December Giovanna had married a young German Swiss, Emil Zannger. As the wedding was in Bombay I could not go but was able to give her the wedding dress and a little towards a "dot". I knew she was disconsolate; it was a lonely wedding for her.

One of the places on my itinerary was Dacca and after it I was to drive the familiar eleven miles to Narayangunj, a thought from which I shrank. "You should never go back," I have often said, but I had to go back. I did not know how far back.

On the morning I was due to go there, my Narayangunj hostess-to-be telephoned. The manager of one of the jute works had died and he was to be buried that morning as is the custom in a hot country—it was April—and, of course, every European in Narayangunj's small community had to drive into Dacca to attend. As I was booked to leave on the midday steamer for Calcutta it was impossible to postpone my visit and, "Would you mind", she asked, "being received by the Babu in charge?" Mind! I could not have been more relieved but had no idea what was waiting for me.

Indians do not change; their clothes and customs are timeless and there was not one Westerner in the little town to disturb this. As I walked through the bazaars and the jute works, along the river, past the Club, the bamboo-built church and school, the houses I had known, it was as if I had gone back thirty or more years and was seven, eight, nine, ten, eleven, twelve, again. Everything was the same. I had lunch on the verandah of one of the houses waited on by white-clad servants who might have been our own; on the way to the ghat we passed the gates of our house. I could see the top of my cork tree over the gate; it was in flower; my secret hole would surely be there. For a moment I hesitated. "Go in. Go in," the Babu urged but I could not bring myself to do that.

Most uncanny of all was the steamer; it was one of Fa's double-decked paddle-wheeled steamers with the first class forward on the upper deck, where I was the only passenger.

There was the usual clamour from below: steerage passengers with their bundles and tin boxes, goats and crates of chickens: coolies padding up and down the gangway, heavy loads on their heads: crew shouting. There was the familiar steamer smell of hot oil and gunny sacks: of human sweat and of goat: the smell of sun-warmed decks and of the river itself. Then came the sound of a bell, the steamer gave a warning hoot and ropes splashed into the water as they were cast off. As the paddle wheels began to turn I stood at the front rail.

Usually, as I knew well, the steamers draw away from the ghat, then turn in a wide circle to go upstream but now, for some reason, the steamer backed. She backed further and further so that I, looking at the town, its banks along the river, its houses, mosques, temples and bathing steps, saw it grow smaller and smaller until it was like looking at it down a telescope, smaller but more and more clear until it was out of sight.

As the steamer turned I went to my cabin and began to write.

Now on the quay at Liverpool that miserable morning I had two things; rolled up, under my arm, was the Agra rug and, in my suitcase, a finished book, the manuscript of *The River*.

We could start over again.

# GUIDE
# TO THE COLOUR CODING
# OF
# ULVERSCROFT BOOKS

Many of our readers have written to us expressing their appreciation for the way in which our colour coding has assisted them in selecting the Ulverscroft books of their choice. To remind everyone of our colour coding— this is as follows:

## BLACK COVERS
Mysteries

\*

## BLUE COVERS
Romances

\*

## RED COVERS
Adventure Suspense and General Fiction

\*

## ORANGE COVERS
Westerns

\*

## GREEN COVERS
Non-Fiction

# NON-FICTION TITLES
## *in the*
## Ulverscroft Large Print Series

# FICTION TITLES
## *in the*
## Ulverscroft Large Print Series

| | |
|---|---|
| Enquiry | *Dick Francis* |
| Flying Finish | *Dick Francis* |
| Forfeit | *Dick Francis* |
| High Stakes | *Dick Francis* |
| In The Frame | *Dick Francis* |
| Knock Down | *Dick Francis* |
| Risk | *Dick Francis* |
| Band of Brothers | *Ernest K. Gann* |
| Twilight For The Gods | *Ernest K. Gann* |
| Army of Shadows | *John Harris* |
| The Claws of Mercy | *John Harris* |
| Getaway | *John Harris* |
| Winter Quarry | *Paul Henissart* |
| East of Desolation | *Jack Higgins* |
| In the Hour Before Midnight | *Jack Higgins* |
| Night Judgement at Sinos | *Jack Higgins* |
| Wrath of the Lion | *Jack Higgins* |
| Air Bridge | *Hammond Innes* |
| A Cleft of Stars | *Geoffrey Jenkins* |
| A Grue of Ice | *Geoffrey Jenkins* |
| Beloved Exiles | *Agnes Newton Keith* |
| Passport to Peril | *James Leasor* |
| Goodbye California | *Alistair MacLean* |
| South By Java Head | *Alistair MacLean* |
| All Other Perils | *Robert MacLeod* |
| Dragonship | *Robert MacLeod* |
| A Killing in Malta | *Robert MacLeod* |
| A Property in Cyprus | *Robert MacLeod* |

# MYSTERY TITLES
## *in the*
## Ulverscroft Large Print Series